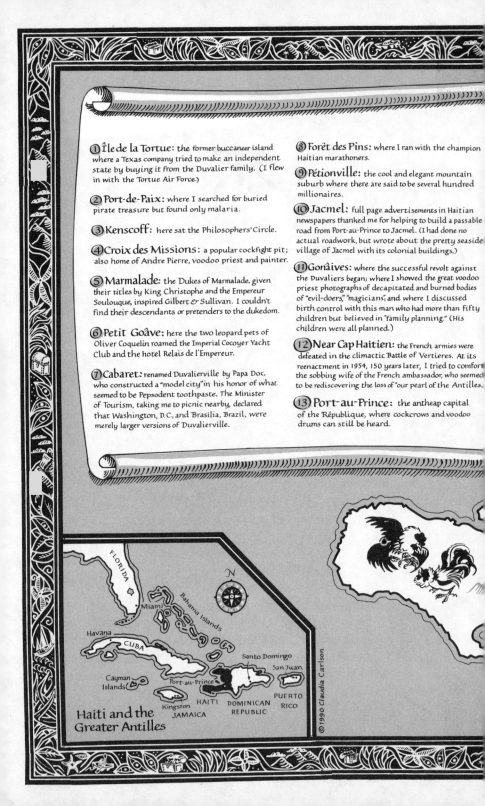

① **Île de la Tortue:** the former buccaneer island where a Texas company tried to make an independent state by buying it from the Duvalier family. (I flew in with the Tortue Air Force.)

② **Port-de-Paix:** where I searched for buried pirate treasure but found only malaria.

③ **Kenscoff:** here sat the Philosophers' Circle.

④ **Croix des Missions:** a popular cockfight pit; also home of Andre Pierre, voodoo priest and painter.

⑤ **Marmalade:** the Dukes of Marmalade, given their titles by King Christophe and the Empereur Soulouque, inspired Gilbert & Sullivan. I couldn't find their descendants or pretenders to the dukedom.

⑥ **Petit Goâve:** here the two leopard pets of Oliver Coquelin roamed the Imperial Cocoyer Yacht Club and the hotel Relais de l'Empereur.

⑦ **Cabaret:** renamed Duvalierville by Papa Doc, who constructed a "model city" in his honor of what seemed to be Pepsodent toothpaste. The Minister of Tourism, taking me to picnic nearby, declared that Washington, D.C., and Brasilia, Brazil, were merely larger versions of Duvalierville.

⑧ **Forêt des Pins:** where I ran with the champion Haitian marathoners.

⑨ **Pétionville:** the cool and elegant mountain suburb where there are said to be several hundred millionaires.

⑩ **Jacmel:** full page advertisements in Haitian newspapers thanked me for helping to build a passable road from Port-au-Prince to Jacmel. (I had done no actual roadwork, but wrote about the pretty seaside village of Jacmel with its colonial buildings.)

⑪ **Gonâives:** where the successful revolt against the Duvaliers began; where I showed the great voodoo priest photographs of decapitated and burned bodies of "evil-doers," "magicians," and where I discussed birth control with this man who had more than fifty children but believed in "family planning." (His children were all planned.)

⑫ **Near Cap Haitien:** the French armies were defeated in the climactic Battle of Vertieres. At its reenactment in 1954, 150 years later, I tried to comfort the sobbing wife of the French ambassador, who seemed to be rediscovering the loss of "our pearl of the Antilles."

⑬ **Port-au-Prince:** the antheap capital of the République, where cockcrows and voodoo drums can still be heard.

FLORIDA

Miami

Bahama Islands

Havana

CUBA

Cayman Islands

Port-au-Prince

Santo Domingo

San Juan

Kingston
JAMAICA

HAITI

DOMINICAN REPUBLIC

PUERTO RICO

N

© 1990 Claudia Carlson

Haiti and the Greater Antilles

Herbert Gold's Haiti

ALSO BY HERBERT GOLD

NOVELS

Birth of a Hero
The Prospect Before Us
The Man Who Was Not With It
The Optimist
Therefore Be Bold
Salt
Fathers
The Great American Jackpot
Swiftie the Magician
Waiting for Cordelia
He/She
Family
True Love
Mister White Eyes
A Girl of Forty
Dreaming

SHORT STORIES AND ESSAYS

Love and Like
The Age of Happy Problems
The Magic Will
A Walk on the West Side—California on the Brink
Lovers & Cohorts: Twenty-Seven Stories

MEMOIR

My Last Two Thousand Years

REPORTAGE

Biafra, Goodbye

A DESTINATIONS BOOK

BEST NIGHTMARE ON EARTH

A LIFE IN HAITI

HERBERT GOLD

INTRODUCTION BY JAN MORRIS

A TOUCHSTONE BOOK
Published by Simon & Schuster
New York London Toronto Sydney Tokyo Singapore

TOUCHSTONE
Simon & Schuster Building
Rockefeller Center
1230 Avenue of the Americas
New York, New York 10020

Copyright © 1991 by Herbert Gold

All rights reserved,
including the right of reproduction
in whole or in part in any form.
First Touchstone Edition 1992
TOUCHSTONE and colophon are registered
trademarks of Simon & Schuster Inc.
Manufactured in the United States of America

1   3   5   7   9   10   8   6   4   2

Library of Congress Cataloging-in-Publication Data
is available

ISBN: 0-671-75516-1

*With grateful friendship to Jean Weiner, Jacques Large,
Al Seitz, F. Morrisseau-Leroy, Shimon Tal, Shelagh
Burns, Issa el Saieh, and to some who cannot be named.*

CONTENTS

	Preface	ix
	Introduction by Jan Morris	xi
Chapter One	1953: The Golden Age of Strange	1
Chapter Two	Americans in the Port of Princes: The Early Fifties	13
Chapter Three	Loupgarous/Werewolves/Hobgoblins	37
Chapter Four	The Renaissance of the Fifties	51
Chapter Five	Combat de Coqs	69
Chapter Six	Castaways	75
Chapter Seven	Land Without Jews	91
Chapter Eight	The Philosopher's Circle	109
Chapter Nine	The Darkest Ages	123
Chapter Ten	"Here Is the Young Leader that I Promised You"	157
Chapter Eleven	In Haiti, They Run *From*	181
Chapter Twelve	Minglers	203
Chapter Thirteen	The Perfect Dear	219
Chapter Fourteen	The Uprooting: 1986	233
Chapter Fifteen	After the Dawn Came Another Night	251
Chapter Sixteen	Wonder of the World	283

OTHER BOOKS IN THE DESTINATION SERIES
Introductions by Jan Morris

Alice Adams
Mexico: Some Travels and Some Travelers There

Fergus M. Bordewich
Cathay: A Journey in Search of Old China

Gordon Chaplin
The Fever Coast Log: At Sea in Central America

M. F. K. Fisher
Long Ago in France: The Years in Dijon

Thomas Keneally
The Place Where Souls Are Born

Aaron Latham
*The Frozen Leopard:
Hunting My Dark Heart in Africa*

William Murray
The Last Italian: Portrait of a People

Mary Lee Settle
Turkish Reflections: A Biography of a Place

PREFACE

This is an account of my times in Haiti, from the years of the early fifties when I lived there as a young student to my most recent visit in 1990 as a less-young traveler. I have changed some names and identifying details. As in the past, some of my Haitian friends will not be happy with my reporting; but they know I keep coming back because their country is still the magic island.

Haiti was the first independent black nation of modern times, winning its freedom from France with a slave revolt against Napoléon at the height of his power. Here is the first sentence of a primary school reader still in use in the 1950s:

Nos ancêtres, les Gaulois, avaient les yeux bleus et les cheveux blonds.

Our ancestors, the Gauls, had blue eyes and blond hair.

INTRODUCTION
by Jan Morris

ONE OF the astonishments of our time has been the existence, 500 miles from Miami, 200 miles from Puerto Rico, fifty miles from Jamaica, of the endlessly amazing Republic of Haiti, the left-hand end of the island of Hispaniola. For sheer improbability nothing can touch this francophone black State, which came into existence as the result of a slave revolt, which had an Emperor once, which was occupied by the United States for twenty years between the world wars, which "Papa" Doc Duvalier ruled with a mad hand, and after him "Baby" Doc, which is the land of voodoo and glorious native art, and about which indeed almost nothing is ordinary. Religiously fantastic, politically grotesque, artistically explosive, sexually wild, inhabited by 6½ million people of great beauty and dangerous charm, throughout our lifetimes Haiti is like a work of fiction. Indeed, when Graham Greene set his novel *The Comedians* in Papa Doc's Haiti of the 1960s, much of it was straight reportage.

Not many foreigners know this country well. Although Haiti has enjoyed its moments of touristic prosperity, and has intermittently attracted the more louche, raffish, or idiosyncratic of travelers, few visitors have stayed in the Republic for long. They have generally been too frightened, whether of crazy dictatorships, the eerie possibilities of voodoo, or AIDS. A day or two at a safe hotel on the coast, a trip to a conveniently arranged voodoo ceremony, downtown to buy a couple of bright pictures, and for most callers it has been back to the airport or the cruise ship.

Not for Mr. Herbert Gold, the author of this extraordinary memoir of Haiti. Through the years of a distinguished writing life Mr. Gold has been repeatedly drawn to spend long periods in the Republic, sometimes *en famille*, sometimes alone. First as an impecunious student, later as a celebrated literary person, he found himself irresistibly attracted by what he found there, and he immersed himself in every aspect of Haitian life—so totally that he was once invited to be the Haitian Consul in San Francisco. *Best Nightmare on Earth* remembers a thirty-seven years' acquaintance with Haiti, and it is hard to think that any other writer in English could reflect upon the country with such a combination of authority, art, and infatuation.

Even Haiti has its areas of normality, and these Mr. Gold affectionately evokes. What could be more beguiling than the Cenacle des Philosophes, the Circle of Philosophers which met each afternoon in Judge Noh's coffee trading post to discuss the world, the flesh, and the devil? What could be more entertaining than to jog through the Haitian highlands pursued hilariously by the entire complement of a local school, teachers and all? Many delightful people appear in the pages of this book, people of brave integrity, too, and one is made conscious of a quality more intense than the general run of patriotism, amounting to a truly passionate love of country.

Love is always more passionate, of course, when it is laced with forgiveness, and the fondest patriot would not deny that in Haiti there is a great deal to forgive. The countryside is lovely, the general sense of tropical *dolce far niente*, so beautifully evoked in these pages, must permanently tug the exile's heart, but alas, *au fond* it is the weirdness and the horror of the place that makes Haiti so compelling to outsiders. Mr. Gold, who obviously loves the country dearly himself, hides none of it, from the pitiful poverty of the ordinary people to the frequent enormities of their rulers.

Even after thirteen chapters of this book it comes as a shock to read of a man burnt in a city street as a werewolf—in 1986, 500 miles from Miami! To this day it is said in all seriousness in Port-au-Prince that Papa Doc procured the assassination of his brother-President John Kennedy by sticking pins in a voodoo doll. To the age-old oppression of superstition has been added, down the decades, the terror of political despotism, and the whole cauldron has been kept on the boil by constant infusions of corruption, ambition, villainy, and fantasy.

Fantasy certainly; for better or for worse, the strangeness of Haitian life seems to be made stranger still by irresistible elements of color, beauty, and fun. Mr. Gold himself, though he has experienced almost the whole range of emotions in the Republic, seems to have had any amount of fun there, on and off; and it is the power of his book that, weaving as it does a complex way between character and situation, aberration and normality, then and now, fear and joy, misery and enjoyment, it manages to interpret the most peculiar of States in familiar human terms of empathy, compassion, and even admiration. As nightmares go, so Mr. Gold tells us in his title, his life in Haiti was the best.

"We are very much interested in Haiti," said the American Secretary of State, William Jennings Bryan, in 1913, to the Ambassador from Haiti. "Tell me about the country and who the people are. Where is Haiti?"

". . . ."

"Dear me, think of it! Niggers speaking French."

CHAPTER
ONE

1953: The Golden Age of Strange

IN PARIS I met the teasing, laughing, flirting, Haitian bride of a black American friend. The lady, a singer and dancer, was the daughter of a poor family which lived in a cinder-block house a short walk from the National Palace in Port-au-Prince. "Haiti has a National Palace?" I asked.

"It doesn't have a tin roof," she said. "My mother's house does."

And then the inexorable winding down of my G.I. Bill and Fulbright sinecures brought me back to my hometown, Cleveland, the Paris of northeastern Ohio, to await the fame and riches which would surely fall from the heavens (New York) after publication of my first novel. The novel came out; I hurried to the Post Office in the Public Square; my picture failed to appear on the new three-cent stamp.

I had a wife, two babies, no good prospects to support them. I remembered the laughing Haitian singer and dancer. I went to the library to look up scholarships and fellowships and applied for one to take me to the Université d'Haiti. In due course, I was on a ship traveling from New York to Panama, with a stop in Port-au-Prince.

Steaming south along the coast on a white Panama Lines vessel, I watched a tall, imperious Haitian, with an aquiline nose, impeccably dressed, pacing the deck. I admired his self-possession, and as a very young man enraptured by everything different from Cleveland, Ohio, I wondered about his manner of proud exasperation. A quality I had not developed and could only admire from afar was the talent for being elegantly pissed-off.

3

In the way of travelers, eventually we spoke, and we became friends for the next quarter of a century. As the years went by, his exasperation grew. Haiti gave him plenty to be exasperated about, although he would not leave his country except for brief visits.

This tall black man pacing the deck, Jean Weiner, was an electrical engineer. His family, from the town of Jacmel, had been in the coffee-exporting business. A certain molding of his face and the prominent nose carried on the look of one of his grandfathers, a Jew from—as his name suggested—Vienna. Later I met other good Roman Catholic or voodoo-believing Haitians with ancestors among the wandering Jews who at times had pressing reasons to make their lives in this hidden and unlikely place. Educated in Paris and the United States, an angry and generous soul, Jean was my first friend among the class of Haitians called the elite—African and French and Haitian all at once, and negotiating their lives and their history with unique charm and difficulty.

When the coastal waters began to turn tropical, Jean changed into a white linen suit and began to groan about the island where I was coming to spend the next year—the next year and, as it turned out, a part of every next day and night of my life. "Ah, Herb, go back, go home while you can!" he said, and I laughed, treating this as a joke.

In fact, Haiti was not bad to me. Haiti was mostly bad to Haitians.

The white Panama Lines ship passed the Île de la Gonâve, where uncounted people lived without electricity, machinery, or contact with the larger world of Port-au-Prince and the mainland. I had tried to prepare myself by reading everything I could find in English and French and so I said, "Oh yes, the *White King of La Gonâve*," remembering one of the romance-drenched books. These accounts were normally illustrated with woodcuts of drum-beaters or voodoo ceremonies, all staring eyes and licking flames.

"You think you're ready," Jean Weiner said. "My dear friend, you are not ready."

The bay of Port-au-Prince was like a black mirror reflecting the heat. Frantic boys in burned-out log canoes were begging for coins alongside the ship, diving into the murk and coming up gasping for more, another, *vite, à moin, vite!* Jean extended his long arm to offer me the entire city, spread out in a yellow-gray haze along the wide, wide bay—a low jumble of thick-walled colonial buildings and corrugated tin sheds nearby, and the smoking slum of La Saline, then the irregular slopes with spots of gardens, cloud-shrouded mountains rising into the distance above the town.

I landed with household goods for four; my family would follow by airplane when I found a house. The tropical rush, noise, heat, and harborside dust gave me a dizziness of expectation. I braced myself to sink into clamor as a team of port officials, sweating primly and stubbornly in clothes made for another climate, asked for my papers. "Passport, please!" The startled customs chief looked up, smiling, and waved me through with a welcoming largeness. He was, he declared, an immense and devoted Haitian *amateur* of my distinguished cousin's music.

"Who?"

Victor Herbert . . . evidently a cousin of Gold Herbert.

"*Mes-z-amis!*" said Jean, shaking his head. "It's too late now. Welcome to the Land of Unlimited Impossibility."

Jean's son, Ti-Jean, delivered my goods in a pickup; and I settled for a while at the Grand Hotel Oloffson, which was then a rundown gingerbread mansion, catchall home for an international collection of wildballs—drunks, criminals, the sexually obsessed, crazies, remittance folks, mistresses and gigolos and bemused adventure-seekers. Over the years it would become my favorite place in the whole wide world, even after it was cleaned up, decorated, prettified, with many of the fat scurrying rats chased from the premises.

I was supposed to give a series of lectures on literature at the Haitian-American Institute. During the first one, someone asked about the place in world literature of Jacques Roumain, Marxist poet and novelist, author of *Rulers of the Dew,* a book about the conflict over land between the rich and the peasants.

I was new to the politics of Port-au-Prince. Rashly I remarked that Jacques Roumain wasn't the equal of Dostoyevsky or Tolstoy, and this provoked a crisis in Haitian-American relations. One of my best new friends wrote a front-page editorial in the *Nouvelliste,* the oldest daily newspaper, denouncing me as a racist for not acknowledging the preeminent sublimity of the Haitian writer. Laughing, he presented me with an advance copy, and then embraced me, saying, "This is tragic but not serious, like so much of our lives." The American and Haitian authorities jointly decided it would be prudent to cancel the rest of my lectures.

An American cultural affairs officer recommended long siestas. "Build up your strength for the evening," he crisply advised, and taught me the Creole word "bamboche," which combines the notions of dancing, drumming, drinking, flirting, and celebrating into a single concept which could be translated as . . . *bamboche.*

"Just stay, study, come to know our beautiful country," said his Haitian counterpart in the cultural affairs office of the Haitian state department. During the rest of my year and a half as a silenced lecturer, he and I exchanged formal dinners and perspectives on the great world. It was not bad work for a writer. My then-wife had a harder time, since at that time women were several centuries behind in elite society. She raged at the Haitian wife's conversation, which was mostly on the order of: "Est-ce que vous aimez le Brillo, Madame?"

It sounds no more fascinating in English. *Do you like Brillo, Madame?* The lady believed, as my wife did not, that a woman's place was to control the keys and discipline the servants.

The cultural official explained that he had the joy of a large family, sixteen children—"cinq de ma femme, onze dans le peuple." Five by my wife, eleven "in the people." He denounced my new friend Fortuné Bogat, a Haitian millionaire, and explained that Bogat had grown so rich because he was fair-skinned.

"But he's much darker than you," I said, and we argued about that.

I was receiving a lesson in the complexities of Haitian racism. Traditionally, mulatto had gotten ahead of black, but a rich black man was seen as mulatto. Therefore, obsessive eyeballing was a never-ending process. The permutations of Haitian pride seemed infinite and too subtle for American taste. The Cercle Bellevue in Bourdon, to which we were frequently invited as guests, did not offer membership to either whites or blacks. The bylaws were strict in protecting mulatto purity. A North American black visitor was called "un blanc noir"—a black white person—because only Haiti really counted. In this feudal world, the triumphant mulattoes, along with a few proud black families, spoke French, lived luxuriously, and ruled over the millions of the poor, uneducated Creole-speakers. Of course, when they made love, joked, grew angry, or commanded servants, the elite also spoke the language of childhood, that rich and spicy Creole. The handsome and graceful Haitian air force officers who courted visiting tourist women (sometimes lined up at the bar of the Oloffson to pick this northern fruit off the tree) as children may have had *ti-moune* ("little one") servants to tote their books to school for them. Later, the servants rode in the backseats of their cars to the tennis courts, carried their rackets, chased balls.

The complex injustice of Haitian class, money, and color distinctions gave daily experience a continual quality of incomprehensible parody. In the early fifties, under the reign of the laughing, drinking, womanizing President Paul E. Magloire (a black man ruling under the politics of *doublure,* doubling, in which black frontmen represented the mulatto power structure behind the scenes), Haitian life seemed impossible, trivial, charming, corrupt, desperate, "tragic but not serious." It was a tragedy that people could dance to.

The times were not trivial, but rather, as James Joyce said in another context, quadrivial.

MY BABY daughters from Paris and Cleveland did not have an American nursery-school rearing during our year at the little house in the Bourdon district, down a dirt road near a ravine off the Pétionville road from Port-au-Prince. Their favorite friend was a child next door whose mother came to us and said, "You like our daughter?"

"Very much." She was a lovable little girl, her hair done in braids with an assortment of ribbons.

"Please take her with you when you go. Give her a chance."

We explained that this was not possible, we could not separate her from her family, it was inconceivable to us.

"I love my daughter very much. I am willing to let her go home with you. I give my permission."

"Please," we said. "It's impossible."

"She will learn to clean your house. She is a good girl. If she does her work well, you could also send her to school."

"*Please.*"

Our neighbor gazed at us with grief. She didn't understand how people who seemed fond of her child could be so cruel, choosing to deny her a chance in life. Puzzled, just wanting information, she asked: "You are racists, Monsieur et Madame?"

OUR FRIEND Felix Morisseau-Leroy, poet, playwright, a "master-of" from Columbia University, a laughing high-liver in the warm-hearted bohemian style, used to drop by for a chat and a rum-soda. He had, still has, the talent for pleasure in life that is also pleasure-giving for others, so he was always welcome. Personally, he wasn't always happy. Once he came breathless to our door. "Morisseau, what's wrong?"

"I had a bad dream."

This made perfect sense. Even in the golden age of the mid-fifties, politics was a bad dream, the conditions of life were bad dreams, the future was a nightmare. A person didn't have to fall asleep to see demons. But after a rum-soda, he calmed himself and benignly watched my daughters, Ann and Judy, at play with their cats. "Do they speak Creole?" he asked.

"English and French," I said.

He asked them about their cats and their chicken in Creole and they chattered back happily. My wife and I stared at each other. Our daughters had learned a language behind our backs; from their friends in the neighborhood, of course, and from the servants, who were careful to speak only French with them in our presence but used the natural language of children at other times. We used to hear Gabrielle singing traditional French children's songs to them, "Bateau" and "Rossignol," and wondered if they also knew Creole songs. Of course they did. Creole is the medium of the people's life with each other. Morisseau, who wrote poetry in Creole and adapted Greek tragedy into Creole, proved a point to us. We had better learn the language. Later my wife translated his Creole version of *Antigone* into English after it was performed before enthralled crowds who had never heard of Greece. ("This is a story which happened a long long time ago . . .") In his version, Tiresias was a voodoo priest and Creon a rural police chief and the tragedy became a familiar Haitian tale.

ALAICE FILS-Aimé-de-Dieu was a key member of our new family apparatus. When the children's pet chicken disappeared or expired due to excessive hugging, he found an identical new one. As the houseboy, he was supposed to perform the car washing, the garden clearing, miscellaneous errands; he was supposed to shine my shoes. Once, astonished to find him handing them to a shoeshine boy in the street, I asked what the devil he was up to. "Ce mon secreteh," he said—it was his secretary. In office for a year, he had grown to consider shoe-shining beneath him. Out of his own funds he hired one of the boys who patrolled the streets, pounding their shoeshine boxes to attract trade.

Before arriving in Haiti, I had first been a poor student, then a would-be writer, gradually working my way up to lumpen proletariat. Now, like Alaice, I had become a pioneer of the trickle-down theory. At first, my wife and I thought not to have any servants. It turned out that foreigners could not live this way. Then we thought to hire only a couple, but to pay them twice the normal rate. We found a couple who happily agreed to this plan. We were American liberals and egalitarians.

But they would not perform certain tasks, no matter what we paid them. ("C'est pas mon travail"—it's not my work.) We liked them. We negotiated. They were content to have their tasks limited to their specialties, their salaries appropriately reduced. We finished with a "staff" of four, and our friends among the Haitian elite wondered how we could manage with so few.

After intense resistance, sometimes lasting as long as two or three days, foreigners ended by accepting the system. Haitian communists have servants; I know a Maoist, educated at the Sorbonne, whose "ti-moune"—little one—carried his briefcase for him.

One day, Ann, my eldest daughter, came running upstairs. "Daddy, somebody is talking in Alaice."

In Alaice?

She had been playing with her chicken near his room and heard a tumultuous voice coming from his mouth while he slept. I hurried downstairs. In his dream the normally shy and smiling young man was tossing—no, was being tossed—and from his mouth was pouring a stream of violent abuse of Alaice Fils-Aimé-de-Dieu, the lowest of the low, cursed on earth and in heaven. It was the hoarse and cruel voice of Ogoun Feraille, god of war. Ogoun was very angry. Alaice was possessed.

I shook him awake.

Dazed, despairing, in pain and fright, he explained that the god was punishing him for not visiting his mother, who lived in the north, near Cap Haitien, which at that time had no good road link with Port-au-Prince. I gave him some money and sent him off. I wondered if we would ever see him again.

In a few days he came trudging through the garden, dusty and weary, but with his smile returned. He had visited his mother. He had propitiated the god. Everything was okay now. How did he make peace with Ogoun? "Ti rum, ti gateau"—a little rum, a little cake, left at the altar in the "hounfor" (temple), where the family worshipped.

Alaice knew he deserved Ogoun's wrath, but the harsh god forgave him. Voodoo, which for most visitors was a weekend or festival entertainment, entered our lives in unexpected ways. It protected our house against thieves. It defined boundaries for behavior. Not only the poor believed; everyone was touched by the art, music, and practice of a view of the world coming from the ancient African spirits. When my daughters suffered rashes or bites, Alaice and Gabrielle, our cook, treated them with leaves and murmurings. Ann and Judy were soothed and calmed. We weren't sure if it was the wetted herbs or the murmurings which did this work. If there was magic here, my wife and I were in favor of it.

The writer Pierre Marcelin took me to all-night ceremonies and shrugged when I said, "This is more than an entertainment for you, isn't it?"

"We need another life," he said. "This life on earth has too many shadows."

"Haiti's flooded with sunlight."

"We need some shadows for our sunlight, mon cher."

P ORT-AU-PRINCE, with its thick-walled colonial buildings near the harbor, climbed the hills into mist and mountains. Visitors came to photograph the gingerbread dream houses which seemed to be made of spun wood. There were also the cinder-block dwellings, and the houses—*cailles-pailles*—that were huts composed of boxes, debris, mud, straw, and tin strips. Chickens, goats, and donkeys plied the streets, as did small black creatures I first thought were smart quick dogs. They were pigs. When the sun went down, the roads cooled a bit, and then streetlamps glowed in the advanced districts where there were streetlamps, and schoolchildren marched back and forth beneath them, studying their books. Few houses had electricity. The evening came, that rapid tropical nightfall. The romantic French crepuscular twilight is brief in these latitudes. In Port-au-Prince in those days, drums pulsed a person to sleep at night. I learned to separate the sounds of voodoo drums from those of dances and partying. The smells were those of people, emulsifying vegetation, and charcoal smoke. Why was it a kind of heaven? After all these years, I'm still answering this question.

Those first weeks in Haiti marked out the elements of an inexhaustible set of interlocking puzzles: unimaginable poverty, unpredictable appeal; friendship and fear; a culture which is impenetrable and profoundly hospitable; desperation and humor; corruption in politics and generosity in friends; a collaboration and suspicion between classes unlike anyplace else. The complex strains between black and mulatto seemed more like a racial than a class separation.

In my mid-twenties in those years of the mid-fifties, I was navigating among new gods, new languages, a very old and new world of magic and love, need, celebration, and suffering, with a goofy thirst for all the experience I could drink down. At an age when other young parents like my wife and me were also navigating the shoals of marriage in the fifties—"togetherness" was the American voodoo put forth in this postwar American dreamtime of prosperity and insecurity—our family was thrust onto an island of absolute strange. My wife and I went to ecstatic ceremonies instead of the movies. Our children were learning three languages, English, French, and Creole. Our friends were men and women a universe away from our midwestern rearing, our student loafing.

I didn't feel that Haitians were alien because I liked so many of them so much. How could I not? They were troubled and full of fun— just what a fellow needed. They had the gift of the Caribbean morning sun on dew, to bring all of creation into sparkle. Although my wife and I didn't know it yet, our marriage was a fragile vessel to set sail amid the persuasive, steady Haitian drumbeat of pleasure and risk.

Years later, I'm still explaining Haiti to myself. Probably I'm still explaining myself to myself, too. But as they say in that land crumpled in God's hand, beyond the mountain lies another mountain. And beyond any explanation lies another explanation.

CHAPTER
TWO

Americans
in the Port of Princes:
The Early Fifties

The little fellow does what he can;
the big fellow does what he wants.

—Haitian proverb

Every creature in the sea eats people;
it is the shark which bears the bad name.

—Haitian proverb

MY WIFE and daughters had come out of the coolness of an airplane onto a road where donkeys plodded and peasant women, market-bound, were carrying their loads of vegetables or coffee on their heads. My wife noted that this was different from Paris and Cleveland. Ann and Judy rode with the easy curiosity of children into a new world. An airport beggar greeted us by putting out her hand, "Geev-me-fiave-cents-Meester," and then joined us in laughter because I had no hand free of babies, goods, papers. Beggars had not yet become desperate and insistent.

What nourished wayfarers was the taste for strange. The traditional joys of tropical tourism—swimming, sunning, rumming, sexing, and writing postcards home—seemed to make contact with the known world, but this Garden of Eden had fallen into deep disrepair. The Republic of Haiti, a Caribbean island nation the size of Maryland, mountainous, sea-bordered except for the frontier it shared with the Dominican Republic, was so densely populated, even then, that the visitor found it difficult to relieve himself by the side of the road without a crowd of peasants materializing out of the brush to observe his achievement. Born of a slave revolt unique in history, the chief characteristic of Haiti's career has been a nervous alternation between occasional reformers and ephemeral tyrants who have used their rank as the means to personal fortune. Freed from some of the stunting of colonialism, Haiti has given birth to many gifted and powerful individuals, but the nation has never succeeded in developing a stable government serious about educating the illiterate mass and consistent in attempting to raise the standard of living of one of the world's poorest and most long-suffering peoples.

In principle, Haiti was a black nation, French in language, Catholic in religion, democratic in government. In practice, Haiti in 1953 was a collection of 3½ million blacks ruled by a largely mulatto upper class; its business was controlled by the so-called elite and by foreigners; the people spoke Creole and, except for about 8 percent of the population, did not understand, read, or write French. The people were profoundly rooted in the celebrations of the voodoo pantheon. Defiant plantation slaves named Macandal and Boukman were among the precursors of revolution in the late eighteenth century—they were also *houngans,* voodoo priests, summoning revolt with drums and fires. They were tortured and broken by the French; they burned and tortured in return. After independence came in 1804, against a Napoléon Bonaparte at the height of his powers, Haiti adopted a model constitution—interrupted by brutal kings, emperors, and ephemeral presidents just passing through. Occasional reformers and patriots kept the ideals of justice and freedom flickering. By the 1950s, under elegantly inscribed laws, Haiti was democratic in form and a military dictatorship in fact.

Some of the first leaders of the Haitian slaves against their French masters had fought earlier at Savannah in the American Revolution. The motives for rebellion in Haiti were the misery and the sublime injustice of slavery. The genius of Toussaint L'Ouverture, the philosopher slave, and the other leaders who finally brought victory in 1804 was kindled by the same ideas of the Rights of Man that justified the turmoil in Paris and Boston.

Despite ideals shared in the declarations of independence for the United States and Haiti, official American policy, often made by slaveholders, remained deeply hostile to the new black nation. Haiti's black slave leaders, Toussaint L'Ouverture, Dessalines, and Christophe, and later the mulatto general Pétion, acted with skill, persistence, and a spirit of self-sacrifice, first in expelling the French, then in initiating the new state among the ashes and ruins.

Thomas Jefferson expressed the fear that Haitians might invade the United States in order to free American slaves. During the first hundred years of Haitian independence, the United States stayed aloof from the affairs of Haiti, which was treated as an untouchable among the nations, except to warn away any Europeans who seemed to be looking for naval bases in the Caribbean. Haiti's commerce and official culture were still linked with France. The Haitian ruling class preserved sentimental ties despite the bitterness of slavery, the blood-baths of the war for freedom, the crippling ransom eventually paid for the lost plantations. The sons of rich Haitians, perhaps bearing the blood of both Norman nobility and Guinean princes in their veins, went to school at the Lycée Stanislas and the Sorbonne in Paris.

Then, in 1915, the integration of Haiti into American hemi-spheric affairs began with the military occupation of Haiti by Ameri-can Marines. The public explanation for the occupation involved disorders in Port-au-Prince. President Vilbrun Guillaume Sam, follow-ing a massacre of his political opponents in prison, had just been torn to bits by a mob in the street; presidents before him had come and gone like the wind, poisoned, blown up in their palaces, regularly subtracted from office by irregular means. The more compelling reason for the American Navy's steaming into the harbor concerned a debt which the National City Bank of New York wanted to make sure would be col-lected and which was, in fact, paid out of the customs receipts.

A just appraisal of the occupation, finally ended by Franklin Delano Roosevelt's "Good Neighbor" policy, should include progress in public health, road building, fiscal organization. A medical school was developed. At the same time, the Haitian spirit was affronted by an occupying power which chose Southern Marines for duty in Haiti because "they know how to deal with darkies." The memoirs of American officers and diplomats during this period make depressing reading. The Paris-educated elite, accustomed to being the master in its own house, suffered insults; the peasantry suffered from the forced labor gangs organized by the Americans to build roads—this seemed close to the slavery which Haitians have never forgotten. Military force was a poor teacher of the democratic process.

After years of sentimental efforts to relate the Haitian to the French economy, the occupation ended with Haiti now fixed as an economic pendant to the United States. Coffee, the chief money crop, finally found its natural market.

How comfortable was Haiti in this conjunction of its destiny with a profoundly different culture? Not very.

Where was the place in Haitian life of the Americans living in Haiti? On a distant edge.

In this "tropical paradise," formerly "pearl of the Antilles," the foreign resident was as free as a person could be, almost exempt from normal laws. He was also constrained and excluded from the secret life which surrounded him.

The long shadow of the United States was a protective mantle for the American visitor. He felt it when he made a traffic error and was whistled down by a cop who then, seeing he was American, waved him on if his victim could walk away. The Haitian government charged the United Nations $150 for a baby killed by a careless chauffeur. This may have been a fortune to the bereaved parents—to most Americans, a rather inexpensive baby. That immensely moving Haitian hospitality—almost any peasant who had it offered coffee to a stranger, and if he needed a place for the night, the peasant would put his family outdoors and give the traveler his hut—was especially tender toward Americans.

Invitations to the exclusive clubs came readily to the visitor, while *nouveaux riches* Haitians, who may have had every personal merit, were kept waiting until their children made a brilliant marriage into the right family to prove themselves with the elite. An American slid easily as a guest among elite society, there to play tennis or politics with people whose names dated back to the time of the court of Jean-Jacques Dessalines, a brilliant general in 1804, later a ferocious and doomed emperor. A Haitian whose wealth was new, whose skin was dark, and whose family was unknown would be voted down by the admission committee of the Cercle Bellevue. Some upper-class Haitians had dark skins; some lower-class Haitians had light skins; the matter was complicated by history and connection. Finicky genealogists ranked ancestry from black toward increasing infusions of whiteness with such terms as sacatra, griffe, marabou, mulâtre, quarteron, métif, mamelouc, quarteronné, and finally the sang-mêlé who was supposed to have only a validating trace of heroic African blood. The workaday criteria for class distinction were color of skin, angle of nose, twist of hair, curl of lip, although all were proud of their slave ancestors who united to win freedom.

Occasionally American blacks came to visit a society where racism had been eliminated. Sometimes an adventurous black businessman would bring his money for investment, as did one young man who had the idea of importing dry-cleaning equipment so that the Haitian elite would not need to air-ship their uniforms, suits, and dresses to Miami for this service.

Both black and white visitors found permutations of racism for which they were unprepared. I went sailing with the beautiful daughter of a former President who proudly informed me that there were no Negroes in her family.

"Do you mean you're descended from an infinite series of mulattos?"

"Oui."

Yet there were also traditional elite black families which jealously guarded their African purity, such as the Mars family, of which a world-renowned member was Jean Price-Mars, author of the most influential Haitian book, a work of anthropology and history called *Ainsi Parla l'Oncle—Thus Spake the Uncle.* When I came calling, invited for afternoon tea, I found a teasing old man, fond of French puns and wordplay, agreeing vigorously when I said my only recourse was to play the buffoon. He said it wasn't my fault that I hadn't learned French and Creole as a child. He was in his nineties and still had much to do, but he didn't mind taking an hour out of his day to laugh at the visiting American student.

His son, the psychiatrist Louis Mars, wrote a book, *Voodoo et Hysterie,* which argued that voodoo supported mental health by providing socially accepted expression to impulses which cause neurosis and psychosis in others. A person can legitimately change sex during possession as part of a ceremony, enacting the opposite-sex spirit which has come to inhabit his or her body. I saw shy people become bold, repressed people show anger—the warlike cries of Ogoun Feraille or the cold murderous rage of Baron Samedi. When they came out of the trance, their friends and family would bathe and soothe them, consoling them for the god's trick. Sometimes they were teased and treated as part of the comedy of voodoo, especially when a powerfully macho man was seized by Grande Erzulie, the great female god sometimes represented as a raunchy Virgin Mary. This is called becoming the god's horse, and is related to the expression "straight from the horse's mouth." You are ridden by the god. You speak the truth the god gives you, whether you want to or not.

Louis Mars, under Papa Doc, took jobs as the Haitian delegate to the United Nations and ambassador to the United States. Better if he had remained a practicing psychiatrist.

Fortuné Bogat, sometimes known as "Le Sénégalais," the Senegalese, was a very black Haitian who had risen to wealth and power from his early days as a taxi driver. Tall, graceful, imperious, and a collector of women, Bogat was a charmer with an edge of ruthlessness. He ran the General Motors and RCA franchises for all of Haiti; he owned property; he had found foreigners willing to invest in mining explorations. They found no precious metals, but Bogat always managed to find something. He was amusing, subtle, both gregarious and very private—a genius at survival. The American investors who toured the extinct volcanoes and picked their way among sliding cliffs and gorges with this guide, took his food and drink, admired his collection of paintings and sculpture, listened to his slow deep voice as it rolled on with a tone of benevolent indifference, and then begged to participate in his mining ventures, got their money's worth in the form of lessons in blue-black charisma. (Of course, it wasn't my money.)

His current wife was an American journalist; he had had wives before her and would have wives after her—the last one, when he was in his eighties, a titled Belgian woman who raised doves. She lived in Haiti because she was married to the ambassador from Belgium, a conjugal detail which had to be remedied before she and Bogat could marry and move the dovecote. The titled Belgian, in turn, married one of Bogat's daughters.

Bogat and I were friends and tennis partners. With his rumbling low voice, the elegantly furrowed masklike face carefully studying my responses, he told stories about politicians, about getting rich, about his sexual adventures; he explained Creole proverbs and meditated on black magic. He described the consternation at General Motors when he visited its headquarters in Detroit, and then how the president of

General Motors begged for shares in one of his manganese mines. "I like manganese, Chico, it doesn't sound as imaginary as gold or silver. . . ."

He recounted the events of Haitian history, many of them better than the truth, as if he had been there. When I asked, "Did you just make that up?" he would answer reproachfully: "Chico, you drink too much lemonade." He stared through his dark glasses and asked if my wife and I would like to go dancing tonight, or to swim at his *caille-paille* by the bay, his beach house, or just share a lobster, rice, and beans for dinner.

He admitted he had made one mistake in his life, an error of impatience, hastily convincing the Haitian government to declare war on Germany before the Americans did. It was the day of Pearl Harbor. But it worked out all right—the United States soon followed Haiti's lead. He smiled in the dark, recalling the impetuousness of his youth. Now, when we played tennis, he didn't need to run very much. He always seemed to know where the ball was going.

My Haitian foreign office contact—call him Albert—was exasperated by my choice in a tennis partner, the "mulatto" Fortuné Bogat. As a man who entertained the president of General Motors on visits to Haiti, Le Sénégalais was *seen* as light-skinned by those whose vision was sufficiently filtered. Envy was a color selector. *Poor mulatto—black. Rich black—mulatto.*

Within the system of classifications of race, mulatto being only the most general, wealth, the proper spouse, or connections could alter the picture. Bogat was feared, admired, resented; therefore Albert saw his blue-black skin as lighter than his own.

The black American dry-cleaning businessman, who lived for years in Port-au-Prince—a blanc who happened to be noir— eventually suffered the frequent fate of blancs who do business in Haiti. He lost his shirt in the dry-cleaning shop.

FOREIGNERS WHO knocked at the doors of Haitian society could find aristocrats like Jean Price-Mars, humorous, wizened, and wise in his old age, the philosopher heir to Toussaint, or Fortuné

Bogat, the cunning tycoon building both his fortune and his fortress of intrigue, or the handsome officers in white uniforms, sought out by the women I named the minglers, or the intellectuals of *negritude,* celebrating their African roots and making voodoo pilgrimages to the magic mountain waterfall, Saut d'Eau, or the idealists dreaming of the sun-drenched paradise which would inevitably be created by the patient and laborious spirit of the Haitian peasantry, or the artists, fun-lovers, and stringent survivors who consented to entertain visitors. What blocked entrance into Haiti, the mysteries of the place, increased the passion of those who were tempted. Haiti was a minotaur at the end of a labyrinth which either devoured the explorer or bewitched him forever. There were those who never went home.

My dearest friend, Jean Weiner, was elegant, kind, and in a permanent stately despair about "poor Haiti," and also about "my poor Herb"—the American boy too innocent to understand what corruption surrounded him. "Don't tell me you went to another party. . . . played tennis with le Sénégalais, that thief. . . . let your wife dance with those scoundrels in our, oh that stupid word, *Maison Blanche.*"

"Jean. I have sinned." Indeed, the National Palace was also called the White House.

He lifted his Benzedrex inhaler to his nose. "I am allergic to the smoke that comes out of people's ears in this place. You too are a *fumiste*—your head filled with illusion."

"Forgive me."

He sniffed and gazed at me with pity, and said, choked with wheezing and laughter, "Mes-z-amis! Quel désastre! You are becoming Haitian."

In case I didn't understand his English, he translated the word "désastre": *événement funeste.*

Port-au-Prince erased the distinction between heaven and hell. It served nicely as both, and included endless chaotic misery along with the grace, that predatory graciousness, of the wealth found as you moved up the hillsides into purer air, the Canapé Vert and Pacot districts, and then farther up toward Pétionville, the suburb of the rich. In town, the gingerbread houses of the old elite seemed to be spun out of spaghetti and lace and sugar candy, mincing and flirting and shivering in the jaws of the termites, an architectural erasure of sense. It was appropriate to a world where people flew like birds, sent messages without wire or words, sang,

> Caroline A-cao, dance till it hurts, O!
> Just dance until it hurts, O!

Streams of the poor wandered through elegant Petionville, like ants in a fine house. Harborside in Port-au-Prince, in the Martissant district, the rich established little outposts of luxury, elaborate fortress and fantasy mansions, complete with walls protected by broken glass and barbed wire. Protective servants lounged at the gates day and night.

Outside their gardens, often only a few steps away, there were *terrains vagues* of rotting mangoes, dead chickens, tangled underbrush, and charcoal cooking fires for the lean-to shacks of those lucky enough to find work as helpers to the blessed. The rich swam through this sea almost as if the poor were invisible. It was said that many elite Haitians could make love without embarrassment in a space where servants provided drinks or food or simply waited to be summoned. A friend asked, "Would you be troubled, mon cher, to embrace your wife in the presence of a dog or a chicken?" He had a Ph.D. in Philosophy and later went to teach at a university in Virginia.

The rich in Haiti today are the traditional land-holding or coffee-trading elite, or those whose now respectable families gained fortunes from long-ago thieving governments, plus the new, Duvalier-enriched military officers and bureaucrats, the Bon Ton Macoutes with their BMW's and Land Rovers, their gold chains, their coke. Pétionville is home to two or three hundred millionaires. A million dollars goes a long way in Haiti, and of course the rich don't suffer the inconvenience of taxes. They can live in a kind of luxury and privilege that makes U.S. multimillionaires envious. Occasionally an American buys a vacation house in Pétionville or Jacmel, often paying more for an imported American kitchen than for the house.

A Haitian tale tells of the creation of the world, when God kindly inquired of the three races of mankind, white, mulatto, and black, what they wanted out of life. The white man spoke up first: "I want riches, power, and dominion over everything." The mulatto considered his options and said: "I want to help the white man." And then the black thought and thought and finally shrugged, answering: "I just came along with these gentlemen."

THE CREOLE and French languages of Haiti were impregnated with Americanisms that set the teeth of visiting Frenchmen on edge. A policeman yelled, "Fais back!" (pronounced "bock"), not "En arrière." The verb for spraying a room with insecticide was "flitter," from the popular product of Standard Oil. The grammar of Creole, modeled on various African languages, was more like a simplified English than like French, although most of its vocabulary comes from French. High status words and phrases, such as "Dry Cleaning" and "Air Conditioning," were usually uttered in English rather than in the French equivalents.

The radio blared singing commercials for American toothpastes and breakfast cereals in Creole; offices, parties, dances, and dinners required clothes that were a real burden in the tropics—but gave the sufferer the badge of European culture that separated him from the peasant or laborer. To drink "visky" instead of the native rum was a manifestation of chic. A common reading of *Time* magazine or a common appreciation of Bing Crosby offered occasions for communion with the forces of power. One of the great primitive painters of Haiti, a man of enormous originality and pride, decorated his house with his own drawings, with paintings and sculpture by his friends, with relics of Catholic and voodoo art, with flowers and plants from his neighborhood—and, in the place of honor on the wall, a full-page photograph of Harold Stassen, clipped from an ancient copy of *Life*. In a voodoo temple, near a menorah with candles burning, I saw Grande Erzulie, goddess of fertility and orgasm, represented by a photograph of the winsome tap-dancing Shirley Temple. Once I saw a Damballa, the great snake god, chief among equals in the voodoo pantheon, painted with stripes and stars. *Jesus bon, mais Damballa puissant.* Jesus is good, but Damballa is powerful.

Ambivalence toward power-holders runs deep in human nature.

An American had little chance against a Haitian in a court of law. The American who started a business in Haiti without Haitian partners would suffer such strange misfortunes as to make him wish he had stayed in Delaware. An official of the Université d'Haiti told me that Haiti must import its automobiles and tractors from the States, but its textbooks and "culture" from France. A younger generation was beginning to notice that students spent their evenings outdoors memorizing Racine under streetlamps because they didn't have electricity in their houses. For many years French law, art, and manners were painted over the realities. Many Haitians could compare the styles of Bossuet and Racine; not enough could set up an electrical circuit. The emphasis on classical training, along with a disdain for technical skills, was an inheritance from the master-slave society of the colonial period. "You Americans tell us to work," the Haitian seemed to be declaring, "but we are masters now." And the master was a cultured gentleman for whom others did the work. "Sweating is a sign of ignorance."

Houseboy was a job of higher status than shoeshine boy. A worker promoted to foreman would not deign to show the men under him how to perform a task which he used to do every day. Getting the job done was foreign to the Haitian way.

Yet national habit is one matter and individual personality another. Every American in Port-au-Prince knew a few angry Haitians who defied climate, custom, and public pressure, arriving at work promptly, rigorous about their jobs, taking pleasure in accomplishment. They had a hard time. It was a reversal of the normal American rebellion against the work ethic.

Haitians sent to the States to study often found a wall of suspicion when they returned. The engineers opened shops, the educators worked as clerks because they no longer fit into "the Haitian way." Columbia and Carnegie Tech were beginning to replace the Sorbonne, but it was the graduate of French schools who won the respect due a scholar and gentleman. An agronomist who defended his American hosts was admonished with the peasant saying: "The fish trusts the water, and it is in the water that it is cooked." Nourished by a history of spite, exploitation, and prejudice, the years of suspicion were not over. Charlemagne Peralte, who led a peasant band against the American Marines and was said to have been crucified against a door, was a national hero.

Among the elite, the fine arts of political gossip and maneuver seemed even more important than lovemaking, except perhaps on Saturday nights. Every American was an FBI spy, a journalist promoting zombies and black magic, or an agent sent to do in the regime. Paranoia didn't mean hostility—they *liked* the shameless exploiter, the lying reporter, and the CIA saboteur. After all, they were guests of a proud and sovereign people. But trivial remarks by American residents, transmitted by that most rapid means of communication, the "telejiol"—telemouth, the rumor system—took on urgent political weight. The American Embassy was a control, for bad or for good, on Haitian affairs. The opposition to the military government, necessarily revolutionary, was rooted in hopes of American approval. During the absence of an American ambassador, no opposition newspaper was permitted. When the Honorable Roy Tasco Davis was appointed, two newspapers took courage again, and lo! their presses were not burned, their editors not beaten or imprisoned. But on January 8, 1954, the police broke up and carried away the printing press and type of *Haiti-Democratique*. A few days later, the editor, the deputy Daniel Fignolé, together with his printers, associates, and friends, was arrested. A student in my twenties, I was asked to intervene with President Eisenhower.

While the political gossip at a nightclub like Choucoune seemed merely playful, another sort of mischief like the flirtation, it also had consequences that affected the millions who lived outside Port-au-Prince in the perishing villages and on the terraced mountainsides with their diminishing fertility. The government just took care of itself. People danced the merengue to blaring horns, whispered in each other's ears, made their arrangements. My friend Bogat held my wife so close as they danced that she said, "Hey, Bogie, are you trying to sell me a Chevrolet?"

He answered: "Madame, I make more money selling parts."

Governance was treated like the pursuit of pleasure, an anarchic individual enterprise programmed for quick gains and diminishing stability. There was a sense of brutal frivolity in the way rulers were chosen, chose themselves, were eliminated, or eliminated their rivals. The good of the nation and of the Haitian people was evoked in exalted rhetoric, a delirium of pious French. It was comic on the surface, but those were real people, real mountains and ravines, villages and floods out there; Haiti was a history of work unrewarded, land destroyed, children born to ever-diminishing opportunities.

Later, after the long havoc of the Duvaliers—the nearly thirty-year terror regimes of Papa Doc, François Duvalier, and his son, Jean-Claude, from 1957 to 1986—the negligent corruption of General Magloire came to be remembered with nostalgia. During his reign, in 1954, a cover story in *Time* depicted him as a Haitian Eisenhower, distinguished by an affable smile, rushing to his office every morning and rolling up his sleeves to practice the arts of democracy and progress. (The chief reporter on the story, whom I drove to the airport, said, "Forgive me, Gold, I know not what I do.")

The corruption was not always negligent. The editor of *L'Aigle* was beaten by police and released to die. *Le Constitutionel,* the only newspaper which dared to criticize the regime, was closed down. Colonel Marcaisse Prosper, the chief of police, frugally managed to build a millionaire's house on savings from his $350 a month job. (He wore a diamond-studded question mark on his tie. When my wife asked him what was the question, he said a woman could never know.) A poster for the national lottery proclaimed: "The best, the only way to insure your old age! Buy a ticket in the National Lottery!" I transcribed this proclamation during one of the all-day drones on a government radio program: "People of Haiti! Here is the truth that you must believe! The General of Division Paul E. Magloire is a conqueror unequaled in history since Julius Caesar and Alexander the Great." An editorial in a newspaper stated: "Le sourire de Son Excellence est la meilleure garantie de nos libertés." The smile of His Excellency is the best guaranty of our liberties.

Two boys, surprised at night putting up an antigovernment poster, were shot by detectives when they tried to flee with the tools of their crime, paper, and a glue pot.

Smiling Paul Magloire was also called Papa. Prudent Haitians got along as best they could, but the lively merengue that became the theme of Carnival in 1954 proclaimed: "Tous les jou' m'sou"—

Every day I'm drunk, without naming its hero. My friend Morisseau-Leroy cited a proverb during this time when Haitians could still make fun of power: "When the rotten tree falls, we goats will eat its leaves."

"Money in Haiti has dried up and blown away," said Jean Weiner. The President responded to government employees offering him a bouquet of flowers: "We thank you for this spontaneous demonstration which has been so well organized." I used to see his personal bottle-holder standing next to him in nightclubs. Morrisseau assured me that he took his role as leader of the nation so seriously that he muttered "We love you" when conversing with his mistresses. But he consoled visiting Americans, "Even in 1804, there were no Communists in Haiti." It was a time of gaudiness. And Morisseau-Leroy wrote a poem in Creole:

> Tourist, don't take my picture
> Don't take my picture, tourist
> I'm too ugly
> I'm too dirty
> I'm too skinny
> My donkey is overloaded
> My house is made of straw. . .
> Your camera isn't used to such things, tourist.

Intelligent people clung to the dream of magical intervention. Some hoped for it, some feared it, everyone believed in it. In the meantime, I imagined the international do-gooders in seersucker suits on their voyages of inspection, hovering over Haiti in multinational hot-air balloons, looking for a starving child to drop a chicken on him. (Normal procedure in Haiti would be for a government official to intercept the chicken in midair and offer to sell it to the child.) The aid bureaucracies established rows of offices near the boulevard Harry-Truman, with chauffeur-driven Jeeps parked outside and the chauffeurs dozing in the heat. A UNESCO project commissioned posters to teach people to brush their teeth; and when the question of toothbrushes came up, they revised the drawings to show twigs or leaves. They also produced drawings to show hygiene after defecation and called staff meetings to debate how to indicate that the washing should be done after, not before. As a resident expert, I suggested putting a happy smile on the face of the peasant crouched in the brush. (In fact, Haitian peasants wash every chance they get.) Staffs native to a half-dozen UNESCO member states lugged authorizing memos back and forth from Port-au-Prince to Paris.

As a recipient of a fellowship to study Haitian institutions, I was interviewed by journalists in Port-au-Prince. This was not a great distinction—they would also interview vacationing starlets, cruise-ship entertainment directors, and a real estate mogul from "Phoenix dans l'état d'Arizona et sa compagnon, la belle et charmante Kitty MacDougal." In one newspaper I was credited with citing Montaigne's remark, "All culture comes from the people." It was immediately telemouthed that the visitor had put himself on the side of "the people" against "the regime," he represented official American policy, he was a paid "fomenter." I was warned by a friendly visiting officer, who complimented me on the warm eyes and gracious smiles of my wife and daughters, that further statements could result in my being "sent into exile."

While the citation from Montaigne is an unexceptional remark, if he really made it, it was not cited by me. The journalist, playing on the subtlety of readers of a controlled press, put the phrase in my mouth for reasons of his own.

Another American resident, philosopher, remittance man, and lover of twelve-year-old girls, wrote in a local newspaper that fear is an obstacle to human progress. He created a sensation among Haitians who took this to mean that they should not be afraid of trying to cast out the Magloire government. Logic has its correct procedures. Fear makes us obey. An American says that fear is bad. Ergo, the secret policy of the State Department is to help us overthrow the regime.

In fact, I think he was only sending a defiant message to his ex-wife in New Orleans.

At first, if I got lost in the maze of unmarked streets near my house, I would stop and ask for the street by name. No one knew it. Then I asked where the new white man lived, and was led home immediately by people who had never seen me before.

A TWO-HUNDRED-pound retired Florida women's prison guard, in her twill sergeant's uniform, could turn the head of a man married to the loveliest Haitian woman. A state senator down for a quick suntan deserved receptions, dinners, and an exchange of fountain pens with the President. A buyer for the notion counter of a department store became a "gros commerçant" and the pale cowboy who turned out Western stories at two cents a word was buttered up as a "grand écrivain de notre amical voisin nord-américain."

A small brown smiling person was the Chief of Staff of the Armée d'Haiti. When I complimented him on his Eisenhower jacket, that short military uniform made popular by an American general and President well-known in his time, the Haitian Chief of Staff misunderstood what I was saying. "You find?" he declared proudly. "Yes, when I go to Café-Societé downtown in your Greenwich Village, ever'body and master of ceremonie say, 'Ooh, eet ees General Eisenhower. Ooh no, eet ees the Colonel André of the Armed Forces of the Républque of Haiti, performing tour of military inspection on behalf of his beautiful countree!' "

I struggled to get a clear mental picture of Sheridan Square rising to pay tribute to the Haitian officer.

My pretty young wife and I were invited to a party at the National Palace, in which the munitions for the army were kept under guard by the President's henchers. After the party, we were offered a ride home by Colonel André. But I was abruptly pushed into one chauffeured military Buick while my wife was urged into the limousine of the Colonel. Oh-oh, I thought, this will be a contest of wills, the Hero of the Haitian Military vs. The Nice Girl from Detroit.

She arrived home an hour later, grumpy but probably not as annoyed as the Chief of Staff. Yes, he had attempted seduction in the limo, and things got a little difficult. So she stuck her finger down her throat and threw up on his Eisenhower jacket.

The Colonel was irked with us for weeks. In those days, a person had to send his "jacket-Eisenhower" by plane to Miami for the careful dry cleaning that fine garments deserve. But our friendship resumed, due to the intimacy of the world of Port-au-Prince, our desire not to go into exile, the Chief of Staff's patriotic will to preserve good relations between two great Caribbean powers.

THE THOUSAND or so American residents, mostly located in the capital, fell into several categories. First, the commercial and diplomatic residents who led the familiar life of American officialdom abroad. They were assigned to a job; did it; then went home. Contact with Haiti was kept to a minimum. The American country club had recently admitted its first Haitian members, but the usual social life of these Americans was one of Ping-Pong and poker, sewing bees and bazaars, and as little socializing as possible with the locals. Of course, the avoidance of relationship was a kind of relationship. Haitians suspected race prejudice, and it did nothing to improve feeling between the two peoples, but American businessmen and diplomats lived like this all over the world. They solved the problems of living in Haiti by not really living there.

Then there was a small number of former Marines and American Army men who stayed on after the occupation. These men, usually marrying and otherwise Haitianizing themselves, were perhaps the most secure of the foreigners.

Another group included the American women who married Haitians. Living in a black world did not retire the problems of intermarriage. These women had families, friends, and their own pasts abroad, and they were usually unprepared for the homegrown race prejudice. What did the American woman do when her husband forbid their coffee-colored children to play with the black children next door? She was marrying into a culture that provided continual alienation. These rebellious women also sometimes found themselves the envy of their American friends, having taken exotic, French-accented husbands with special attributes of attractiveness and fortune. The Haitian upper class that was interested in lightening its children's skin was an elite of considerable charm and, often, ability.

A small group of Americans merely floated on the island. The bohemians attracted by sun, sea, glamour, and cheap rum generally did not stay long. The perplexities of life in a world that was African and French and something else besides, difficult to penetrate, usually sent them back to the more familiar exotisms of Mexico or Europe. While the qualities of weird, magical, and primitive were tourist attractions, they presented challenges to the usual American cheap & easy rider abroad. Café talkers had trouble finding a café. Elite snobbery mostly excluded foreign men in search of casual adventure. Creole maidens were lovely, but their fathers were all crack shots. Peasant girls, or the ones found in the bars named after American presidents—the G. Washington, the A. Lincoln, the W. Harding— were more popular among sailors and lethal drinkers.

I suppose my wife and I, with our two little girls, were members of a subcategory of the bohemian floaters—the international students, anthropologists, askew Francophiles or wanderers in Africa or the Caribbean, artistic seekers who had answered the rumor that here was a place like none other. A French composer came one summer in his winter tweeds, wan, frustrated by love, blocked in pores, chain-smoking, assiduously spreading the word that he was a misunderstood genius. When the rumor finally got around in its distorted form that he was *not* a genius—it took a year—he went wanly home. An American painter lived in a cottage near the Grand Hotel Oloffson and supported her Haitian poet lover by making "voodoo paintings" for tourists. She called herself "Carole Carcassonne," and when her grown children came to visit, they asked, "Ma, what kind of name is that? Why don't you call yourself Feffer like the rest of us?"

"I'm having an experience," she said. "Treat me with respect. I'm a mambo."

"What the hell's that, Mother?"

"A female voodoo priest. I'll put a charm on you if you don't behave."

Another lover, a fellowship student like myself, threatened the wife of a French UNESCO official with suicide unless she shared his revelation. Forms of homicide were favorite means of persuasion among foreigners frustrated by language difficulties. They had danced the merengue together and he took this as a kind of promise.

She referred the scholar to her husband, who listened patiently to the American graduate student's avowal and threat, took it under advisement, and then answered, "Eh bien, Monsieur, allez-y. Je recommande la mer." ("Go ahead, dear Sir. I recommend drowning.") It took work for Americans to connect. We were honored, too-much honored guests whose slightest mistakes were disillusioning to our hosts. Inadvertent slights, such as forgetting that the novelist Jacques Roumain belonged in the company of Dostoyevsky, Tolstoy, and Flaubert, resulted in jittery little wars. Any island is a walled city, and this one was walled by more than the sea. It was a society supported by nerves and daily pleasures, with little hope for the future; an intense, a tragic way to live. I still need little sleep in Haiti.

Americans separated from their own realities were similar everywhere. They got a little goofy. They needed to decompress, and then perhaps, if travelers and not tourists, to compress in a different way. We forgot about Arthur Godfrey and the New York Yankees. Television had not yet come to Haiti. U.S. newspapers arrived late or not at all, especially if there was news from Haiti in them. At the university I used to see the editors of the Haitian newspapers lined up to get their money from the government; it came from the education budget.

We had to find sources of distraction different from the warm bath of American routines. Haitian art, poetry, literature, and dance were based on rich traditions in Africa, in voodoo, in a tragic and glorious history. Along with the intense smells and weathers, the storms and languors, there came the thought that not only Haitians live on the brink. In the postwar Eisenhower fifties, blandness had not spread as far as this island.

Longtime American residents ran the risk of mere expatriation, moving off, opting out of families and society, becoming distant from themselves. A whiff of vagueness in the expatriate is familiar to travelers everywhere. Pompous self-importance seemed more virulent, and was a frequent entertainment among the failed diplomats who were sometimes sent to ambassadorships to Haiti as farewell gifts just before they slipped into retirement—sometimes after they had slipped into senility. I took a census of ambassadors with little rivulets of saliva running from the corners of their mouths.

Sometimes officials posted to this nonessential sovereign nation found a peculiar satisfaction in selling their clothes and being picked up drunk and naked in the brothel called La Frontière. Maybe it was the heat, the humidity, the responsibility, or emulation of Haitian skills at improvising both survival techniques and a good time. People tended to make the best of things when they didn't make the worst of them.

In 1954 I watched the reenactment of the battle of Vertières, which had taken place 150 years ago, in 1804. The wife of the French ambassador burst into tears at the loss of this "perle des Antilles"— still another pearl fallen out of the French crown—while the Haitian spectators applauded the gallant act of the French general, who stopped the battle and sent out a fresh horse for Toussaint L'Ouverture, whose mount had been shot out beneath him. The pageant was enacted on the actual grounds of the battle, in the north near Cap Haitien. In rehearsal, the first actor had been shot by the marksman whose job it was to shoot the horse. Now the understudy shot his own horse with a concealed pistol.

While the French ambassador's wife wept to discover that Haiti was no longer a French possession—the news seemed to come slowly to these outposts—a local photojournalist ran about taking pictures of celebrities and those who thought they were celebrities. Film was expensive and I knew this operator was stingy. He kneeled, snapped, went on to the next happy dignitary. "What are you going to do with all those pictures?" I asked.

He whispered in my ear as he passed on to the Guatemalan Chef de Mission: "No film in the camera."

Since Haiti was not a major post, many countries tended to send diplomats at the end of their careers or not scheduled to have much of a career. Under President Eisenhower, an American ambassador paid tribute to his Haitian hosts at a banquet by rising and, in lieu of a toast, singing Stephen Foster's "Old Black Joe."

But the official receptions, outings to celebrate Pan American Day, the Fourth of July, Bastille Day, Christmas, Carnival, various birthdays of heroes and spouses of heroes, dates in the glorious past and inaugurations of glorious projects for the future were nearly continuous. My friend with the empty camera definitely wanted to be invited.

For Americans and other foreigners, Haiti offered the kind of freedom called license. The brilliant irreality—real enough, of course, for those whose entire lives were on this island—tended to deepen sleep or violently wake a person up. I was one of those wayfarers from elsewhere, vexed by dreams.

IN THE cool of an afternoon, I was walking up into the traditional Pacot district, hilly and flowered, with walls like those of Fiesole or Jerusalem, hidden gardens from which chattering and laughter could be heard. There was an open gate and I looked in, past a trellised corridor of vines, toward a courtyard where a cracked and eroded fountain stood. There was no water, but a bit of green moss clung to the stone, remembering water. I heard doves from a dovecote. Charcoal smoke arose from a stove in the courtyard, dinner being prepared, and the lady of the house, or her daughter, suddenly appeared at a window.

I was ready to shuffle and apologize for prying, but she just smiled and waved. We didn't know each other and wouldn't meet. I shrugged and she shrugged. I fell in love and she disappeared from view.

And then I continued my walk, coming back in time for dinner with my wife and daughters.

CHAPTER
THREE

Loupgarous
Werewolves
Hobgoblins

W HEN I hiked the mountain above Port-au-Prince, in Kenscoff, Furcy, and the Forêt-des-Pins, I was never alone. There were stretches of woods in these cool highlands, but they were inhabited by people tending coffee bushes or vegetables, their onions or tomatoes, alongside the precious streams. Or there was the clang of machetes cutting down the trees to burn for charcoal or to make room for a few more vegetables—also making more room for the erosion that was killing the mountain. Sometimes I heard the rhythmical chant of a *coumbite,* the cooperative work ritual, as neighbors cleared a bit of land or put up a hut for a new family. The hills also gave birth to new rocks as the earth at its slow boil cast them up, and again the coumbite set out, singing and drumming the ritual songs, to clear a space once more.

If I stopped to do anything interesting, such as sniffing the still-sweet air, eyes appeared to watch me. If I decided to pee, naked children, perhaps with a stick of sugarcane in their mouths, marveled that the forest was full of such miracles.

When I approached the house of a peasant—the caille-paille, that hut of straw held together by mud and hope—there was a ritual of greeting in the best of form.

"Honneur!" called out my host, the master of the caille-paille, bowing.

"Respect!" I replied, bowing in my turn.

By appearing in this place, I was already his guest. I was made welcome, good comfort shared. If there was coffee, I drank that dark rich brew. If there was *clairin*—a raw white rum, cloudy and suspect, often mixed with grapefruit juice to make a *coktel,* or mixed with honor and respect to make an aphrodisiac—I drank this, too, although even the most devoted veteran of Haitian hospitality seldom regrets the lack of clairin abroad. Most people, especially in the country, led lives barely touched by history and the restlessness normal to cities.

Yet spirits, werewolves, spooks, and hobgoblins, the beasts of the Haitian hills, haunted this overcrowded little patch of island. The demons did service for those who harnessed them; they also served themselves. My house was robbed once by someone who stole a pair of shoes, a knife, some sugar and flour. Instead of installing locks, Alaice, our houseboy, put a lizard in a cage at the front door, letting it be known that this was the soul of a burglar the *blanc* had captured. There were no more thieves in my house. Another time, visiting a *hounfor,* voodoo temple, I inadvertently stepped into the sanctum sanctorum, where no unprepared soul may venture. "Now you will die!" sadly announced my host.

"Before I die, let me see Damballa Ouedo."

"Unblessed you cannot see Damballa! Too much for mortal eyes!"

"But I'm to die anyway, so what harm is there?"

The priest appreciated the logic. He shrugged and unrolled the portrait of the great snake god from its ritual lodging in a Coca-Cola bottle. It was that photograph, clipped from a magazine, dog-eared, frazzled, and woebegone, of Harold Stassen.

A mixture of Christian and African beliefs, voodoo is a religion with rich ceremonies, rituals, observances, and consolations. It offers a view of the world and a hope for the future. And alongside voodoo there is also the parallel world of white magic and black magic, the system of curses and devils.

During the early fifties, the mahogany-burning train that kept a daily schedule—sometimes—from Port-au-Prince to Saint Marc made its last run, and thus ended the history of railroading in Haiti. I spent a day on the train, along with crabs on strings, pigs, goats, turkeys, geese, chickens, and the market ladies riding herd on them, and talked with Monsieur Luc Pierre-Paul, Conducteur-en-Chef de la Compagnie des Chemins de Fer de la République d'Haiti. The title gave him the right to use his teeth on the tickets, since his punch had been out of order for thirteen years. He denied the foolish rumors about evil spirits interfering with the train. "That's the superstition of foreigners! President Vincent chased all the witches out of Haiti. Of course, we do have to watch out past Trou Zombi, where the souls of the poor departed railway workmen live. If we forget to salute them as we go by, they come out and put their hands on the couplings and bump us all together. A disgusting racket it makes, and disturbs the chickens. But there are no zombies!" He put up his finger against the suspicion that witches or zombies could interfere with his train. A few jealous ghosts, yes; but superstition, no. "He who spits in the air will get saliva on his nose."

One afternoon, after tennis with Fortuné Bogat, we went to his automobile and found a chicken on the front seat of his Buick, feathers plucked out and the carcass painted blue. This was a serious curse. Bogat went into a foaming rage, falling to the ground; and then, a few moments later, recovered and dusted himself off. "But you don't believe in black magic," I said.

He stared at me and shrugged. "Of course I don't. But it's bad for business if people know I've been cursed."

He was a millionaire, flew his own plane, adeptly entertained American tycoons and extracted investment for imaginative mining ventures—a clever, worldly, charming operator. "Le Sénégalais" was a good tennis player and a great dancer; I liked tennis with him; others—the women I called the minglers—liked to dance. For a few years his wife was an American journalist.

Did he believe in black magic?

Did he think he believed, and not believe? Or did he believe, and think he didn't believe? His eyes were suddenly red and swollen.

The Haitian parent still warns his family against the werewolves that cruise at dusk in automobiles without license plates, leaping out to gobble up the souls of unlucky children. Kids at a birthday party automatically choose the piece of cake farthest away on the plate— why be turned into a zombie? A woman of the elite makes fun of the *baka*, the *loupgarou*, those imps, werewolves, and malevolent spirits of the dead, and the tricky voodoo *loa,* gods; she was educated in Paris and had an automatic dishwasher in her kitchen; but one evening, this lovely and witty person told me she saw with her own eyes a peasant woman kneeling and praying in a field, carrying a plate in her joined hands. A star shook itself loose from the sky and fell into the plate.

"No, no, this is not superstition," she insisted. "It's just that the Haitian prays harder than most people. Our need is greater."

PIERRE MARCELIN lived and drank in a small house in the hills above Port-au-Prince. With his brother, Philippe-Thoby Marcelin, he wrote three novels, *Canapé-Vert, The Pencil of God,* and *The Beast of the Haitian Hills,* translated into English, praised by Edmund Wilson. He came of an elite family that included Supreme Court judges, ambassadors, and presidents among his ancestors, but he had turned his back on the usual preoccupations of a society that preferred Saturday nights at country clubs or dancing at the Choucoune in Pétionville.

He passed these years in isolation from his family and class. He said he had written all his books. He preferred to stay in his little house—more like a cottage or hut—and he walked the country roads. He had become the collector, he said, of conversations. He listened and asked. The ambassador-judge-president's descendant embraced his African history, not in the western way of his novels, making romance of Haitian folklore, but as a country gatherer and rememberer. Sometimes I strolled with him; we went to voodoo ceremonies together. Often we just sat in his hutlike little house as the tropical day rapidly closed down, and remained sitting by the light of an oil lamp or by no light at all, and he sipped from his glass of rum and described what he had recently gathered.

And then sometimes on those nights in 1953 and 1954, he picked up his *cocomacaque,* his stick, and we walked out to gossip about black magic and loupgarous with whomever we might meet on the mountain paths.

Haitian loupgarous are not werewolves in the European tradition. They are once-human beasts whose souls have been devoured. The demons continue to use the bodies of men when it serves their purposes. Your best friend might turn out to be a loupgarou, which sometimes accounts for deceit and betrayal. An unworthy neighbor gets rich while the rats are eating your corn? He's a loupgarou. The coffee speculator manages to buy your few handfuls for sixty cents? Loupgarou at work. A thuggish layabout wins the love of the prettiest little girl? Watch out, a loupgarou will do anything.

The peasants were so accustomed to their lives of marauding struggle that they viewed any good luck with suspicion. A man has the money to build a new house because he's a loupgarou. And then if a baby falls sick, the loupgarou is eating a soul. Sometimes a house goes up in flames when the neighbors suspect a traffic in souls with the devil. Even a rich loupgarou might keep his traditional straw roof, and it burns nicely.

Black magic helps to explain injustice. Therefore it also helps to preserve the sense that justice exists, is even possible for poor people.

There are three ways to become a loupgarou: by voluntarily joining them, by having one's soul gobbled up because the usual charms have failed, or by becoming a zombie first and then being transformed into a loupgarou. Zombies looked to me like what others might call catatonic schizophrenics. They are pretty depressed, unavailable to the normal human pleasures, such as gambling, loafing, singing, or lovemaking. A man accused of making a zombie, stealing his soul, has a lot of explaining to do. In addition, he must keep salt from the lips of the slave or it will really die. R.I.P.

Sometimes a zombie is changed into a loupgarou to do an animal's job. Sometimes a loupgarou devours a soul just for the fun of it. It's a satisfying revenge on an enemy. The loupgarou is a spiteful creature and it pays to protect yourself and your children.

The peasants are thoughtful; they know the gods would not normally permit speculators, usurers, and petty officials to grow sleek on their flesh. They are pious; Jesus and Damballa Ouedo, the great snake god, will not permit the wicked to go unpunished. The peasants are kind and hospitable. Only a loupgarou is mean and unwelcoming.

From the hills around Pierre Marcelin's house, almost every

night but especially on weekends, we could hear the drums sounding their invitation to voodoo ceremonies. On important evenings, the dirt roads were streaming with men and white-dressed women hurrying to worship. Black magic is not a part of voodoo in the same way that superstitious charms and curses are not a part of European religions—reputable folks deny them.

One Saturday night, driving along a road to a dance in honor of Papa Guede, the *loa* of phallic delight and comedy, we picked up a hitchhiker. He was carrying a stick with fresh clothes wrapped around it. The road was rough and the springs and axles of my Chevy were getting a severe test. The hitchhiker shook his head over some vicious jolts thrown in our path by loupgarous, but encouraged us with many confident smiles because the magic of General Motors and other foreign gods was riding bravely over the local demons.

Loupgarous are threatening, the prospect of being changed into a zombie is scary, but life provides protections. Both Christianity and voodoo can save a person in the everlasting. Salt, a woman more clever than the demon, or a determined Chevrolet can overcome the teasing of earthly enemies.

During one walk, a farmer told us he had seen a neighbor's bull with an unmistakably human expression. I wondered if maybe it was just a sad bull. "Then how," he demanded, "do you explain that he also had a gold tooth?" I admitted this was a problem. "So they sent the bull away to Gonaives, I'm not sure why, because we were on to the loupgarou. . . . "

If you meet a pig at a crossroads at midnight, it is very likely a loupgarou. You might try taking some earth in your left hand and holding it against your brow and saying, "Earth"; then against your chest, saying, "In earth"; then against your right shoulder, saying, "To earth return"; and finally against your left shoulder, saying, "Thou art dust, to dust thou shalt return." This might help. It should be followed with the prayer, "Jesus Christ, go thou before me, with me, after me." Drawing a circle on the ground and inscribing within it the letters "JMS" while chanting "Jesus, Man, Savior" is also recommended. I also saw these letters in indigo on the doors of houses. A person can't be too careful.

Watch out for the *cochons-sans-poils*—literally, pigs without body hair. They resemble big creamy Iowa pigs, but they are loupgarous. The doggy black Haitian pigs are the good guys.

Sometimes a horse, a sheep, especially the ones who baa at night, an owl, even a glowworm or bats can be loupgarous. One fellow, gaunt and wizened under his oversized straw hat, told us he had seen goats leaping about the road near the cemetery. Fortunately he knew the proper words to keep himself from harm. He didn't say what he was doing near the cemetery at midnight.

In the city, a "masters-of"—he had studied at Columbia University—reported sightings of the loupgarous who roam the streets in unlit cars with no license plates. Sometimes pathetic cries could be heard. Some of these city loupgarous carry macoutes, straw sacks for carrying away children, women; or if they don't want to bother with the whole person, just the soul. One female child-devouring loupgarou was known as "Little Casket" because . . . "I suppose you won't believe this, *blanc,* it's too horrible for you" . . . she went about with a little box for her prey.

"Do you know about the *gros-bon-ange?*"

I didn't know.

This is the body's double, something like the soul, but more like a shadow-cadaver.

"Do you know about the *Zobopes,* blanc?"

I was ignorant. They dress in red, they drink blood, they do horrible things, maybe I shouldn't know about them.

There are also the *bisago-ouete-peau,* the night-flying loupgarous who leave their skin behind in some nice cool place. A good friend of my friend happened to awake one night and his wife was gone. He got up to look for her. Oh-oh. Her skin lay empty near a jar of water. 'Ah, so my wife is a loupgarou. I'll teach her a lesson.' He seasoned the skin with salt, pepper, a dash of pimento. When she returned from her *vol* and stepped back into her skin, she felt a terrible burning and itching. She began to jump and yell.

Her formerly loving husband took up a wooden needle, spat three times, and shouted: "Renounce! Renounce! Malediction!" and then, filled with grief, he beat her. He was very angry. She dropped her skin and fled. He cried after her: "Go on, loupgarou, see if you can do anything, even live without your skin!"

Somehow he calmed himself enough to finish his night's sleep. But in the morning he found his wife's body beside the jar of water.

"I already told you about the cochons-sans-poil, blanc. I'll spare you a really sad story, although the ending was not so bad."

But then he told me a sad story anyway, this one about the "vlin-bindingues," loupgarous with long white gowns, tall white horns, who bend and straighten up and leap in gangs, although they can also take the form of a crow flying past. One poor fellow sold himself to this group in order to provide his young wife with riches, and he succeeded, he gave her all sorts of good things, but then he discovered that she had stolen another luxury—a lover. He brought home a gang of loupgarous and presented his wife with a claw, a pen, and a bottle of red ink. "Write your name on this claw!"

She knew what was up. She threw herself at his feet. She wept and wept. She did not want to be a loupgarou.

"I sold my own soul for you, but you betrayed me. Now write!"

"I can't, I can't, I can't!"

Well, blanc, I can see you don't believe my story. But I can prove it is true. The man is my cousin. The unfaithful wife ran to hide with her parents, but that very night she went mad, she went empty, she never spoke again, blanc. You see? She should have shown respect. She should have behaved herself.

JEAN WEINER didn't approve of my new friends. He put his Benzedrex inhaler to his nose—"I am the only man in this country allergic to sun and charcoal smoke, do you think I'm really Haitian after all?"—and said I was turning into the worst kind of Haitian he could imagine.

"What's that?"

"Anthropologue!" he cried, choking and laughing, and then apologizing for the tears that ran down his face. *Mes-z-amis!* Such are the tears of selfish laughter!"

IN BLACK magic, death is confronted and dramatized, along with the early premonitions of death—fear, defeat, enemies, loss. Thus death is made social and shared, our loneliness is relieved, the ceremonies bring communion. In voodoo the gods are propitiated together, under the guidance of the houngan but with inspiration permitted. Then the god rides the communicant; he or she becomes the god's horse; the god's words pour from the horse's mouth. The function of voodoo is to serve the gods, reconcile ourselves with the powers, to celebrate, to share life and eternity. The function of black magic is to manipulate the gods, and make them serve us.

Voodoo and black magic seem weird to outsiders. They are both weird and ordinary to believers. This awe, this familiar awe, provides some of the relief from suffering and turmoil. It brings festival to Saturday nights, and holiday nights, or whenever a believer calls up the spirits.

Mardi Gras, the Haitian Carnival that is a shrewd, guileful, and dead-earnest African joke, sets forth Haitian need in all its pain. During this traditional Christian occasion of comedy, masquerade, permitted excess, the Haitian smuggles himself back to Africa and voodoo. It is also a festival of rage. When the Christian celebration stops, it does not stop. Rara continues, the Rara bands roam the streets—a voodoo form of Carnival. The two religions collaborate in a place where many gods are needed. The Haitian mobilizes his wit in a rag-end, needle-and-thread, papier-mâché rebellion against the African ancestors who sold him, the French who bought him, the Americans who commit the sin of having power now. And most of all he laughs, sings, drums, and dances against himself for being caught by his own weakness and error.

Haiti is poor in all natural resources but the energies of imagination. The Haitian is in trouble with the world. Carnival and Rara are a way of acknowledging trouble and exorcising it. Laughing, the celebrant performs grotesque parodies of the attitudes of prayer. His need is great.

The paradoxes and terrors of Haiti's past are expressed in the weird distortions of life in Port-au-Prince. Chickens sometimes invade the grounds of the Palais National. A psychiatrist imported insulin shock as a cure for alcoholics. Businessmen perspired passionately in woolen suits, convincing themselves that they are in Paris or New York. I've seen proud clerks wearing spats and celluloid collars. Yet thieves enter houses naked, their bodies oiled, so that there was nothing, or very little, to hold them by if they were caught. Luxurious chauffeured automobiles carried women to the smart shops while the beat of the drums, heard on the edges of the city, announced a *cérémonie* in the hills for that night. The government stole from everything—including the voodoo religion.

And the hunger was—is—everywhere. At any hour of the day or night, wherever you go, people are stripping sugarcane, peeling bananas, crunching bits of fried pork, buying food, selling it at every corner, eating, and being still hungry. Even the skinny spitting Haitian lizards work their mouths constantly.

Carnival is also the chance to take revenge, against hunger. The distinguishing ritual is "déguisement"—that masking which is an unmasking. The man who fears starvation wears a bow tie made of a herring. The drinkers wrap themselves in straitjackets and follow a keeper who is really Papa Guede, god of sex and comedy. The boy who has watched people posing for snapshots in the Champs de Mars dresses himself in a sunsuit and struts belly-forward in his dream of an American tourist.

The thick press of the carnival band smells of decaying flowers. Bannered, bearing trays of candies and cakes, holding thousands of tiny kerosene lamps aloft, the bands go dancing through the streets in the evening. Drums and whistles greet the tropical night. The entire mobbed city sways under its yellow-gray twilight skies. The *vaccins,* bamboo reeds, make their hoarse piping and the drums drum and the dancers are taken by the dance.

But despite the insistence of the merengue rhythm, everyone knows what is the true justification of carnival: *déguisement.*

A bull rolls on the street, jazzing its legs, its papier-mâché horns quivering, and the automobiles of the elite cannot pass.

A man with a stocking over his head carries a sign that gives him the success of laughter wherever he walks, and therefore brings a transformation of his fate: MY FORTUNE IS LOST. I AM MISERABLE.

The Mardi Gras winds to its climax in a procession before the President of the Republic and his entourage, who watch Baron Samedi, guardian of the cemetery, leading the dead into the other world. Whispers follow the parody of wealthy Haitians, mincing and airily gesturing, magnificently overdressed except for the detail that they have no pants.

Memories of Africa and slavery stir awake once more. The mass ritual of love and sacrifice is also an exorcism of disease and death. The gigantic sick tongue turns from side to side as its bearer patrols the streets. The voodoo pig family, and the Indian chiefs annihilated by the followers of Columbus, are brought back to life. The watchers cheer the splendid military uniforms that are passed down from year to year, some of them originating in the days when the Haitian army had thousands of generals. The drums are carried down from the hills into the streets of Port-au-Prince.

And the play is complete. The thousand all-in-earnest caprices of the Haitian imagination are given their roles. The devils take the air. What irony in the fact that, watching the festival, for many years sat President-for-Life François Duvalier, former doctor, excommunicated Catholic, with his carbine across his knees. Dressed all in black, like Baron Samedi, impassive and cruel, like Baron Samedi, he was said by the telejiol to *be* Baron Samedi, and immortal. He welcomed the rumor. "Papa Doc Forever!" was the title of the carnival anthem one year.

Despite fear, it is carnival time, and everyone drinks. No one is drunk. All is permitted if sufficiently disguised. Do what you like—and anyway, what is life? The cocks crow all day. The dogs bark all night. Bark and crow yourself, or spit like a lizard. You are a free soul, a Haitian. Life is the happy pursuit of death. Love and birth are a *déguisement* of the fact of mortality; laughter is an act of defiance.

Carnival and Rara play themselves until exhaustion, and then the bands disappear into Carrefour, into Croix-des-Missions, into the slums of La Saline and Brooklyn and Cité Soleil, into Bourdon and Pétionville and all the ravines and hillsides and unmapped corners of

Port-au-Prince. Baron Samedi and the male bride and the man with the herring tie go back to the difficult work of making do with a single lonely identity. Nevertheless, the hobgoblins will have their times again as the months turn round. Their need is great; they cannot be denied.

If the Haitian has no food, no property, no chance for the future, no power, no protection against the whims of his rulers, well, he can still, with his complicated modesty, both claim and offer to others the first privilege of a free soul. Honor. Respect.

I CAME TO know a neighbor of Pierre Marcelin who lived down a muddy path hidden by dense leaves. "There are many problems in life," he said. "I see you want to understand."

"I'd like to."

"Well, these problems cannot be solved. But we can solve them."

I must have looked puzzled.

"If you think this is not true, if you do not understand, although I can see that you are listening carefully, then you are not a Haitian."

"I am not a Haitian."

"Oh, le pauvre blanc." He took my hands to comfort me.

CHAPTER
FOUR

The Renaissance of the Fifties

I ASKED PREFÈTE Duffaut why he began to paint. One night a woman appeared to him in a dream—his sister or the Virgin Mary, he was not prepared to say which—and commanded him: "Prefète! From now on you are a painter!"

First he painted on wood, on pieces of wood or planks or board; then he learned to use canvas. Life on earth was a mysterious interlude for this young man who wore odd shirts with tassels and embroidery, and tirelessly painted versions of his home village, Jacmel, water and mountains and dream bridges, Jacmel islands on towers or winding into the sky. He was calling back the home place he loved, elaborating it into a celestial Jacmel. His success bred little Duffautlings, imitating him, and years later he seemed to be imitating himself.

For Jasmin Joseph, a brickmaker, mere oblong solid bricks didn't do the trick. He began to make light-filled bricks with fantasy animals where solid mortar might have been. These sculptures—see-through bas-reliefs—were used as walls in buildings designed by Albert Mangones, a Cornell-trained architect who produced elegant houses for foreigners and wealthy Haitians, houses straddling streams, with orchid-filled atriums, guarded by dream creatures baked in a kiln by Jasmin Joseph. The brickmaker's gargoyles protected the houses against both harm and boredom. Later, still protecting the world against solemnity and boredom, Jasmin Joseph began painting his animal metaphors.

The visions of former artisans, clerks, yardboys, voodoo priests came to be sold and exhibited all over the world.

DeWitt Peters, the American teacher who had fallen in love with voodoo designs and the decorations of tap-tap trucks (the common transports), drove me to the village of Croix-des-Bouquets where there was a cemetery with graves mounted by weird cast-iron crucifixes, as jagged and threatening and agonized as barbed wire. Sometimes there seemed to be figures straddling the mounds. Looking closely at this intricate ironwork above the tombs, I saw the voodoo symbols worked into the patterns. They were the creations of André Liataud, a wizened and illiterate artisan, thirty years in the trade of making conventional funeral decorations, who one day decided that no, the crucifixes should be another way, bringing in all the gods, and he made them so compelling *his* way that even the local parish church was decorated with his work. Why shouldn't there be a rooster on the cross? God suffers for all suffering, Liataud believed.

Now, of course, hundreds of artists work in rusted iron, and it's the visitor who suffers, trying to choose his purchase. The tradition of making things out of whatever materials come to hand has been a vigorous one in Haiti. At the Marché au Fer, the Iron Market, Pet Milk cans were fashioned into chandeliers, candlestick holders, toys, woven and spun and textured with color and the reflections of light.

When I read Edmund Wilson's essay on Anthony Lespès, praising his novel, I decided to try to meet Lespès. People knew him, remembered him, but nobody saw him. He lived in the hills above Port-au-Prince, on a secluded farm with unwelcoming dirt roads, no working telephone. He was a fierce and dogmatic Marxist who had studied architecture, engineering, agronomy, and now was engaged in scientific chicken and pig farming. I sent him a message, asking if I could visit, and in due course received an invitation to lunch and directions up the ruts and jolts of the mountain.

I suppose his isolation reflected some bitterness. "I stay out of the way," he said.

"Is that what you want to do?"

"I think it is better for me if I try to continue to live. Better for my chickens, who give me plenty of company—they answer when I call—and perhaps better for my nation, too."

He was a compact, leathery, brown-skinned man, courteous in the traditional elite fashion, ironic and slightly elaborate in his speech, a man who found it prudent to do most of his political discussing with chickens. He was proud of his pigs. He was trying to develop more economic methods of penning and feeding. He had a small library of manuals in French, English, and Russian.

His judgment of the class from which he came, that airily Francophile little group of dandies and dandettes, went beyond disappointment to contempt. A couple of revolutions back his opinions had earned him a vacation in prison. While locked up, he wrote a novel that even his political opponents seemed to admire. He wanted nothing to do with Port-au-Prince, but hoped an example of scientific farming might help his country in a way that his writings could not. He still believed in words. He was preparing a new book for publication "someday," and as we ate under a trellis in a garden, he smiled and said: "I'm raising poetry and pork. I can market the pork."

A
T THE Théâtre de Verdure, an outdoor concert pavilion, I met a skinny thirteen-year-old who played the flute for the Troupe Folklorique Nationale. No one knew where he found a flute, an instrument barely known in Haiti, although pipes made of bamboo and American Marine whistles are used in voodoo ceremonies, Carnival and Rara bands, and the volunteer cooperative work teams, "coumbites." The boy had been improvising fantastic melodies, accompanied by the drums of such masters as Ti-roro, an ageless performer who played the drums and the buffoon for tourists, and Ti-Marcel and Celestin.

Some of the writers, Felix Morisseau-Leroy, Jean Brierre, Roussan Camille, Pierre Marcelin, his brother Philippe-Thoby, Jean Price-Mars, and others were known to foreign residents, partly because of their elite origins. The creativity of ordinary people was a continual revelation. We don't expect the poor and illiterate to have a sense of form, style, the talent for communicating their joys and sufferings. The stories told by peasants, the songs improvised by servants, accompanied by swish of broom or percussion of hand against pot, the teasing of the nearby world made the passing of time a continual re-creation of reality. Life was judged and interpreted by a people whose survival on the edge did not yet defeat them, and perhaps, despite all their trials, never would. With what delicacy of feeling flowers were set out everywhere, even if the only vase was a rusting Pet Milk or Crisco can. People confirmed the joy of being alive—still alive despite everything—with continual eruptions of playfulness, as if Carnival and Rara could be made to inhabit the entire year. ("To nod your head *yes* won't break your neck, friend.")

Wayfarers greeted each other on the roads, stopped to tell the story of the day, went about their business after clasping hands. A former president remarked about the cultural parodying of things French: "When France sneezes, Haiti gets the whooping cough." The laughter of his friends, joining the yipping of dogs and the kokoriko of the cocks everywhere, was the daytime equivalent of voodoo's violent putting together of what the troubles of life sundered.

The men on the road gangs danced to the music of shovels. Last night they may have been twitching and exalted in a voodoo ceremony. Tomorrow they might be running in the streets to drive out a president.

Amid the conflicts and sufferings, a renaissance of art was taking place. Seldon Rodman, an ardent publicist, described a festive occasion: the return of a painting from a framer to the Centre d'Art, escorted through the streets of Port-au-Prince by a singing, strutting, cheering crowd.

DeWitt Peters was the catalyst for this folk movement. He saw the possibilities of the decorations on a door, on a café wall, tap-tap buses, on a few bits of board or canvas. He hunted up the artists, gave them materials, a few dollars, and spoke like the actualization of Prefète Duffaut's vision: "Paint!" The first generation of painters, Obin, Hyppolite, Bigaud, Bazile, Gourgue, and others, became famous, are collected internationally and by museums. The Obin brothers had already been painting their visions in Cap Haitien; Hector Hyppolite, a voodoo adept, had been making his designs as an expression for the gods. What the Americans did was bring them rewards and an audience from abroad.

Without foreigners like DeWitt Peters, founder and director of the Centre d'Art, Seldon Rodman, involved as a journalist, collector, and gallery owner, and Bishop Alfred Voegeli, who had the courage to commission the murals for the Episcopal cathedral in Port-au-Prince, the gift of Haitian painting might have been lost. The cathedral murals marked a crucial step in the evolution of the artists. The project gave them both freedom and responsibility for a sustained personal effort. Duffaut placed a religious procession on a road in Jacmel. Wilson Bigaud joined voodoo symbols and the teeming poverty of twentieth-century Haiti in a portrait of a lounging, prissily cigarette-smoking Haitian bourgeois. Philomé Obin depicted the great figures of the gospel—all but Judas—as black. Judas looked like a slick New Yorker. Obin was telling us something.

Later, Seymour Bottex, a painter from Cap Haitien, depicted a Nativity with a lonely Joseph standing off in a corner, eating a banana. This painter was a deep thinker. He chose the right fruit. He discovered the joke of a husband's irrelevance when his virgin wife gives birth.

Just as Haitian exiles, doctors, teachers, engineers, have nourished French-speaking communities in Africa and Canada, Haitian artists have exported their discoveries to other Caribbean islands. On visits to Jamaica and Martinique, I found painters doing "Haitian primitives." In Martinique the popular music on the radio was sung in a Creole I could understand—often traditional Haitian songs and the year's Carnival music, complete with Haitian political satire. Relatively prosperous under French rule, the culture of Martinique seemed tame despite a few distinguished individuals like Aimé Cesaire and Edouard Glissant. It seemed that freedom, even as ambiguous as it was in Haiti—perhaps only the myth of freedom, the legend of the slave revolt—lit the fires. Martinique had a functioning national electrical grid. But after the pepperiness of Haiti, the people of this French overseas department appeared docile.

In most Haitian painting there is a tension between the formal weight of traditional "primitive" subjects and the brilliance of the tropical palette. In the stuff turned out for cruise-ship visitors, Haitians learned to do palm trees, beaches, bare-breasted Creole maidens; but oddly enough, in the heaps of paintings stacked up in the Marché au Fer, among the schlock and imitations, innocent treasures of personal obsession could be discovered. The uncharted area between formal skills and the people's visions, which kept Haitians separated from themselves for centuries, was beginning to find expression. Voodoo ceremonies still included Latin ritual and the mincing steps of the court dancers at Versailles among African paroxysms and stylizations. When I visited André Pierre, painter and priest, in his *hounfor* (temple), he had a menorah with lit candles on his altar. This transplanted people, with its infusions from other transplanted cultures, was living at a rich crossroads.

Admiring a new work by Wilson Bigaud, I asked why he put a snake on the roof of a house. The snake had ducked its head down through a window and was gazing at the girl inside. Bigaud smiled sweetly, intending to be helpful. And so he was: "My imagination told me to. That's what I saw. *Moi je suis le peintre.*"

Me, I'm the painter. And so he was. He meant what another Haitian friend said more explicitly: "We're for purifying our water, but we want to drink *our* water. We take from others how to do what we already want to do."

This generation of painters—Philomé Obin, Wilson Bigaud, Castera Bazile, Prefète Duffaut, Enguerrand Gourgue, Jasmin Joseph, who came just after the precursor, Hector Hyppolite—explored familiar scenes from daily life, familiar fantasies from Christianity, voodoo, or black magic. Gourgue especially dealt in devils and zombies. The power and energy were not achieved by opinions about the world. They expressed what they lived, their reality.

I used to watch voodoo priests stand with a handful of grain, pause a moment, and then with swift precise gestures trace symbols and images on the packed earth floor. They were painting or sculpting with the grain guided through their fingers. From these ritual *vévés*, god-inspired flour drawings in the temple, to deliberate creation of images by artists planning and judging their materials—this was a significant step. It was the passage from celebration of a historic passion, a group myth, to individual response. The sense of personality broke through. Their success in communicating with foreigners created opportunities for corruption of the original impulse, of course; it also gave isolated souls the chance for exhilarating achievement. Sometimes the painters chose to work in group houses or in courtyards near galleries, seeking patronage, approval, and shared learning. Sometimes, as in the case of Gourgue, the painter hid out and carried his labors to town like a Madame Sara toting her vegetables down from the hills.

I bought a painting by Gourgue of a zombie being led by a peasant out of the graveyard under a glowing midnight sky. It was ominous, unsettling, a convincing nightmare. Through the vicissitudes of divorce, the painting disappeared, but many years later I found it in the permanent collection of the Milwaukee Art Institute. I tried to trace its path to Milwaukee, but the route was as devious as the myth of the zombie itself. The donor just repeated, "It's mine." I explained that I was only curious. I wasn't accusing him of illegal acquisition. "I gave it to the museum. It was mine," he said. "But *before* you had it—I'm not saying you did anything wrong—it came from someplace." The Wisconsin philanthropist shook his head. "I've always had it," he said. Perhaps, indeed, like other elements of voodoo and Haitian black magic, it had always existed. But it was a discovery to learn that Milwaukee and my divorce were all part of the Haitian empire.

Gourgue used to visit me, and sometimes invited me to his house in which he not only painted on wood and, later, canvas, but also on the walls and furniture. It was a house filled with unloosed demons, who had tormented him until he found the courage to paint them. These creatures of a private and menacing world had closed in on him, but he foiled them by raising his magic brush. He came to a truce with the demons because others recognized them, therefore recognized him; joined him; were also plagued and could overcome the plague as he did.

He even grew rather rich off his work, was prudent in his spending, took a Spanish wife, moved to Spain. The victim of demons made them work for him. This seems appropriate for a painter of zombies.

There seemed to be a pattern of facial expression in Haitian painting, different from the exaggerations of other folk painters. Often the eyes were done as disturbing emblems, looking in rather than out. The mouths could show many emotions, the tilt of the head, the attitude of energy or resignation, the shapes and modeling suggested humor, pain, fortitude. But even when the mouths were taken by laughter, the eyes might be fixed white or black spots, cold with a speculation about what was not yet known or unknowable.

Many of the artists were balancing between starvation and mere hunger. A few managed to sell to tourists, dealers, and collectors. Some caught sight of Duffaut's Jacmel or the Obin brothers' Cap Haitien and turned out imitations and forgeries for the cruise-ship day visitors. Except for a few, like Gourgue, the Obin family of painters, and Hyppolite, who profited after his death (that is, the people who owned his masterpieces grew rich off them), most of the early generation eked out the few necessary dollars as day laborers, yardboys, clerks, teachers, or spongers. Jasmin Joseph still made his bricks.

Jasmin Joseph also painted dozing brown Haitian bears with his own face—there are no bears in Haiti—being lectured by white rabbits—rabbits are not indigenous, either—wearing what looked like blue nylon shirts and horn-rimmed glasses, some kneeling, all piously carrying identical books that looked convincingly like the Good Book. These bears are Haitians, aren't they, Jasmin? And these rabbits are white missionaries? "No, these are bears and these are rabbits," he explained, smiling with sly discretion.

I noticed that one of the most sleepy, most bored bears had exactly Jasmin's face. "Tu trouves?" he asked.

When Americans began to visit the country as tourists, looking for Strange, as adventurous travelers do, and finding Very Strange, as travelers in Haiti are bound to find, Haitian art came into fashion. It was entertaining, sometimes moving, and the best of it transcended the categories of folk and primitive art. The Japanese may be pioneers in electronics wholesaling, but at least they came after the Americans, French, and Germans in collecting Haitian art. Painting and sculpture became a major item in city markets that also sold rice, beans, and scraps of metal; art became an export to rival the fading coffee trade.

Every Haitian event is celebrated in painting. There are weddings and funerals, schoolhouses, terraced fields, children playing, fantastic villages, exploding flowers, scenes of bourgeois concerts, historical images of defeats and victories, dreams of bliss and dreams of perdition—the entire career of a people. Even Africa is recalled in mythic evocations.

The acts of daily life, even the acts of geography, form a continuum of astonishments. The land is so steep with mountains (Haiti means "High Place" in the Arawak Indian language) that people have been known to die from falling out of a cornfield. These days, people who have no food are still able to use cocaine, which finds its way out of the transshipments from secret landing strips. AIDS is ravaging the country.

The artists have plenty of grief to portray. When the Duvalier kleptocracy was overthrown, the most popular poster was taken from an underground painting. Anti-Duvalier paintings had been made in secret, as writers in the Soviet Union published their work in samizdat. The painting shows Baby Doc in a white wedding dress, standing on rocks with what looks suspiciously like a tail emerging from under his dress. He is shooting himself in the head. It is a comment on his marriage to Michelle Bennett, a thin version of Imelda Marcos, who swept the treasury clean—not even sparing American aid for the starving—and helped to drive a beaten people into revolt. The painting has a fine sly irony, a mad humor in its cheerful colors.

The poster hangs in my bathroom, opposite a poster from Petainist France, in which the word "Collaboration" appeared for the first time with its now indelible meaning.

WHAT HAD seemed an impossible situation in Haiti has gotten worse. Yet the artists are still depicting what they call the "Boulevard of Millionaires"—that desolate portside street in the capital where people live, die, give birth, sell their wares, among a dense crowd of donkeys, garbage, debris, a frightening and hellish world. Among the painters, there is both the shrug of stoical acceptance and compassion. The gaiety of color and bold figuration makes its own statement: We still have the sun, music, love of kin, hope.

ARTISTS ARE liars about life, bringing their fantasies out of dreamland, attempting to enforce them on others. The great lie becomes a true lie, a way to understand our lives—the lie about

Hamlet, about Cezanne's apple, the lie about human grace when Leon Destiné danced, the lie about control of blood and breath when Celestin drummed. In Haiti, bragging came to seem like unborn storytelling. The *délire verbale* of both street talkers and the poet Roussan Camille expressed the magic power of words to create reality. The government statistician Maurice Lubin's map of the poets of Haiti, dense with dots, an inundation of cries for love and freedom, seemed an accurate chart of the situation. Verse was chronic.

Visitors learned to thread their way through this poetic reality. A Haitian never said no. Ask him to dinner and you had to judge by the way he said yes whether he meant yes, no, or maybe-if-convenient. Each person told the truth that really mattered to him—that he sincerely wanted you to like him—but the signposts in discourse were as meaningless as the random numbers sometimes attached to houses on a road. After all, words were merely French or Creole or English or Spanish. Was it his fault if you cooked just because he said he would love nothing more than to come to dinner? All he wanted to transmit was his undying affection.

Some believed this intermingling of yes-no-maybe was a relic of slave times. The slave could not say no to his master, but he could forget, go slow, follow another master. It was a smiling, most agreeable method of resistance. It was literature. It eked out domains of freedom within the subtle slaveries that persisted under other regimes and conditions.

From the lies and brags of survival and self-respect sometimes came those more complex brags that dramatized and improved dusty reality. The brag uses delusion to sing that life is worth the trouble. Sometimes the poet heads for glory; sometimes he is just a person who has saved his money until he can print a card that lists his profession as Poète–Anthropologue–Ethnologue.

Haitian creativity was a result of all the meetings of the African past, slavery, and the French, the heroic outburst of independence and the long anarchy that followed during times of vindictive international isolation. Periods of confusion—like the absurdity of the Emperor Soulouque, a senile warlord who established his Dukes of Marmalade and Duchesses of Lemonade that inspired Gilbert and Sullivan—were followed by moments of individual brilliance and lapses into passive shock. In the mid-fifties, with a flowering of the arts, it seemed that a culture that was uniquely Haitian, supple, singular, fitted to history and experience, was being created. An audience in Europe and the States began to welcome Haitian writers, painters, musicians, dancers. Jean-Paul Sartre, Edmund Wilson, and André Malraux declared that the rest of the world could learn from this renaissance. The rule of General Magloire, while erratic and corrupt, did not chase the most gifted sons and daughters of Haiti into exile. Effective in extracting money from relief organizations, churches, the United Nations, and Uncle Sam, the regime even left a surplus for the arts.

I N MEMORY it seems like a golden age. At sunrise I saw hummingbirds running down the light. The garden smells were sweet, Ann and Judy ran in for good morning kisses, there was mango, papaya, warm bread, and dark-roasted coffee at breakfast. At night the drums rocked and rolled us to sleep. It was as soothing as low thunder, and no more ominous. For recreation, I would go to ceremonies on weekends. Once, walking with Pierre Marcelin, I stumbled, due to enthusiasm or a rock underfoot, and the chant "Bat tambou, bat tambou"—*beat the drum, beat the drum*—was changed to "Blanc tombé, blanc tombé"—*the white guy fell, the white guy fell.* When I got up, it seemed that the whole world was laughing.

The peculiar play of French and Creole together, one the language of education and connection with the outside world, the other the language of feeling and childhood, seemed to generate what Edouard Glissant called "délire verbale," that verbal delirium in which earnest old-fashioned French harangues, pompous and unreal, filled public discourse. Some of the poets were bringing Creole into their French or using Creole, the linguistic fact on the ground, in their writing. Its spicy reality put some limit to the endless nonsense of official French in a place where, for most people, French was *merely* official.

I contributed to a magazine called *Conjunctions* which was inspired by Jean Price-Mars, that hilarious old sage, author of *Ainsi*

Parla l'Oncle, the *Golden Bough* of Haitian anthropology. His family was one of the few traditional elite *black* families, pridefully guarding its blackness instead of marrying its sons to white or mulatto women. His intellectual goal was to convince a Frenchified elite that their African, peasant, and slave roots mattered, that they might even want to serve their people and nation. Many played the role of Paris boulevardiers in Port-au-Prince.

The artists, chronicling and judging the Haitian comedy and tragedy, found plenty to tell in daily life. The traditions of sociability could be depicted along with the fear of strangers and the periodic national explosions of wrath. In those days Haiti lived under a gaudy corruption that sometimes murdered but also allowed freedom for gossip, slyness, and judgment by those who didn't interfere with President-General Paul Magloire's personal pleasures and profits. He seemed modest and loving compared to what came next.

The work of Felix Morisseau-Leroy—imagine a combination of Arthur Miller and Lenny Bruce—is read throughout the French-speaking world. Later in exile in Senegal, he was the director of radio and television broadcasting, another symptom of the Haitian brain drain. When I visited him in Dakar, he wept when we spoke of Haiti.

I remembered the time back in Port-au-Prince when he came banging and shouting at my door and demanded to be let in. *"I'm frightened. I have bad dreams."*

THE DILEMMA of the sophisticated artist making his life in a primitive culture is dramatic in the case of an architect, whose medium requires capital. Albert Mangones was a lean young man with a Rive Gauche face, harassed, poetic, and in need of a haircut; he slept in his studio when he was planning a house and on the job when he was building it. The most original of the Haitian architects, adapting his North American training to the conditions and beauties of his native island, he designed tropical houses that were both clean lined and playful, using streams for cooling, Haitian artists as artisans, bringing flowers into atriums, constructing overhangs for ventilation and against storms to reduce the need for glass. In a park in downtown Port-au-Prince he designed the Théâtre de Verdure, open to the sky. He displayed inventive Haitian craftmanship, such as Jasmin Joseph's clay-sculpted ventilation blocks.

MANGONES COULD have worked successfully abroad. He preferred to work in his own land, but asked: "How can an architect function when workmen have no experience with precise drawings, fitting doors or windows, using T squares or levelers? That is the problem we try to solve. We improvise. We do our best."

Later, he became the official regime architect under the Duvaliers, doing official buildings of no distinction. His career took a sad turn, bent by history, into what was called collaboration. A former friend called him Papa Doc's Albert Speer.

The best writers were trying to express the conflicts between a static peasant culture, country people following African traditions, and the feudal society inherited from the days of the French plantation colony. Jacques Roumain, ethnologist, poet, and political desperado, wrote one novel before he died "of alcohol and chagrin." He had been in jail for Communist agitation; he had been sent into exile as a consul in Mexico City, the mild doom practiced by relatively tender regimes. *Gouverneurs de la Rosée,* was published in English under the title *Masters of the Dew.* In this novel, a farmer's passion for water was translated into something like the quest for the Grail. He was a man for whom Water meant all art, beauty, truth. The pressure of the modern world on a man who had modern ideas about irrigation and land use set up a series of events that finally killed him, just as these ultimately political conflicts finally killed Roumain himself.

The novels of Pierre and Philippe-Thoby Marcelin all proceeded from the meeting of science and superstition in Haitian life. When Pierre took me to voodoo ceremonies, we were both visitors from another world, he from a mulatto family of judges, diplomats, and privilege, although he had sunk into poverty by the mid-fifties. In *The Pencil of God,* the hero is a city Don Juan against whom black magic curses were pronounced. He doesn't believe, he doesn't believe, he *doesn't* believe—and then he dies of the curse. His childhood convictions are stronger than his urban sophistication.

The books by Jacques Roumain and the Marcelins, following the line advanced more theoretically by the Creolizers in the group called "Les Griots" and in their master text, Jean Price-Mars' *Ainsi Parla l'Oncle,* made a break with the faded tradition of Haiti as a faded province of French literature. Earlier writers tended toward sepia nostalgia for a past they never had, an inappropriate nineteenth-century longing for lost lives and loves that had been prelost by European poets. The language of the new generation remained French, of course, but sometimes the prose rhythms were Haitian, the manners and the news of the world came from observed life, and Creole was introduced into dialogue. This shocked some older Haitians who liked to think of themselves as tan Frenchmen. Language was beginning to reflect reality.

THE POETS Émile Roumère, Felix Morisseau-Leroy, and others took a further step in throwing off the weight of France. After beginning a literary career in Paris, Morisseau-Leroy became a prophet of Creole, the only language understood by all Haitians, the tongue of childhood, joking, anger, and lovemaking even for an upper class that often hated to acknowledge it. He argued that Creole could provide Haitians with the emotional resonance for a great literature. Besides adapting Greek drama to Creole realities—and directing and acting in productions he brought to the countryside—he composed his own poetry in Creole, published newspaper columns in Creole, conducted a furious campaign in favor of a language which had only just begun to be written. Modestly, he pointed to the examples of Rabelais, who gave modern French its direction, and Chaucer, who in *The Canterbury Tales* did a job of propaganda in favor of English during days ("not so long ago, my friend") when cultured people wrote in Latin. Morisseau took precautions against his earnestness by making sure that life was also a series of comic adventures for himself.

In 1953–1954 the literary monthly, *Conjunctions,* expressed this vitality and ferment. The first issues included stories, poetry, reviews, polemics about Creole, and essays on such varied subjects as hydroelectric power in the Artibonite Valley and the relationship between French surrealism and James Joyce. A community of writers was growing up, based in Port-au-Prince but with contributers from the north, Cap Haitien, which had recently been connected to the capital by a passable road. My wife and I joined the procession, led by President Magloire, from Port-au-Prince to the Cap, celebrating linkage of the two major cities. Previously, it seemed easier to go to New York or Paris than from the south to the north of Haiti. There was a mood of optimism; the word *renaissance,* applied to the painters and sculptors, seemed appropriate to the cultural scene. The playboy President even served as a subject for satirical Carnival songs without necessarily having the satirists killed. This was great progress.

The national folklore troupe performed regularly at the Théâtre de Verdure, no doubt inspired partly by the recent tourist boom; the "Ballet Affranchis," "Dance of the Freed Ones," stylized the merengue, the popular dance enjoyed at noisy bamboches, blow-out celebrations in the city and country, and at Choucoune, the nightclub on the central square in Pétionville where the elite performed its weekend rituals of courtship and display. These late-night sessions were entertaining but exhausting combinations of political gossip and sexual intrigue, relieved by energetic wiggling as the band played traditional songs and recent Carnival favorites. At that time I had a wife who liked to dance.

The merengue was originally performed by house slaves who witnessed seventeenth-century contradances at the formal balls of their masters. First for their own recreation, then as freed people, the former slaves adapted the French dance to African steps, introducing drums and sometimes the *vaccins* or bamboo pipes, developing a style that has the strict grace of the minuet, plus a freedom, litheness, and a Haitian touch of malice in the parody of their former masters' restrained jiggling. In the folklore troupe version, the men advanced, retreated, up and back, touched their partners, fanned overheated behinds with leaves; bowed and scraped and simpered. It was fun to dance and to watch.

Max Wilson, Ph.D. in Philosophy from Columbia University, an expert in epistomology, the philosophy of the origin, nature, limits, and possibilities of human knowledge, spent a few years trying to find a crevice for himself at home in the Université d'Haiti. (The brother of one of the President's mistresses, a Cuban guitarist, ran the School of Music.) Max eventually left to teach in a college in Virginia. At his goodbye party, we grieved for the departure of Haiti's foremost epistomologist. We drank, we embraced, we shed brotherly tears. "But this entire nation is an epistomological dilemma," he said.

Haiti's problems were not being solved by its many talents. This "golden age," this "renaissance," was a mere respite in a long attractive disaster. The artists were telling the story of Haiti and also, at their best, the story of the balance within unbalance of all peoples. Moment by moment in the days and nights of Port-au-Prince, visitors felt an immediacy of need, the bravery of Haitian striving, a ferocity of the will to survive, all of it properly confused by smells, music, and laughter.

In my twenties, during the Eisenhower doldrums in America, I had enough sense to know I was privileged to attend this thrilling byway of history.

CHAPTER
FIVE

Combat de Coqs

AT CROIX-des-Missions, outside Port-au-Prince on the Saint Marc road, stands a small wooden and thatched structure with an open roof and a set of benches circling the dirt pit. On Sunday afternoons a crowd gathers here to drink *clairin,* discuss the ways of the gods and women, and bet on the wisdom, skill, and talent of roosters whose vocation is to peck out each other's eyes and fracture each other's skulls.

These are not ordinary birds, of course. The chickenly qualities of meekness, plumpness, and talkativeness have been stripped away. They are fighting cocks, of aristocratic, perhaps even noble breed, meat-fed, proud, expensive, trained, trimmed, cherished for battle. On this Sunday afternoon at the cockfights, I am the only foreigner. For about sixty seconds the habitués turn their attention from their roosters' spurs to my skin of a blinding lack of color. They blink and return to important business.

The man next to me explains himself in English: "I am an educated gentleman like you, sir, I have been to America. I only come here because they invite me. I come because it would insult them if I stayed away."

He passes me his bottle of what he elegantly and fastidiously calls rum. It is *clairin.*

There is no hurry for the match. The handlers stroke and caress the birds, pinching their heads, smoothing their tail and wing feathers, wiping their beaks. There is a ritual of proud impatience.

One man challenges another. He questions his virility, his parentage. They set their cocks a short distance apart. There is a stylized exchange of rebukes. When the challenged cock shows the proper spirit, tugging at his cord, and when the challenged man feels that the gods are with him, he accepts.

The bets are shouted out over an auctioneering rattle. A raucous stomping and applause hastens this first act.

The bookies run and slap hands. Everyone waves gourde notes and dollars. The referee shouts to clear the pit. No one moves. The referee screams. He jumps threateningly. He pushes. He is pushed. But the event has its own rhythm and he is part of the dance. Eventually, when the betting money has been kissed away, the ring is cleared.

The owners prepare their fighters. They comb and clean the feathers and show an especially tender concern for the spurs. They lick the rooster all over with their tongues. They take its head in their mouths to clean it. They examine its eyes critically. The eyes of a rooster are like splinters of dull agate. All this is performed very slowly and deliberately: *ritual.* They take a mouthful of rum and lift the cock's wings and spray rum over its body. Another mouthful, and the same for the other side. Another, and they blow rum into its head and eyes and at the rear. Lovingly, like patient lovers. Very considerate courting of all the rooster's fighting and feeling parts.

Then each handler examines his opponent's bird to make sure that the spurs are legally prepared, no poison has been hidden on the body. He tastes its feathers. If there be poison, let me suffer it.

The men stand waiting, affectionately tucking their roosters close to their bodies, until the referee gives the signal. They murmur encouraging words. Covertly they watch the adversary. The din from the crowd is deafening, and the fume of bodies and excitement is visible, steam rising to the open roof. I point to a bird, and hand over ten gourdes, two dollars. The banker shows huge white teeth and with a trombone slide of laughter, says: "Blanc conné!" The white man knows.

The cocks are put down. They peck in exploratory fashion. They seem to be blind unless the enemy is directly in front of them. They are negligent assassins. Just a few stretching pecks. They have an almost languorous air of chickens in a yard, but still they turn, they peck, they peck again at each other's heads. They lock necks. They hide like lovers under each other's wings. Gradually they anger. Short furious cries are urging them on. They leap into the air and peck at each other's heads, aiming for the eyes. As they come down, wings hissing, they seek to jump over each other, driving the spurs back behind. Blood and feathers give them ideas. Suddenly the idea of murder floods these capsule heads with their bright silvery beaks. Now the beaks are pink.

Feathers begin to scatter. A scrawny neck is laid bare in patches. They fan the air, rise, turn, leap, squawk, fall back, go jerking to look for each other. Spots of blood are staining the dirt. One handler has his head in his hands and is swaying, praying, pleading for a lucky blow. One of the cocks is now gaining a clear advantage, more blows, faster. The other rises passionately despite its hurt squawk and occasional stumbling. The more powerful one is now pecking straight for the eyes.

My neighbor turns and says in English: "I see that you are holding your stomach. Primitive, is it not? But once I visit a prize fight in Chi-caw-go"—and he shows his teeth with appreciation of his witticism at the expense of bloodthirsty North Americans.

Suddenly the weaker cock sprawls, stunned. A roar goes up. The winner, avid now, leaps upon the struggling mess of feathers, wings whirring, beak chopping, spurs tight. The referee kneels to see it; the crowd comes to its feet. The defeated trainer rushes forward for his bird.

Ko-ko-ri-ko! The winning trainer beats his breast and screams: "KOO-KOO-REE-KOOO!" He staggers about the pit amid the mess of feathers and gore, holding his bird aloft, kissing and kissing it.

The loser tenderly retrieves his cock. He blows rum into its beak. Too late. Dead. Those who have won are collecting their bets and congratulating each other. The losers are shaking their heads and wondering how they could ever have made such a mistake, how the gods could let them down once again, how their desire and need could have been ignored one more time.

Two men are hissing and spreading their arms for silence. The loser's owner has something to say. His bird has just had its eyes eaten and its braincase broken. This love-lavished battler that had carried the burden of his ambition is now good only for the frying pan. What words can mitigate his shame? He accepts the glass of consoling *clairin,* but shakes off the sympathy of his friends, wiping his eyes with his sleeve and raising his hands:

"Listen, you!" (A hush comes over the huddle of men.) "Listen, let me tell what has just happened to me, otherwise you will not know. I came with my cock in a sack to win lots of money. I promised my girl a trip to Jérémie. You know what women are. Well, I spread this cock's wings and I sprayed him with rum and I licked his beak in mine and I bet everything I had. My old father's money, too! And my mother darling's! My cock fought bravely, friends, yes you know it, and he fell down, he lost, yes you know it, but I don't go home empty-handed. Not me!"

"What?" someone cries, shaking a fist. "You bet against your own?"

"No, no!" He is laughing and bawling. "I don't go home empty-handed, dear friends—*I still have the sack!*"

With the surge of laughter that rewards him, he is no longer entirely defeated. All these men know what failure means. He has communed with them. He has made a work of art—a work of laughter—of his defeat, and therefore he has also won.

He is muttering to himself as he carries away his sack and the lump of bird. "My cock lost because he was an honest politician in an earlier life." His eyes are red and grief-stricken, but his palm is slapped by his friends. They have lost together.

The man who had been to Chi-caw-go follows me out into the silver-gray late afternoon sunlight, where women are selling little bags of *griots,* spicy bits of grilled pork, and a crowd is watching a man plead with a donkey that has died to get up and be his friend once more. "Say, Meester," asks the man from Detroit, "did Primo Carnera ever win the championship from Louis Joe? Would you care to visit genuine voodoo that only the experts get to see?"

CHAPTER SIX

Castaways

AFTER NEARLY a year in Haiti, I persuaded a friend, a dentist from Detroit, to come for a visit. He is an ardent tennis player and was convinced to make the trip by a combination of name-dropping and winter doubles—a match against the Army Chief of Staff and a senator. The senator kept his own court and permanent ballboys to do the hard work. We began under the midday tropical sun, winning our first match. Although we were tired, courtesy demanded another couple of sets. We were winning again as I whispered to my friend, "Lighten up. We've got to lose before we can quit."

He found this difficult. He was an upward-mobile oral surgeon who rushed the net. As the afternoon wore on, we both looked for the abrupt equatorial nightfall to rescue us. I had my daughters to attend to, and a regime of study and writing. My friend's blisters were bleeding, but he seemed incapable of letting our host take the match. The unforgiving sun finally dipped below the horizon and we thought the contest would end. Lights flashed on—the senator kept his own oil generator. The situation was worse than a botched root canal. We played until we lost.

In this prefeudal, premechanical world, where straight lines are rare because straight lines hardly exist in nature, some had the benefits of civilization. The senator, part African and part German, with both Nazi relatives and African ones, preferred to dominate at tennis. That was a straight line. His first son was named "Hitvelt," after

Hitler and Roosevelt, because he had wanted to be a winner, no matter which side came out ahead.

A few days later, I heard a rumor of a police raid on a house where opponents of the Magloire regime sometimes met. As part of his winter vacation, I offered my friend the dentist a taste of totalitarian oppression; they didn't have much of that in Detroit. Wearing our tennis shoes, we stood watching in the shade of a tall coconut palm when the black Buicks roared up, filled with gun-packing soldiers. They saw us, stopped, and broke into excited discussion. We were, it was decided, CIA observers. Bad show. The cars roared away and, on this occasion, the conspirators escaped.

"Great holiday," said my friend, the dentist from Detroit. "Beats Miami Beach every time."

IT WAS easy to float away in the company of an assortment of refugees from reality. Drums throbbed at night from the ravines and hills intersecting Port-au-Prince, along with the barking of the dogs, the cawing, cackling, and crowing of birds and chickens, the sharp rhythms of shoeshine boxes being beaten, and an occasional gunshot. This was Elsewhere Land. The smells were also convincingly unCleveland, unDetroit—mangoes, frying pork, banana leaves, charcoal, and folks. Foreigners were lifted by their money atop a vivid world engrossed by the defiant struggle for both pleasure and survival. Some visitors came with their combs, but found Haiti didn't have much in the way of beaches to comb. They drifted into other lines of endeavor. My young wife and I, with our babies, were also refugees. Although I was supposedly a student at the Université d'Haiti, thanks to that fellowship I found listed in a book at the Cleveland Public Library, we were fleeing the prison of each other.

Other residents had more serious histories.

The man I'll call Colonel Chocolat, a cashiered French officer, marched around the dining room before meals at the tiny hotel Florville in the mountain village of Kenscoff where he lived. He was banned from France for collaboration with the Nazis, but confided in me that the Gaullists were wrong to do this because: "Who has not eaten of chocolate cannot judge of chocolate."

He tramped back and forth, his boots thundering, keeping fit for the next war against Godless Communism and Perfidious Albion. He avoided the paths outside the hotel because he hated to step in donkey shit, but his hands were brown and his pants stained from the melted chocolate bars his family shipped to him from Lyons.

THE AMERICAN occupation of Haiti still provides a textbook model of colonial brutality, including conscription of men to build roads, routine racist degradation, the alleged crucifixion of Charlemagne Peralte, leader of a peasant revolt. The history of "ephemeral Presidents" was used to justify strong-arm governing. Improved health and sanitation, a medical school, a few roads, and a bitter rage were accomplished.

Odd relics of the occupation remained during the fifties. Doc Reser, a former sergeant, now "the white voodoo priest of Haiti," was a barrel-chested old guy with cunning eyes and the habit of going about without his shirt in order to make things easier for a harem whom he allowed to tickle his mat of curly chest hairs. How serious was he about voodoo? For a few dollars he would do a good ceremony, biting off a chicken's head and spewing a mixture of chicken and other people's rum over the communicants; for a few dollars more, a great ceremony. Sometimes tourists commissioned a major bull sacrifice, lining up to share in the mahogany bowl of hot blood while the moaning animal, stumbling and falling, sang its final song to the gods. Like many con artists who have found a good scam, Doc Reser also seemed to have scammed himself, although his sun-washed blue eyes showed a glint of amusement at being a boss voodoo priest, best white god in town. He was also a drummer, painter, and folk healer. For a while he directed the insane asylum.

In addition to voodoo and tourists with money, he was diligent about young girls. He loved lecturing, lounging against a heap of pillows, about the spirits of water, air, and fire—the charms, the

79

ceremonies, and the Marines; and he watched like a drillmaster to make sure I didn't poach on the chesthair-ticklers who surrounded him. In Haitian fashion, he referred to me as a "blanc." I was young enough to accept the contempt of a great maestro. "Give me money," he announced regally, "and I'll teach you my secrets."

"I have friends who do voodoo. I don't pay them."

"I'm not your friend," he said.

"How about if I buy you a couple drinks?"

We sat crosslegged on the floor to negotiate. "A couple *bottles*," he said.

It was, as they now put it in Hollywood and on Wall Street, a done deal, and he told me his secrets: Make a lot of noise. Enjoy war, sex, and long life. Wash your mouth out regularly with rum and check yourself for the clap every morning.

THE MAN I'll call Terry McTeague retired from high-fashion photography because it failed to satisfy his creative needs. In Port-au-Prince, his place of retreat, where he went to heal his wounds from the Manhattan hurlyburly, he found the availability of eleven-year-old girls much more fulfilling artistically. His procedure was a bit complicated. He adopted them at eleven, offered them to his chic friends from New York as party favors, disadopted them at thirteen—this was possible, under Haitian law, with a contribution to Haitian judges—and then married them. When he married, he grew jealous and no longer shared the girl with his visitors. When she grew old, say fifteen or sixteen, he divorced her.

Finally he met his match. One of his ex-daughters, a clever slip of a thing with a joyous smile, turned out to be a free spirit. He couldn't control her. He also couldn't divorce her; she knew how to fight. He had fallen in love with her eleven-year-old sister and the family approved of this new match, but Pouki turned out to be stubborn. She knew her rights and managed to establish them. Pouki (from the French *pourquoi*) periodically asked her friends in the police to toss Terry in jail for a night or two. A Haitian jail is not a place for restful contemplation—even a term as *Vogue* photographer must have seemed more pleasant—and Terry would emerge dirty, hungry, thirsty, bruised, and contrite. This at last was true love, although Pouki was nearly seventeen by now. Her sister pouted and complained, but fate did not give her a turn.

Terry drove a VW, using the baggage compartment as a bar. It was lined with bottles, insulated ice cases, glasses, the mixes. It was no longer a Volkswagen; it was his Flying Tavern. He made provision for every emergency, and provided instant hospitality along the roadside.

Eventually, of course, in the fullness of his happy old age, Terry died. As both his lawfully adopted daughter and his wedded wife—a definite double claim—Pouki inherited his estate, invested it prudently in a whorehouse, and became a popular businesswoman.

On a trip to Haiti during the darkest days of Papa Doc, I visited Pouki to reminisce about old times. She was now an elegant madam in her late twenties, wearing her trademark single gold hoop earring. "Do you have any regrets?" I asked her.

"I miss Terry," she said. "How can one regret one's childhood?"

"Some people do."

"But my friend," she said, "how can I? Because of Terry, I have become what I am today, the envy of a nation. Do I not bring joy and hard currency where it is sorely needed? And for what are you in sore need?"

M Y FRIEND Alois de Bonaire came equipped with a little red 4CV Renault, a little red-headed French wife, and measleslike red dots on his face, sun splotches. He was French and not French— had spent most of his life in Paris—but now, in 1953, he hustled up and down the hills of Port-au-Prince as a gofer for a millionaire Swiss flower grower. The Swiss had the idea of using cheap Haitian labor and flying the winter flowers to the United States for promgoers, lovers, apologetic persons, funerals. The business thrived. It needed a man of charm, languages, and affable energy to make contacts, run errands, get things done. Alois was the man.

He sought to serve me, too, as friend and helper. He talked fast and often. He had been a student at the Sorbonne before my term there; in fact, during the war.

"As a result of those terrible times, mon vieux, consequentially," he said in his mostly accurate English, "I have become deeply interested in the questions of Loyalty, Survival, and Corpulence—the big problem for a true idealist."

"Do you mean Corruption?"

"Precisely! You attack my thought! Fat with greed!" he cried with the good cheer of a man who was finally discovering a soulmate. "Forgive, dear friend, my excellent English."

I forgave. Adrift in a strange place, I too needed a friend. He looked like the clerk in charge of making the arrangements, telling the jokes, fixing the parking tickets. Sandy-haired, skinny, and busy, he considered his profession to be that of *débrouillard*—a wiggler out of tight places. He helped me extract my packages from the Haitian post office; he helped me find my way around. Someday he might become a millionaire in francs, dollars, or Haitian gourdes—probably, as he said, he would grow corpulent in an ideal world. Meanwhile, his metabolism raced. It wasn't malaria. There was something he hesitated to tell me.

Alois was writing a novel, and would I read it?

"When it's done," I suggested.

This is not as safe a response as *No*, but at least some people don't finish the books they want other writers to read. And Alois was my buddy, wasn't he? We sped up and down the hills in his chugging red 4CV. *Beyond the mountain stands another mountain.* That's the geography, and perhaps the psychology, too, of Haiti. He talked about how "childlike" Haitians were, "like chattering monkeys," and when I asked why he lived here, he said he was only waiting to finish his book, migrate to the United States, start a new life. Haiti had been his way station for many years now.

It happened that I met a black New York City police sergeant, sent to Port-au-Prince to help the Haitian police organize a fingerprint lab. Alfonso was a very intelligent, overweight, frequently laughing man with a shiny handsome face—the high-cholesterol Sidney Poitier. He would announce a visit by cupping his hands and shouting, "Herb! Hustle your butt on down! It's your buddy with the big belly!"

And I would hear his laughter echoing over the terrace of the Grand Hotel Oloffson as he ordered a pair of rum punches.

One afternoon, bent over our fruity fortified syrup—the thought of rum punch no longer inspires me—he stopped his regular laughter, which was normally like a lighthouse steadily rotating, shedding its beam at ninety-second intervals. He lowered his voice. He said: "Your friend Al-loise? His real name is von Bonerz, I think it's some kind of Baltic name, some shit like that. . . ."

"Go on."

"There's a piece of paper in a file . . ." And he wrote it on a napkin: *Interdit de Séjour*. Forbidden to Reside. He was banned from France because at the Sorbonne, during the war, he had been a Gestapo informer.

This was why Alois was having trouble getting into the United States, why he found himself among the "chattering monkeys." He had not mentioned this detail.

The loneliness of the expatriate makes him cling to strangers, and I had liked the lively, agreeable, would-be writer. We had gossiped about Paris, literature, women; we had had fun. I wasn't quite ready to accept Alfonso's story.

That evening I met Alois for a nightcap at one of the waterfront bars, Le Rond Point, in the half-festive, half-bereft area known as l'Exposition. Suddenly a fleet of black Buicks pulled up. The President of the Republic, His Excellency General Paul E. Magloire, had arrived for one of his democratic episodes of public drinking. There was also a new girlfriend to show off—the dancer had gone to Chicago to marry a psychiatrist she had met at the Oloffson, the Cuban guitarist had grown too plump. Along with the distinguished President, "The Eisenhower of Haiti," came his usual entourage of bodyguard, medal and apple polishers, and cronies, including what seemed like a good part of the military arsenal of Haiti. Alois and I decided to leave.

The bodyguards lounged outside in the midnight heat, their car doors open. A couple of moonlit fun-lovers were clumsily playing sword-fight with their U.S. Army surplus M-1 rifles. As we passed an open Buick, I noticed that I was a bit tipsy and Alois was definitely drunk; and in some kind of reflex half-joke, I suddenly grabbed him and shoved him toward the bulging Buick. "Okay, you're under arrest," I said.

He jerked straight. His face was white and furious; his face was blotched, his little lips compressed, the blond mustache quivering. Abruptly he was cold sober. *"Don't never do that again."*

We parted without another word. It was an odd way to prove something, but in that instant of fear and rage I knew Alfonso's story was not a mere rumor. Afterwards Alois and I only nodded to each other in passing. I knew; he knew I knew; no explanations.

On a later trip to Haiti, I learned that he had finally gotten his visa to the United States. The rat railway was still running. And only a few years ago I discovered he is now the p.r. representative for a Swiss computer firm in New York, contentedly married to an American woman, but the happy extra man at parties where his hints of aristocratic family, of a title, make him an honored guest. He charms the Upper East Side with tales of his wanderings among the former island colonies of France, where he chose not to live because he required a certain sense of standards.

THE BROTHER of a prominent French publisher lived on a hillside of Port-au-Prince. A recluse, but if anyone happened to ask, he had a clear French explanation for his presence in Haiti. A person didn't even have to ask. He had done a study of global wind currents. When atomic war broke out between the Russians and the Americans, Haiti might avoid the fallout. He made a small sad smile as he shared this news. "If you are fortunate," he said, "the war will happen while you are still here."

"I hope I won't be so lucky."

He shrugged. Frenchmen know that foreigners can't be expected to share the bright clarity of Cartesian logic. When he went out and a storm was coming up, he stood under a big black French umbrella with a bemused expression on his face, listening to the drumsnaps of wind on fabric, wondering if this was it and if the helpful worldwide air currents were still churning in their assigned places.

MOST EDUCATED Haitians seemed to be either poets or anthropologists, but some chose more practical professions, such as hunting for pirate gold. One afternoon a delegation of earnest young men came to me with a proposal. They needed another member for an expedition across the island to the north, a certain terrain near the town of Port-de-Paix, opposite Île de la Tortue, which had been a buccaneer retreat a few hundred years ago. One of the young men had come into possession of a treasure map.

I was honored by the invitation. I asked to see the parchment.

"There are certain arrangments"—embarrassment, halting-ness—"which must be made."

"I'm not in a position to offer an investment," I said.

"Oh no, no, no *money.*" How crass of me. A fellow student and writer, who always called me "cher collègue," explained that he had nominated me as a reckless unbeliever *blanc* who would do anything.

"Thank you, dear colleague," I said.

The delegation was uneasy, their voices shifting from solemn baritones to that odd Haitian sudden falsetto which came with smiles and discomfort. There was a little problem. They intended to be frank with me. The difficulty with the treasure was that thirteen slaves had been buried alive along with the Spanish doubloons in order to guard the cache. The expedition needed a driver (they had one), a jeep (they had it), the treasure map (my dear colleague kept it folded in a little shell case), and someone to accept upon his immortal soul the curse of the thirteen slaves. This would comprise my share in the cost of the expedition.

It took but an instant to decide. Why else was I on earth, if not to seek buried treasure and accept the curse of buried slaves? As far as I was concerned, thirteen souls working in eternal concert against mine were no worse than thesis examination committees or New York editors.

"I'll do it," I said.

"I press your hand, dear colleague," said my fellow student. The other members of the expedition followed, sealing our bargain. Personally, I was also deeply moved by my bravery; or perhaps, since I didn't believe in the curse of the thirteen buried-alive slaves, I was mostly touched by the affection of these sincere entrepreneurs.

"We will find them buried *standing up*," my dear colleague warned. These would be alert two-hundred-year-old watchmen.

A few days later we set out with food packed, winches and ropes for pulling the jeep out of the streams we would be fording, tools, inspiration in the form of treasure map, rum, and good Haitian beer. Our friendship deepened. Those who didn't call me dear colleague called me Mon Vieux, that French term of affection which is inadequately translated as My Old. We bathed in streams and finally, at Port-de-Paix, in the blue, blue Caribbean Sea where pirates had roamed, eaten turtle meat, and banked their booty in the ground with tormented souls to stand watch over it in lieu of bank tellers or stools.

We followed the map, tracing our fingers along various lines indicating streams, thickets, paths, and "terrain inconnu," "terrain vague," unknown land, vague land. As your normal daredevil secularist, I not only didn't believe in the slave curse but also didn't have faith in the antiquity of the map. It looked to me about as authentic as the Harold Stassen portrait of Damballa Ouedo, the great snake god, I had seen in a voodoo temple. But it wasn't parchment, it was goatskin, with bits of hair still clinging to it. My dear colleague admitted that the wrinkles and cracks might give us trouble; eighteenth-century pirate ships didn't carry trained financial vice-presidents for their deposits.

I was happy—again I was happy. I was seeing the country, using pick and spade to dig in sunbaked earth, sharing good fellowship with jolly young adventurers. At night, when we slept in a little guesthouse in Port-de-Paix, I heard soft singing outside my window, crawled out from under the mosquito netting, and went onto the second-floor balcony. A girl was inviting me for a walk on the beach. Failing that, she wondered if I would invite her into my room for a Creole lesson.

Ah no, I said, I'm a treasure hunter who must rise so early in the morning.

The moon was nearly full. It cast a complicated shadow through the iron grillwork. The breeze was gentle. The girl's voice was clear and pure. But nothing in life is perfect. It seems to me now that at that moment, while the young lady crooned upward toward me her tender song of regret and farewell, I was bit by an anopheles mosquito.

My dear colleagues had supplied tools, food, drink, and goatskin treasure map, but they had neglected to tell me that this was malaria country and I should also bring the preventative of that time, Aralen. We did not find the treasure, but in due course the curse found me. The thirteen buried slaves had a lucky winner in my case.

A few weeks later, as I was sitting at the little garden café near the Rex Théâtre in Port-au-Prince, trying to write as usual but feeling dumber than usual, Shelagh Burns, a longtime American resident of Haiti, took one look at me and said, "Herb, you're a funny color, you're sick, go home and get a doctor."

It happened to be one of the frequent five-day holidays, in this case Pan-American Week, and all the doctors I knew were on vacation in their beach houses, mountain chalets, or abroad. But one of our neighbors was both a doctor and a lawyer, although he had never practiced either trade. He preferred to live off family money (they were a coffee family with plantations near the town of Jacmel). He had studied both medicine and jurisprudence in Paris. "Does your heart hurt?" he asked.

Everything else hurt. Not my heart.

"No," I said.

"So much the better!"

"But I have a very high fever."

"Nevertheless," he pointed out, "*your heart does not hurt.*"

He was winning an argument. He had gotten his professions mixed up. He was approaching my illness as a lawyer instead of a doctor.

When I reached a genuinely practicing doctor, I found a man who understood malaria and its treatment. The School of Medicine in Port-au-Prince, during those days before Papa Doc decimated the faculty and put tonton macoutes in charge, provided good training with special expertise in tropical diseases. What was called "malignant malaria" kept me bedridden for almost two months.

My elder daughter, Ann, then four years old, used to help me into the shower and marvel at how a fever could dry me off, without need of a towel, by the time she helped me back to bed. Her baby sister,

Judy, touched my face and then stared at her fingers. My dear colleague from the expedition came to visit with flowers and conversation. As soon as I recovered, he promised, we would all return for the heaps of doubloons. Various markings and goathairs also indicated the presence of diamonds, rubies, and *possibly*—there's always a risk in these matters—the secret aphrodisiac which Ponce de León sought mistakenly in south Florida. There was nothing wrong with the map, although it may have been mislabeled, east for west, south for north; or perhaps it was only that there was another crew of stand-up cartographer slaves who had thrown a "monkey's ranch" into our plans.

"I didn't know your English was so good," I said.

"Cher collègue, in time to come I too will have a Master's degree."

WHEN GRAHAM Greene arrived in Haiti, I was a few weeks from leaving. Someone suggested I might show him about and he might buy me dinner. He was doing research for a book—it turned out to be *The Comedians,* first the novel and then a movie—and I introduced him to people who, with slight alteration, appeared in these works. At the time, however, he seemed more concerned with a quest which confused me. He wanted to meet beautiful Haitian women; that was normal. But when I introduced him to the most beautiful woman I knew, he emitted an English fog of indifference which is not really a withdrawal from interest, but rather an active demonstration of it.

He turned to me and muttered, *"Lesbian."* I was insulted at the implied criticism of my judgment, so then I thought of another—a charming, graceful, agreeable, sweet-smelling dancer. His lack of excitement was profound and aggressive. He seemed tan all over—hair, freckles, khaki clothes—all tall and tan and morose. "Dyke," he said.

Our mutual friend explained that he had recently returned from southeast Asia and was recovering from the experience. This was a Haitian explanation. He was also planning to enter the United States from Puerto Rico in order to be expelled at the airport. During the time of Senator Joe McCarthy, he was on a State Department watch list. Looking forward to an international scandal, he was already drafting his protest. He tried some of the wording on me. I was a very young man helping a master in every way I could.

Since women didn't interest him, I tried drink. He bought dinner; it was only fair for me to buy the nightcap. As we sat at the pool of the El Rancho Hotel and his saucers piled up—the waiters, in the French fashion, kept track of the tab by counting saucers—my mind was fully occupied not by the glamour of the visiting champion of gray-hued prose, not by the honor of showing him Port-au-Prince, not by his odd response to the charm of Haitian women, but by the agony of my bankruptcy as it was measured by an inexorably growing tower of saucers.

The next day I asked, "Didn't he realize I can't afford all that?"

Our mutual friend answered somberly: "He just got back from Indochina. He's used to catastrophe."

CHAPTER
SEVEN

Land Without Jews

THE REPUBLIC was a land without Jews except in myth and memory. There was no congregation and no cemetery, but there were a few visitors. There were some visiting American Jews, two Israelis. There was no community, no rabbi, no shared spirit—this lack was nothing new to me. I had lived my life without a Jewish community, with only a few habits dimly revealed in my family.

As a child in Lakewood, Ohio, I had grown accustomed to being a stranger, the emblem of Stranger. In Haiti, I was a different kind of Other. It seemed that a Jew was just another *blanc* within the hidden black world. The paradoxes of status and isolation incited me to look for traces of my fathers and myself in this land where it seemed there were none. In Haiti, I continued a half-conscious search for the Jew in myself, and on a lonely Caribbean island, suffering the deepest poverty and exile from accepted western history, its Christianity underlit by voodoo, a religion that seemed to have connections with Judaism, I found an imagination of Jews; for me and, as I learned, for others.

In the rank, oily harbor of Port-au-Prince, glistening black boys still dived for coins, snatching at the glint of silver, turning like playful dolphins for the pleasure of the tour ships. The smoke of charcoal fires lay over the white heap of a city built on hills like Naples, Haifa, and San Francisco. The lizards played up walls and across ceilings, darting after flies. Beyond the port, the town was sleepily insomniac, drinking coffee and rum-coca to stay awake, but a long-term visitor also found frantic commerce, subtle sexual gaming, a struggle to stay alive and feel vivid in the heat.

In the hunt for buried treasure, nearly dying of malarial hepatitis, in adventures among white magic, black magic, and harsh strangers, I discovered new possibilities of that stranger which was myself. But the dentist, market women, bureaucrats, and my Haitian friends were all missing something in their definition of me as white like other whites. There was no Jewish community, no Jewish life. Even that most final sign of Jewish history, as of all histories, was lacking—no Jewish cemetery, no Jewish place in a cemetery. A Jew might run and hide, history is full of that, but the cemetery remains, or the place where the cemetery once stood, or the memory of that place. None. No graveyard, no place, no memory of the place which never was. And yet, as it happened, even here, in this lovely, forsaken corner of the world, Jews had come.

Before I found their vivid traces, I found the anti-Semites, refugees from their crimes. The Gestapo informer from Paris who became my friend and companion ("Get me into the States, can't you? Surely *you* can!"), and the Petainist colonel in exile. Odd to meet the evidence of my history first in the form of its enemy, the exiles biting their nails, biding their time in a backwater of time. And I found Haitians like Jean Weiner, as handsome and lofty as a Watusi, with a cackling hysterical laugh when he described the origin of his distinguished Roman Catholic family: "A Jew from Vienna came here to trade in coffee! Left a family of brown coffee merchants in Jacmel, in Jérémie, and another wife here in Port-au-Prince, so now Wei-ner is a fine name for a family *croyant et bien-pensant,* all of us married in the cathedral! I'm the only one who tells the truth, my friend."

His rebellion against the conservative old family consisted in saying, Yes, I am. *I am!*

Through Jean, I met a morose accountant with a degree from a school of business in Philadelphia and a mania for recounting the days of his persecution. Restaurants, doormen, professors, women had all treated him like a *Negro*—"*Moi qui est Haitien!*" he cried. Remembering the purgatory of Philadelphia, he despised Haiti, the peasantry, and the Jews, and his name was Cohen.

When he confided one evening that the Jews are at the root of all the trouble in Haiti and the world, I said to him, "I'm a Jew." He peered at me blankly through his red-rimmed eyes, as if he had never seen one before. "And you, with your name," I said.

"My grandfather came from Jamaica."

"You must have had a Jewish grandfather in there someplace."

"You're making that up! . . . How did you know?"

"Cohen."

"*Cohen?*" he asked. To him Cohen was the name of a Mass-going Haitian accountant. I explained that the Cohanim were priests and he was descended from priests and princes.

"Priests don't have children," he said irritably.

"Do you really think Jews caused all the trouble in Haiti?"

"No, not all," he said, "but the wars, the world wars they started, all the wars hurt us, too."

There was a double ledger for his secret Jewish grandfather and his need to find an explanation for trouble and sin. I could nag at him with facts, scandalize him with my own history, but I could never change his accounting and put Cohen, the Haitian accountant, in touch with Cohen, the man with an ancestor who did not begin the line of Cohens in Jamaica. He had horn-rimmed glasses, owlish eyes with reddened conjunctiva, pockmarked black skin, and a Jew-hating heart that was outraged by the information, which he knew already, that his name meant something drastic in his past. He was not descended from an infinite line of Jamaican mulattoes.

"Priests don't have children," he mumbled, "but of course princes do. That's just a theory you have, however. I've studied the Jews very carefully in Jamaica and Philadelphia."

"If you knew more about the troubles of the world," I told him, "you'd be safer from them."

"*J'en ai eu, des difficultés.*"

"Try to learn what they come from."

I was only confusing the black Roman Catholic Cohen in search of clear definitions.

There were others like him, of course, good Mass-going Haitians with names like Goldenberg, Weiner, Levi, or with Sephardic names like Mendes and Silvera. The legend of Jewish ancestry might make some of them giggle, but it was even more fantastic and unreal than the feudal French names of other Haitians. The Duc de Marmalade was one of the courtiers of the mad emperor Faustin Soulouque, and the hamlet of Marmalade, reachable by burro, still exists in the scrub jungle center of Haiti. Faustin the First (there was no second or other) named 4 princes, 59 dukes, 90 counts, 200 barons, 346 chevaliers. Later the deputies and senators also became barons. I searched, but could never find any of their robes, crowns, patents of authority. In Petit Goâve and Cabaret I found no dukes and no duchesses. Massacre and forgetfulness have ended these lines.

I N JACMEL, a tiny town on the sea with an unpaved Grand Rue, perhaps once a week a police jeep scattered the traffic jams of black Haitian pigs, flailing dust; the *cochons noirs* as skinny and speedy as dogs. There was a *pension,* telephones and electricity which rarely worked, the mud huts of an African village—and in this place, Jacmel, I found a Jewish tailor. A few elegantly carpentered Haitian dream houses floated above reality like candy visions, slats and shutters, parapets and magic cages filled with lizards or birds, but Monsieur Schneider lived in a dwelling only a few boards and nails separated from a *caille-paille,* the country shelter of mud and straw. He did his work at a hand-treadled machine in the dusty street, his head tilted to one side to favor his good eye, his joints swollen and his body twisted by arthritis. He was old and wore rags, like many Haitians, but the rags were sewn into the blurred shape of a European shirt and suit. It was too hot for such formality. He was one of three white people in the town. In the air around him, like the insects and the animals, eddied the members of his extended family, the mixed African and Semitic, some dark and some light, children and adults, wives and grandchildren.

"Mister Schneider," I began, first in English. No English, but he understood what I was asking. Was *I?* Yes. *Oui.* A flood of Yiddish poured out of his head. I spoke no Yiddish. He looked at me as if to doubt my sanity. A Jew I said, and spoke no Yiddish? He tried Creole. We settled on French, which he spoke in a Yiddish accent, with Creole words and phrases. He believed I was what I said I was, for otherwise what gain for either of us? Who needed to tell lies here, so far from the Czar's police? He kicked amiably at the grandchildren—children?—playing about the treadles of his Singer machine. The treadle was cast with ironwork scrolls and art nouveau symbols polished by his bare feet. To do honor to our conversation, he slipped his feet into sisal sandals soled with sliced and shaped rubber tires.

He did not have the look of a person who asked deep questions, but he stared at me from his one good eye. "What's a Jew—?" he asked.

I also wondered.

"—doing in Jacmel?"

His face was shriveled against sunlight, shrunken by age, blotched and deeply freckled. It looked like a dog's muzzle. "Why is a Jew *living* here?" I asked him in return.

"My home," he said. "You call this a life? My wife is dead. I have another wife. My children and grandchildren are here."

"Would you forgive the question? How did you happen to settle in Jacmel?"

He pumped furiously at the machine. He was fixing a seam, a simple matter, but he gave it all his concentration. Then he squinted around at me. I had moved so he wouldn't be staring into the sun. He winked, Jew to Jew.

"And where else?"

Jérémie, Saint Marc, Cap Haitien, Port-au-Prince, Port-de-Paix—that's all. So he settled in Jacmel.

"Were you Polish?"

"Russian."

"So were my parents. Why didn't you go to the United States?"

"Ah," he said. "Because I wished to learn the French and Creole languages, *c'est vrai?*"

"*Non.*"

"Because"—and he spread wide his arms—"I had adventure in my heart?"

"No."

He put down his cloth and he stood up. He put his face close to mine, pulled at the lid of the dead eye as if he were stretching a piece of cloth, and said, "I went to Ellis Isle, maybe your father did too. But he didn't have a sick eye. It was infected from the filth. They sent me away. And then I wandered, no place left, so instead of killing myself I came to Haiti."

"I'm sorry," I said, although it seemed foolish to be oppressed by a sick eye from a generation before I was born.

He started to laugh. It was not the dry, old-man's laughter of my uncles in Cleveland. It was a rich, abandoned, Haitian old-man's laughter. He clutched at his crotch for luck. "You see these children? You see all the brown Schneider children in Jacmel? Many died, my wives often die, but look what I have done. I have proved God is not malevolent. He let me live. He let some of these children live. God is indifferent, but I have shown, not proved, of course, but *demonstrated* that He is not malevolent."

"If you believe, God is not evil, merely all-powerful."

He put his face down. He reached for a packet of sugar and held it up to my face. "If He were all-powerful, then He would be evil. He could not allow what He allows. You like good Haitian coffee, Monsieur? Marie!" he shouted into the caille-paille. *"Blanc v'le café— poté."*

I drank coffee with the tailor and his new wife, who said not a word as she sat with us. He sucked at sugar and sipped his coffee through it.

"I have a few books," he said, "a scholar I was not. My uncle was a rabbi, I think my brother was going to be a rabbi, but"—he shrugged—"I never found out what he became. You're not a rabbi?"

"No."

"It's not so stupid to ask. I heard of rabbis now who don't speak Yiddish."

"I don't speak Hebrew, either."

"Then you couldn't be a rabbi, could you?"

I wanted to give him answers and ask questions, but we made mere conversation. We were two Jews speaking a peculiar polyglot in the town of Jacmel, which few people ever visited, even if they lived in the nearby villages of Carrefour Fauché, Bassin Bleu, or Bainet. At that time there was no paved road from Port-au-Prince, and when it rained, even jeeps couldn't pass the streams. Jacmel was a port at the end of the world, a few rutted streets, a market, survivors. He didn't offer to show me about the village. We sat in his portion of the road in front of his door. His arthritis confined him to his sewing machine and his house of wood, mud, and straw. The house had a floor of hewn slats; it was a caille-paille with improvements. His wife watched us with mournful eyes, as if I might take him away from her, but time was taking him away faster than I could. We had little to say across the years and history between us except to give each other greetings in the town of Jacmel.

When I said goodbye, dizzy with coffee, he stood up painfully, a small thin bent brown man, a creature neither Russian nor Jewish nor Haitian, something molded in time's hands like a clay doll. He put out his hand and said in a cracked voice, laughing at the peculiar word he must have pronounced for the first time in years: "*Shalom!*"

A few years later a hurricane devastated the village, and now, with another generation gone by, I wonder what of Schneider's mark on life can still be felt there. Has one of the mixed-blood Schneiders learned to sew and use the treadle? Have they scattered? How many survive? He had many sons and daughters; something has been sown in this corner of Haiti which was forsaken, like the rest of the world, by an indifferently fructifying God.

I FOUND THE old Russian Jew Lazaroff living with his wife and his library in the hills above Canape Vert. He had a white beard, a shock of long white hair; he wore a linen caftan that vaguely suggested Russian Orthodox priestly garb. His wife was Haitian, silent, wizened, and leathery, with a kind of clay bleaching on her face. There were children in the house, some theirs, some the children of servants.

Monsieur Lazaroff was unused to speaking with visitors; it was a skill he didn't need anymore. He served eucalyptus tea from a samovar, pouring himself. He smiled without speaking when I looked at his books and said, "I've read that. . . . I've read that one."

"Please, if you would like to borrow?"

"No thank you, I have enough to read. You've been here long?"

"Long," he said.

"You plan to stay very long?"

"Forever," he said.

"Why?"

He shrugged. "That's not so far away."

As we walked past the shelves, he ran his hands tenderly over leather, paper, bindings, embossings. "Books die in this climate," he said. "I try to keep them alive."

And that was that. We didn't become friends. He let me see his collection and one visit sufficed. He filled his days with reading these books that he treasured like icons.

The French Calmann, who had suffered under Hitler, chose not to suffer under atomic poisoning. "If that happens," I said, "Haiti won't be safe, either."

"Haiti will be safer. This time I've done all I can."

These flight-obsessed men, cutting their losses, limited their gains to nothing but survival. They served their time on earth in a refuge against bewilderment. Then it happened that I came to know Shimon Tal, the fisherman, who had more than survival in mind. He was an exception among the fishers of souls and souls to be fished (often, of course, the fishers and the fish were identical); the international bureaucrats, United Nations study groups, American military missions, Jesus missionaries, Belgian and Breton priests, chic Episcopalians, CARE officials trying to keep the milk away from the weevils and the politicians, researchers on detached service from the Katherine Dunham dance troupe, entranced addicts dug into a good connection, advisors and profiteers, apprentice white gods, retired white gods, the Swedish geologist looking for gold, oil, tungsten, or hemp—anything salable—Greenwich Village women who loved black men, or at least hoped to be loved in return, homosexuals, political exiles with a purchase on the police, escapees from Devil's Island, the friendly Gestapo informer, wreathed in engaging boyish smiles, and, of course, the wandering students and anthropologists who wore cast-off World War II clothes and were forever looking for an authentic voodoo ceremony, finding a staged one, settling for an authentic cockfight.

A lively American woman, Shelagh Burns, reminded me that I might like to meet a fellow Jew. He was a United Nations fishing expert, an Israeli, and she described him as weathered and quiet as a farmer. "I like him, he's funny. He pretends he's asleep all the time because he's, you know—shy?"

I'd heard of shyness.

She had met him at an obligatory meeting for a UN official; he was hiding from the foreign colony. The notion of a shy Israeli, teaching this island people to fish, made me curious. Maybe he wasn't shy, only embarrassed.

I didn't find him at any United Nations or American Aid drink-fests, but eventually we met. I was visiting the Damiens agriculture station outside Port-au-Prince. His Haitian "counterpart," trainee Monsieur Gérard, a gleaming, very polite graduate of the Damiens School, hung at his elbow as if his every motion gave hints about the puzzling folkways of fish. The counterpart hoped to learn how fish bit and bred, swarmed in schools and took to the rushes, by studying this foreigner's gestures. We toured the ponds—carp, tilapia, fry, mature fish—and Tal explained about protein starvation and the bounty that could be provided by the sea and also by rivers, marshes, ditches, and ponds.

Then he asked to visit my family. When he did, without Monsieur Gerard and his thermometer, grain samples, and Hebrew-French phrase book, he looked like just another lonely middle-aged Jew, far from home and missing his wife and children. His face was sunburned and peeling; there were broken capillaries, sunburn upon sunburn. Pale smile lines radiated from corners of eyes, corners of mouth. It was a face of hard work and conviction. His family waited on the kibbutz back home. He was doing this service and he would use his pay to buy an earthmover. In Israel he had built ponds to raise fish—*pisciculture* was a new word to me—refining the techniques taken by Yugoslavs from the ancient Chinese. In Haiti he was also planting tilapia, the African shmoo-fish, in streams and ditches, besides constructing a few experimental carp ponds for venturesome Haitian businessmen.

"They are a wonderful people. They are so beautiful. But there are certain problems—" And he shook his head. There were difficulties in organizing fish ponds, threading a way through bureaucracies. "But they are a beautiful, wonderful people."

He meant the perfume of Haitian women, the great gold hoops of earrings, and the sliding, enticing walk of those women. There were wonderful things in Haiti. A sensual walk didn't help to clean the ponds or keep the spry safe from the voracious frogs or feed the grains into the stream at the proper steady rate.

"—a wonderful, wonderful people, anyway. But they don't know anything about fish."

He was lonely and I was married, with small children in the house, and thus he became uncle, grandfather, guide, and patron, in return for a place to sit and talk. "We can learn from these wonderful Haitian people," he said. "They know how to dress so beautiful. They can sit and do nothing and smile so. We need to learn some of that, too."

In the meantime, Monsieur Gérard, his colleague, learned to plant fish in the ditches, flooded fields, and waterways. I traveled with them by jeep into the markets of Les Cayes, Saint Marc, Jérémie, and up the mountain from Port-au-Prince to Kenscoff—pine and euca-lyptus, a sudden spring in the perpetual humid August—and every-where tilapia could be bought for a few pennies in the marketplace. Tilapia is a stubborn little African fish that grows eagerly in salt, brackish, or fresh water, in ditches, streams, rice fields, ponds, and puddles, breeding handsomely, provided only that the water remains warm. It had not existed in Haiti; Tal brought it from Africa. Now it grew throughout the island. Tal guessed that the fish, installed near the mouths of streams giving onto the Caribbean, had been carried to the mountains by birds; or perhaps eggs had clung to the birds' wings and then been dropped upstream in mountain sources.

We stood in the market at Saint Marc and looked at some cooked fish in a pan. "*Combien?*" I asked.

"*Deux cob.*"

"*Qu'est-ce que c'est?*"

"*Poisson juif.*"

They had never seen a Jew, but they knew by the *telejiol* that this fish was to be called Jewfish. In another village it was called *poisson israélite.* And in another, *poisson Assad,* because it had been found on lands belonging to a man named Assad, a Lebanese.

Tal played with my children, sat with my wife, told us his trou-bles, and said, "Someday you will visit us on the kibbutz." Amid the drums of voodoo ceremonies, the crazy golden age of Haitian prosperity—generals in Eisenhower jackets tailored in Jamaica, much aid from elsewhere—it seemed odd to remember the nation of Jews far away and for which this man longed. "It is not so much luxury, but it is nice," he said. "If they let us live, you will see swimming, culture, fine things. This could be a beautiful, wonderful country, also."

I took ill with malaria and he sat by my bed. I thought I might die, but he was smiling and knew I would live.

He told me about the other Israeli in Haiti—Morgen, a tomato farmer. He called himself an Israeli, and therefore Tal considered him what he said he was, though he spoke no Hebrew. He grew tomatoes with cheap Haitian labor. He planned to ship them to Florida. He would get rich on delicious little year-round Haitian tomatoes. He borrowed money and took the required uniformed Haitian partners. Sometimes they came to inspect the fields and took a bite from a tomato, and when the juice ran down the lovely front of the Eisenhower combat jacket, an aide ran forward to wipe.

Suddenly there were new taxes. Why new taxes?

Taxes, everyone knows about Haitian taxes, but Morgen didn't know. It was a game they played with foreign businessmen—not so much with Brown & Root, not the big companies from Texas, but with the tasty little innocents like Morgen. Morgen didn't know what he was doing.

However, if he improved the balance of the partnership, an arrangement could be made about the taxes. How to do that? A colonel, squeezing deliciously into a tomato, little pink seeds on his chin, suggested that his share be doubled.

"But twice 50 percent is 100 percent!" cried Morgen.

The colonel made a lightning calculation. "Yess," he said.

"That leaves nothing for me!"

The colonel's lips bubbled fresh tomato juice. He agreed. Yess.

"Impossible!" Morgen wailed.

"Possible," said the colonel, a student of advanced Haitian mathematics.

Morgen found himself one midnight being awakened by gentlemen in a police Buick. He finished the night in jail. He passed a few more days there. A Haitian jail is as bad as a Syrian one, especially when a man's partner is not only an army colonel, but also a police colonel. A Syrian jail might be worse, but a Haitian jail is bad enough.

Tal found the correct channel for the money and got him out. "Go home, not to America," he said. "Son, you're not a tomato rancher. Don't try to do something you can't, such as raising tomatoes in Haiti."

"I'm not really an Israeli," said Morgen. "It's very complicated."

"Well, be one. It's your last chance. You're no bargain, Morgen."

Tal sat by the bed in which I was recovering from malarial hepatitis, smelling the damp ticking of my mattress, and told me that the poor fellow was just a confused Jew from middle somewhere-else who thought he could purify his soul with tomatoes and dollars. He had a tattoo on his wrist. A survivor, but a casualty. Tal shook his head mournfully. "The trouble we get into," he said. "In Israel it's different, different trouble. I don't think we can make anything with Morgen, but he's tired. He thinks all you have to do now is grow the tomatoes. He should go home to rest."

Amid the smell of mangoes and woodsmoke, the hot winds off black history, the humid simmering of Port-au-Prince, I had found a few black Roman Catholic voodooesque Jews. The traders of a hundred years ago, 150 years ago, yesterday, had wandered so far, trying their luck, and died after planting their brown Cohens, Goldenbergs, Weiners, Levis, Schneiders on this forgotten island. In the mulatto population of Haiti there were also French, Germans, Danes—one family of beautiful coffee-colored girls with Scandinavian faces, finally achieving the smooth tan that Danish women always want—and gloomy Poles from the village of Casals. And Jews.

Amid the descendants of, among others, the gloomy Poles who had survived the Revolution of 1804, there was also the beautiful Dr. Goldenberg, plump, brown, *diplomée* from the Cornell Medical School. "They use makeup," Tal said. "They walk so. They dance so. Our women can learn from them even now," said the man who disseminated the Jewfish. He would have liked his daughters on the kibbutz to learn the secrets of Creole grace from the languorous *doctoresse*, Felice Goldenberg.

One morning he rousted me at dawn to come watch the carp spawn in a tricky pond. Monsieur Gérard also stood there, beaming with the pride of a parent. "Look!" said Tal. "There will be good spry!"

The Israeli and the Haitian shook hands over their successful collaboration. In a place deprived of sufficient protein, the young carp were great riches.

COHEN, THE anti-Semite, found a business to suit his temperament. He imported Manischewitz Kosher Wine, sweet and thick, and advertised it for use on Saturday nights. *Kosher* was the magic word he blandished, magic first of all for himself. He understood the Haitian tradition of fear of the white stranger and longing for his potency; the mysteries of the alien people had disturbed his own soul. Fountains of youth and aphrodisiacs were popular in Latin and Caribbean places. "KOSHER!" screamed the newspaper announcements. The anti-Semite, Cohen, felt pleasure surge through his body at the menace and promise of the Word. He would profit from it. "KOSHER! Guaranteed to be KOSHER! Try it and see! Try it tonight! If it doesn't turn out to be KOSHER, your money back!"

HAITI WAS a land without Jews, no rabbi, no place of worship, no community, and yet one Jew, Shimon Tal, made it a Jewish place for me. In the cemetery there were Jews, with crosses over their graves.

When I recovered from malaria, I wanted to take Tal to Jacmel to meet old Schneider. "I'm waiting for that," Tal said.

Our jeep bucked and churned over rocky dry streambeds into the isolated town. I asked myself how the squinting Jewish tailor, dry as a pod in the sun, survived that Haitian male vanity that leads every man to seek to be the *coq du village*, the village cock. Well, for one thing, he seemed to be the father of most of the nearby children. He rode with the vanity. He removed himself into himself, and observed his children, blood of his blood, growing their own souls, compounded of Schneider and of Haiti. And old as he was, teasing with me, he had touched his own balls for luck against the stranger.

Suddenly the leaning nightmare craziness of Jacmel appeared—dust, chickens, speedy black pigs in the road. I expected to find the tailor sewing in the street, as I had first seen him. But it was an overcast day and maybe he was indoors. *"Où est Mónsieur Schneider?"*

"Pas conné," don't know, said a child, and ran. I was sure it was one of his sons. He stood as far away as he could, giggling and shouting, *"Pas conné."*

Of course he knew.

"Où est Schneider?"

In his house, open to the street, the sewing machine stood dusty on a base of slats in the corner. He had died and was forgotten—weeks dead. He had died and was not forgotten. There was a ceremony that night for the rest of his soul.

In the *hounfor,* the temple outside town in the brush, an all-day ceremony was going on, three drummers urging the congregation into a whole series of possessions by the new god Ibo-Juif. Tal and I joined the stream of communicants. Evidently Ibo-Juif was a happy god. The celebrants were drinking the blood of a bull recently slaughtered, catching the thick flow in pans laid at the slit belly. Gleaming brown boys, all named Schneider, danced about us, with firm tiny erections after so much excitement and laughter. It was a slaughter and homage for the disappeared tailor from the Ukraine. His Haitian family danced, seeming to climb in the air, hauling invisible ladders after them as they climbed, and only the wife sat exhausted by her weeping in a corner of the zinc-roofed shack. Waves of drumbeats swept over her grief. The boys grabbed their genitals for luck and consolation in the time of the death of their father.

Tal and I stood silent. Then Tal's lips were moving. He ignored the need for ten men, he ignored his own atheism. He was murmuring the prayer for the dead. Later I told him he should have held himself at the groin in that all-purpose Haitian curse, blessing, and reassurance of power in the midst of ultimate powerlessness.

WE RETURNED to Port-au-Prince almost without speaking. I stood in a stream to guide the jeep forward over a mud bank. Tal showed me how to spin a jack tool when a tire blew out in a stretch of dried ruts. By the time we reached the outskirts of the capital—market women, dogs and chickens and pigs in the road, peddlers, the mobs of hungry-eyed children staring with dead sugar stalks in their mouths—we could talk of other things. His family, my family, fishing, the Artibonite dam project which would stand as an uncompleted ruin when the Magloire government fell. And the good sense and luxurious walk of the mocha-colored *doctoresse,* Felice Goldenberg.

"At least they sacrificed a bull," Tal said. "Not a pig."

CHAPTER EIGHT

The Philosopher's Circle

DROVE A narrow rutted road nearly straight up the mountain from Port-au-Prince, first past the districts of Pacot and Bourdon—already it was cooler—and then past the village square with its church, the rich suburb of Pétionville, and then up, up, past the streams of market women, goats, burros, donkeys, trudging on their errands, past the cluster of houses called La Boule and the mountain chalet restaurant, Le Perchoir, with its view of the harbor below, past banks of flaming bougainvillea and rich tangles of vines and ravines littered with automobiles that had made their final wrong turn, past children in blue uniforms on their way to school, past peasants smoking their pipes and holding out bunches of flowers for sale, and finally arrived in a place of cool streams, water bouncing off rocks, clear air, birdsong, eucalyptus.

The village of Kenscoff was only a half hour from Port-au-Prince—perhaps a little longer, since I planned to return to my wife and daughters and not leave my Chevy *bogota* tumbled into a ravine. It seemed like a Swiss mountain hamlet. For every kilometer of winding climbing road, the temperature was said to drop one degree. The elite, arriving for weekends, would climb out of their cars, stretch and yawn to adjust to the altitude pressure change, put on their cableknit ski sweaters, and say how good it was to be a Haitian in Haiti, where a person can have everything.

The people who lived up here grew sweet vegetables, tomatoes, lettuce, onions, carrots, and carried them by donkey or in baskets on their heads down to the markets in town. They also grew coffee and sometimes I could smell it roasting. I looked down from Kenscoff and saw Port-au-Prince extended along the Caribbean Sea, ships in the harbor, sailboats made of burned-out logs and random swatches of fabric, mists, charcoal smoke hovering over the dense smudged slum of La Saline, and distant rocky islets in the Bay of La Gonâve. The city I had just left seemed as far away now as Cleveland, Ohio, and the imaginary world I was trying to conjure up.

In Kenscoff, high on its cool mountain above Port-au-Prince, Judge Noh, the coffee merchant, summoned the finest intellectuals of the village to keep him company every afternoon amid the mounds of beans, the scales, the steel barrels. The group included a retired Haitian senator, a doctor-lawyer (degrees from Paris, but never practiced either trade), a schoolmaster, an occasional honored guest. Sometimes the guest was the Breton village priest, although the Philosophers were all nonbelievers; sometimes it was the American writer who stayed in his friend Jean Weiner's cottage nearby, tapping at his Olivetti Lettera 32 as lizards jumped from the carriage and eyes that were seeing their first typewriter peered into the open door at this strange foreign metal tambour.

I spent three- or four-day stretches in Kenscoff, escaping the heat of town, perhaps escaping family, too, while I worked at writing a novel to be called *The Man Who Was Not With It*. Despite my yearning for privacy, I also needed sociability, the opening and the shutting of the mouth to utter companionable sounds.

"What is Haiti's role in the world?" was the subject announced for one afternoon's session of the Cenacle des Philosophes. Judge Noh suggested a preliminary answer, mild and Aristotelean: "We are not so powerful as the United States, nor so mighty as Russia. Therefore we must perform the act of the hyphen—the *trait d'union*—between these giant nations." *Gigantesque* was the word he used about Haiti's rivals for power.

"Naturally, the third force," said the doctor-lawyer, who also believed in green shoes made of male catskin, for the benefit of his virility. He had studied in Paris, but had done his learning in Haiti. "We are non-aligned. We Haitians do not choose to dwell in a world of right angles or parallel figures."

On other days, as the sun went spinning through the eucalyptus branches and the smell dropped from the leaves, we discussed whether the Christian God recognizes the voodoo gods as cousins; we debated the deforestation of the coffee bushes for cooking fuel, the origins of Creole, the mission of France and of her sons in slavery. The Philosophers of Kenscoff, descended from both slaves and slaveholders, brooded continually upon the ironies of their destiny on this island cast loose in the Caribbean Sea. Monsieur Dissaint, the schoolmaster, looked at his knuckles and said, "God disposes."

His friends were grateful for the lack of disquisition. They forgave the taking of God's name in cliché.

Mostly we stayed away from Haitian politics, which traditionally created fatalities, and sex, which seemed permanently settled for these gentlemen, although a joke was appropriate now and then among the fellowship of thinkers. Madame Noh appeared with trays of little cups of dark Haitian roast, and disappeared to get the cakes and more coffee, and the philosophers plied their trade as the lines of peasant women wended their way on the dirt paths nearby, heads burdened with Kenscoff vegetables, children trailing, dogs trailing, chickens darting. For us, the Cenacle provided a nice break in the day. Occasionally we waited while Judge Noh weighed a tin of coffee beans and counted out payment into the gray-black palm of a peasant from Kenscoff or Furcy or the misty slopes of Forêt-des-Pins.

I took my meals at the little Hotel de Florville, where the Vichy colonel was passing his last years, doing his calisthenics in the dining room, disciplining himself in public as an example to the colonies, marching back and forth, swearing vengeance on those who had dishonored the Maréchal. He was still forbidden to return to France. For some reason he chose to decline among black non-Frenchmen, explosively correcting the waiters' and chambermaids' grammatical errors. Every afternoon I would stroll up the road, my day's work done, toward the philosopher's circle. By that time I was hungry for the coffee and companionship after a long morning of cockcrow, chicken gabble, Creole laughter and funning, and privacy over my notebook and Olivetti portable.

As different from home as any place could be, Haiti had become something like home, with the complications, responsibilities, and fretful connections of a home place. One day in Kenscoff I received the unexpected visit of a plump American woman, wife of Chican, a Haitian businessman. She wanted me to hide her. She had been having an affair with a handsome detective who was the President's chief torturer, and she suddenly felt guilty about it—"guilt" was her word—because her husband had grown suspicious. "What else does *he* do?" she demanded. "What kind of double standard is this?"

I was not honored by my appointment as confidant and protector.

"*He* thinks I should just stay home and diet—but he married me because he liked *zaftig*—"

During her analysis of the situation a figure appeared at the doorway with a drawn pistol. Husband was red-eyed, possessed by demons, seemed not to recognize his old friend. "Don't shoot!" I said.

"Shoot if you prefer," said his wife, valiantly taking her stand behind me. The bullet would pass straight through my body into hers, so that she could carry with her a witness to the injustice of the double standard.

The pistol wavered. She dodged. The pistol searched another path. The overweight adultress was nimble. Unless he could shoot around corners, there was no way to plug her without plugging me.

"I have an appointment with philosophers," I said. "Why don't I leave you two alone to discuss things? Make yourself at home. Have a glass of water."

The husband, beneath the adrenaline and purplish capillaries and churning bile, remembered that I was his North American tennis partner, not the regime torturer, and let his snubbed weapon droop toward the tile floor. His eyes gazed warmly into mine. "A mere et cetera," he said, and I decided he might not kill her. I remembered the pistol license he had shown me: "—*must be used only against burglars, wild animals, snakes, assassins, et cetera.*"

At the Cenacle on the coffee porch, where today there also sat a visiting merchant from Jérémie, cousin of Judge Noh, I wanted to propose the topic, "Should a Wife Involve an Innocent Acquaintance in Her Husband's Intention to Murder?" However, the philosophers were already engaged in more cosmic debate about the policies of

UNESCO in rural education. I drank my coffee in silence until the judge asked, "You have an opinion? So silent today, my dear friend?" I offered an opinion. I ate a cake. I returned to my chalet and found that the husband and wife had disappeared together, leaving one automobile behind. The next day an employee appeared on the tap-tap from town to drive the Buick back down the mountain, first shooting me a long, slow reproachful look.

"You have the automobile of Messieur?"

"It's parked out here. You're sitting in it."

"You have kept it all night?"

"Right where he left it."

"Au revoir, Messieur."

"Bon voyage," I said.

In the transmission-eating, brake-destroying way of Haitian drivers, he floated the automobile onto the grade and let it roll down the mountain road without starting the motor. This contributes both to gas economy and lowering the rate of population growth by populating the ravines with wrecks.

THE PEOPLE in these mountains smiled with gentleness, and greeted the stranger with kindness, but their lives were not necessarily gentle and kind. When they celebrated a festival by sticking a pig, they did it with the same laughter with which they responded to a comic song or my mishap when I stumbled on the path. When the blood ran at a ceremony, the drums pounding, clairin sprayed from the mouth of the mambo or the houngan, they stared with awe at a dying animal and consumed it as they did their lives, avidly. When we drank the steaming blood of a still-alive bull, its life running into wooden bowls, it was an emblem of their fate on earth, a great and important ceremony, and also vital nourishment they were rarely able to afford.

They touched the world very closely, hungrily, with pride and desire. At first I felt mostly the tropical juice and smells of Haiti, the fun in the drums, loudness, and laughter. Then the pain that came along with unremitting need led me to regard their disastrous governance. The village of Kenscoff was an escape from the edginess of Port-au-Prince, the capital of a gathering chaos. In Kenscoff, sleepy and subdued, alone, resting in the brief tropical twilight, I sat on a rock and waited for night. Sometimes in the glow of moon and starlight, strolling alone on a dirt path, I would hear the soft sounds of peasants in their huts, the appeals of children and the answering solace of mothers and fathers, discussing in the dark the events of the day before they lay down on straw. Then, a little later, I heard the high keening of the night wind coming through the canyon, a noise from space, it seemed, a reminder that the universe is parent to everyone, even these strangers on the mountain. The rock I had sat on an hour before seemed to disappear into the darkness, almost reversing its progress of being born out of the shiftings of earth. And then the next day it was cleared by a *coumbite* and the place where it had been was planted in a dream of future eating. It took imagination to think that this people might find their way in a world that only seemed to be what it had been.

I PICKED UP my mail at the American Embassy in Port-au-Prince, in its old house on the Champ de Mars, near the Rex Théâtre and the Rex Café, where I read my letters and ate fairly responsible ice cream from a fairly clean spoon. The letters from what used to be home often wondered when I might return. That was an interesting point. I was in no hurry; I wasn't sure I could sleep without the proper stereophonic balance of cockcrow, barking dogs, and voodoo drums. I needed the smells of rotting mangoes, charcoal fires, and a sun-drenched people. I needed to be where I was, it seemed, so why move? I still had work to do, perhaps partly to burn Cleveland, Ohio, out of my face before I let it back.

But after more than a year in Haiti, I was becoming one of the castaways. I had absorbed the style of the nonbeachcombers on this island without good beaches. One morning I was sitting at the little café in the garden next to the Rex Théâtre, on the Place des Héros, which was called by Haitian wits the "Place des Zéros." The National Palace, huge and white, stood nearby. As my writing material I used the backs of old menus. I was wearing cut-off jeans, sandals, a T-shirt, and was very tan.

A middle-aged American tourist couple was pacing back and forth in front of the Rex. Someone hadn't shown up to meet them. The visitors were growing agitated. They stared at me and then, leaning on each other, dared to approach. The lady began: "We wait friend. Friend no come."

"That's all right, you can talk English."

She paused, amazed, and then continued. "Friend no meet twelve o'clock. We go hotel. You see friend, big person like so, you say—"

"Ma'am," I said. "I understand. I'll tell anyone looking for you that you're back at the . . . what hotel is it?"

Trickling perspiration, bewildered, they started to walk away. Then they consulted with each other and turned, "Excuse! pardon! so sorry!" cried the husband. "How did you learn your English?"

"I was born and raised in Lakewood, Ohio," I said.

Joyfully they gazed at each other. "A scholarship!" said the wife. "Our American government wanted to teach you American ways!"

It was time to think about going home. After acceptance of the idea that Haiti lay at the center of reality, perhaps we should consider once again that other far universe of underground drains and uninterrupted electrical current. I came to say goodbye to Judge Noh, his wife, and the Cenacle des Philosophes. The day was hot, even in Kenscoff, and the eucalyptus trees were dropping their pungent sap. To celebrate the occasion, we lifted little glasses of Rhum Barbancourt along with our coffee although the Kenscoff Cartesians preferred the pure reason of black roast to the intuitive leaps of amber rum. The schoolmaster cited that great saying of Valéry: "Au revoir."

"You will carry the wisdom of Haiti back to your country?" the judge asked. "That Union makes Force, but not only Union?"

Nothing could deter me.

"And not forget our sufferings, also?" inquired the doctor-lawyer.

I swore.

"Then we too shall never forget!"

We all drank.

M Y FRIEND Roland Devauges and I were stranded when our wives decided to return, respectively, to France and the United States. Surely it was time for us to go home too, but not this minute. It was summer 1954.

Roland was a French anthropologist, teaching at the Université d'Haiti and writing a monograph on the structure of Port-au-Prince. In due course we planned to follow our wives, but in the meantime, we had our appointed tasks to finish. This hard duty involved staying up late, dancing, drinking, forgetting our sworn vows, and careful analysis of the entire situation, in the traditional folkway of temporary bachelors. As a frugal Frenchman, Roland instructed me in "sun laundry"—hanging shirts to dry in the open air, letting scientifically valid tropical rays do the work of cleaning by oxidation that is ordinarily, in less knowledgeable societies, entrusted to soap and water. My malaria had given a tasteful yellow glow to my skin; his research into the cumulative effects of rum was doing the same for him. We enjoyed, in the waning weeks of our time in Haiti, one of those intense friendships between men that are rare after adolescence. We were not boys without women. We were grown men in trouble with our wives.

It turned out that the publisher whose advance I counted on decided my book wasn't what he expected. Instead of sending money, he sent a long letter of advice. This may have been part of the curse put upon my soul by the thirteen slaves from the treasure hunt. The publisher was generous with suggestions.

I wrote back graciously, "Fuck off, asshole," and with stoic acceptance punched a jagged hole in the wall. We young writers know how to accept sincere criticism.

My true friend Roland lent me money for my ticket. I got home, returned the money, and then lost track of him. At the Musée de l'Homme in Paris, they said he was doing research in Africa.

Thirty years later in Paris, criminally jetlagged, I was walking at three A.M. in St.-Germain-des-Prés and stared through a window at a group of celebrants closing a brasserie. They were drunk and disorderly in the classic mode, and when they glimpsed me, one of them rushed out to grab my arm. "Didn't I see you in Mauritius or on Gorée or in the Seychelles?" It was a group of French anthropologists on home leave. I had a drink and another, although this is not the prescribed remedy for dehydration and jet lag.

"You work in Africa?" I asked.

"Vive l'Afrique!"

"Do you happen to know a friend of mine, Roland Devauges?"

"Ah," said one, "in the Congo, I think. Zaire."

"Maybe," I said.

"Great lover of African women?"

"That's the one," I said.

He beamed. "Died two years ago."

It was as if the debris of my youth tumbled in on me. It was now official. Friends part; people die; it'll happen every time. But for me Roland is now forever the young man who sun-cleaned his shirts and lent me $200 to come home on. And was the lover of a dancing "doctoresse," as he called her—a grandmother when I last visited her in Port-au-Prince.

L EAVING BY ship in the summer of 1954, I had troubles in the customs house with an officer who wanted to put mysterious taxes on our belongings. Captain Champlain was that cool official, known the world over, the one who makes others sweat. The sun beat down murderously on the zinc roof; fingers turned slimy as I tried to fill out forms; he knew exactly what he wanted and the heat could not touch him. Amid the shouts, groans, and shrieks of stevedores, the dust and reek of the port, he remained calm, wearing military khakis and a khaki tie with Colonel Prosper's question mark embroidered on it. He waited until the answer to his question would dawn on the *blanc*. He grinned, showed his teeth, and his charmed face looked as if it could open up and send the flies reeling in his breath. I argued for my rights against the taxes he had invented on the spot, export duties on my own shirts, inspection duties, *impôts de passage*. I called out the names of friends in the military, in the government. Finally he shrugged and said, "Give me half the tax."

"That's ridiculous."

"A third."

"No."

"Then ten dollars," he burst out, "to repay me for my time which I have wasted. I've got to get something from you." And he grabbed himself for magic against defeat by a foreigner.

I gave him ten dollars, and hoped all my suitcases got on board. During my year and a half, I had learned the basic techniques. Take money from pocket, hold it between two fingers. Recipient extends palm and pauses a moment submissively. His eyelids fall. He looks dreamy, I look nonchalant. Bill touches hand. Hand closes; the heat of two bodies invisibly shimmers; an incomplete communion is celebrated through the intermediary of cash.

Tal was there to say goodbye, and Captain Champlain inclined his head. "That is why I make things so easy for you. Monsieur Tal has brought us the *poisson israélite.*"

"Thank you very much," I said.

"You are also Israelite?"

"He is an Israeli. I'm an American."

"The Republic of Haiti declared war on Germany twenty-four hours before the United States. Then you joined us, you North Americans. And the Republic of Haiti voted for Israel in the United Nations—I know my history—though it is said that certain Zionist agents purchased the vote of Haitian diplomats. Alas, the Foreign Service seems to have been corrupt in that period—"

I had heard the story.

Courteously, with a tiny bow, he opened the door and we stepped out of the cookery of the customs shed—zinc roof, heat reflecting crazily, like scooting mites across the eyes—out onto the wharf, where the gang bosses' screams of abuse took the place of mechanized loading equipment. Captain Champlain fingered the raised question mark on his tie. "One of our first visitors was a Jew," he said. He grinned happily. "Christophe Colombe." And roared with laughter. The ten-dollar bill stuck out of the pocket of his *veston eisenhower.* "Columbus brought syphilis to the island, destroyed the Carib Indians, and made room for civilized Dahomey people, also Ibos, Yorubas. *Je suis philosophe, non?* Personally, I happen to be descended straight from an Abyssinian prince, and we go back, as you probably know, through Sheba to the King of the Jews."

I RETURNED TO the States, became a university teacher, became unmarried, found my year in Haiti receding into the past and forward into the future—a part of my dreamlife every night, sounds, smells, colors, tastes, smoky fires, pleasure, and the laughter of friends. It had been the most vivid time I knew. Jean Weiner and I wrote to each other that we would always be brothers. Haiti seemed more than a match for me. I too treasured my griefs.

CHAPTER NINE

The Darkest Ages

WHEN I came back in 1963, now as a journalist, during the evil early days of François Duvalier, which were followed by the evil middle days of his reign, and then by the evil final days, the nation where black freedom was reinvented in modern times had fallen into a political agony equal to its poverty. Torture, killing, and fear to no purpose, it seemed. The land crumpled in the hand of God was being crushed in the mad doctor's fist. Dressed in funereal black as Baron Samedi, the god of death, Papa Doc sometimes committed crimes justified only by the rationality of puns. A house was attacked by the tonton macoutes at night, three generations killed, torch put to everything, even the dogs executed, because the family bore the same name as an enemy of the President— the same name, but unrelated.

Those murders were not a mistake. Papa Doc did not make mistakes. Irrational fear, chaos, black magic, and triumphal unpredictability were part of the little country doctor's plan for his domain. The exterminated family and dogs should have had another name.

It was shrewd of François Duvalier to call his personal gang "tonton macoutes," using a term from Creole which means Uncle Knapsack or bogeymen, devils who steal souls, stuff them into their bags, carry them into oblivion. These bogeymen came out of folklore into history. The macoutes were Papa Doc's version of brownshirts and the Waffen SS, except that their usual uniform was blue jeans, T-shirts, sunglasses, and they carried clubs or pistols. They were loyal only to Papa Doc. In return, they could rob, steal, extort, torture, and murder at will. Gladly they accepted the privileges of papadocracy.

By 1963 American aid had been withdrawn. The American military mission was gone. President John F. Kennedy became the great enemy of the Rénovation Nationale. Frequently the lights flickered and went out all over Port-au-Prince. The streets were emptied at night except for roaming bands of macoutes, serving the President, Dr. François Duvalier, "Our Doc Who Art in the National Palace," as his rewriting of the Lord's Prayer put it. He was considering crowning himself king or emperor.

When I arrived in November, the hotels were empty. I asked the cab driver at the airport to take me to the Oloffson and he said, "Fermé," and took me to a gloomy house which rented rooms. By the next morning, the telejiol had worked and Al Seitz, the American proprietor of the Oloffson, heard I was in town. He came to visit and said: "Why don't you come home?"

"You're closed."

"I'll open if you come."

"You can't do that . . . What do you want to charge me?"

"Anything you want to pay."

So I went back to the Grand Hotel Oloffson. I had returned to Haiti to see what had led into this dark age. Although a slow learner, I was beginning to notice that justice is one of the scarcest resources on earth. Haiti's struggle and hope were being punished in one of those explosions of evil that punctuate human history. Haiti's submission to its new slavemaster bewildered me. If I couldn't make sense of it, perhaps I could at least bear some kind of witness.

Infected by the disease of extreme curiosity, a common affliction of the addicted traveler, I hoped to find explanations or at least evidence that could lead to explanation. But to confess the truth: I just plain loved the place, the dream and memory of Haiti, its permission to alternatives in explosions of personality, as in the rituals of voodoo, and the cultivation of fantasy that Haitians manage to continue even in their turmoil. Haiti's jokes, songs and stories, paintings, and laughter could not be extinguished, I believed; they were also a part of my metabolism, and for them to disappear would amount, for me, to a kind of suicide. I had fallen asleep too often to the steadiness of drums resounding over the hills. I loved Haiti as one could also love a woman—despite the pains she inflicted. That's the truth. I have no excuses.

Alone in a hotel filled with ghosts, I began the process of trying to find old friends, particularly Jean Weiner. In a day or two, other guests arrived, a Haitian coffee dealer from Jérémie and an English Red Cross doctor with his wife who kept me awake with their violent nighttime quarrels. They beat each other as if they were all their enemies rolled into one available spouse. The doctor appeared in the morning with a freshly blackened eye; his wife appeared with scratches down her arm. The doctor had a bottle of lotion which he dabbed at her wounds—fingernails are almost as bad as dog bites, he told me.

The Red Cross doctor's wife spoke for both of them: "We'll both take the French toast and the orange juice if it's fresh."

At night we ate by the light of oil lamps on the wooden terrace of this gingerbread fantasy house, built as a palace for the family of one of the ephemeral presidents of Haiti. Al Seitz, a cigar-smoking New Jerseyan, formerly a football star for the University of Alabama, was the model for the character played by Richard Burton in the film of Graham Greene's novel about Haiti, *The Comedians.* He was not the normal hotel keeper. When I noticed that he left the money on the desk and locked the stationery in his safe, I told him he had things backward.

"Everything's backward around here."

"Is that an explanation?"

"Good as you'll get, buddy."

I searched for friends who had survived and not gone into exile in Africa, Canada, the States, where hundreds of thousands were scattered. The American wife of my friend Fortuné Bogat had gone back to New York, but he was a survivor, with another wife and more coming up.

Jean Weiner had sent his family abroad. Little Ti-Jean, growing up, was studying to be an electrical engineer like his father. Jean preferred to stay in Haiti, hiding in a house in the scrub hills beyond Bourdon. "Behind the mountain stands a mountain," he said, "and beyond the mountain I stand." The fight and fun had gone out of him;

he was gaunt and stooped. "It's my age," he said, "it's nothing to worry about. It's the times we've had."

"Why do you stay?" I asked.

"It's my country. My friends are killed, so why not me?"

Some who had been dilettantes in the traditional elite manner, collecting luxury goods and ti-mounes to carry their tennis rackets, dancing at Choucoune every Saturday night, merely passing the time, had earned the right to be forgotten. Some had withered and perished without even being tortured. The reasonless tyranny, terror for the purpose of terror, had no real ideology but some grand words borrowed from General Franco, Emperor Dessalines, Baron Samedi, and the usual demagogues' appeal to the disenfranchised—shuffling new thieves into the places of the old thieves. Naturally, not threatening anyone but his own people, Papa Doc did not interest the United States very much. Graham Greene's melodrama, *The Comedians,* was read as a popular amusement. The macoutes roamed and murdered at night, though sometimes a riddled body was left at the airport or in front of the National Palace as an advertisement for the education of passersby.

A COWBOY STORY

The temperature descended one degree for every kilometer I drove up the mountain above Port-au-Prince; and among these green hills, terraced cornfields, singing streams, wooded stretches of pine and eucalyptus, Haiti still seemed like an eccentric paradise. In the morning, cool mists swirled off the jagged peaks, down the gorges. People smiled and called Bonjour as my jeep slowed on hairpin turns. Peasants were washing themselves and their vegetables in the streams. The black Haitian pigs, those nervous unbarking nondogs, ran free, along with chickens and children. Below, the city of Port-au-Prince steamed in its smoke and heat. The bay sparkled.

Paradise was more ambiguous than usual these days. One day I was stopped by a roadblock of macoutes just above Pétionville, on the way to Kenscoff. In their mirrored sunglasses and jean cutoffs, carrying pistols and the clubs called cocamacaques, they declared this a toll road. Usually I gave them money and they gave, in return, a ticket that said "Pour La Relèvement Nationale," with the name and photograph of Dr. François Duvalier printed as validation. And then they waved me on. But some days they were nervous about foreigners with notebooks; one day they were very nervous.

The roadblock stopped me and a man poked a pistol into my face. I understood first that I was not to move, then that I was to get out of the jeep. I was jostled and shoved. "Give me your camera."

I had no camera.

A journalist without a camera was a liar. I must be a saboteur, an imperialist, a counterrevolutionary.

I had a notebook, I said helpfully. "Carnet."

They gathered round to stare. They couldn't read my handwriting. They couldn't read English. They couldn't read French, either. They held it right side up, then sideways, then upside down. Then one of them dropped it, said something I didn't understand, and shoved me against a stone wall. One of the new Duvalier millionaires was building a house here.

I believed they were going to search me. I hoped they were going to search me. I didn't like being shoved against a wall by men with pistols. "Look, I have nothing," I said. I had a few dollars and gourdes in my pocket; I offered to pay the tax, the "national renewal" roadblock tax, and they took the money, but they were not yet done. I was pushed against the wall, my nose scraped, and a semicircle of men, five or six pairs of sunglasses, faced me. My nose was bleeding.

From behind, one of them stroked my arms, which were bare, and my legs. He pinched my genitals. When I squealed, they laughed and said in Creole, "You may go now."

THAT NIGHT, back home on the terrace of the Grand Hotel Oloffson, I asked Al Seitz whom I should complain to. "The mayor would be good," he suggested.

It happened that the mayor often showed up here to do his drinking. Franck Romain was not only occasionally the mayor of Port-au-Prince but also a chief of the macoutes, later called the "Volunteers for National Security." He was relaxed and at his ease, a bulky smiling man who heard me out, thoughtfully sucking his rum-soda. He had an explanation for my problem. Graham Greene's *The Comedians* was the devil's book. "Perhaps," he said consolingly, "they don't like, on that road where so many enemies of the nation come to foment trouble for our beautiful free people . . . writers whose names are colors . . . Greene . . . Gold . . ."

A few days later, armed with my receipt for national renewal and a scribbled note from Franck Romain, I again drove past the roadblock on the Kenscoff road. The same men waved me by without stopping me. By now I was an old friend.

I was on my way to visit a missionary encampment where food was distributed to people on the mountain, along with training in Protestant hymn-singing. The people already had songs, but they needed nourishment. The American minister in charge showed me the CARE milk, the boxes sent by charitable folks in the Midwest, the lines where silent mountain peasants waited patiently for their flour. Then suddenly, from the house, a man ran out and came shouting toward us. "The President is dead!"

"My God, the revolution has come," said the missionary, Wallace Turnbull, and I didn't stop to ask if he often called upon God for emphasis. I jumped into my jeep and sped down the mountain toward the security of the Oloffson terrace. I was sure there would be rampaging, weapons firing, and as I careened down the road, there was shouting and running about; even the goats and donkeys seemed excited; but oddly enough, the guns were silent and the macoute blockades waved me by, grinning. I heard one say: "Ist-wah de covboi."

A cowboy story. This was an odd formulation for Haiti.

The Oloffson seemed deserted. It was a time of repression, murder, fear—matters that tend to inhibit tourism. I came running up the long stairway and shouted to Al Seitz, "Is it true?"

"It's true," he said. There were tears streaming down his face. "They got him in Dallas."

That night the city was blacked out. There was an ominous quiet. These were magic days for Papa Doc and his enemy, John F. Kennedy. The evil ruler of the cemetery always dressed in his mortician's black.

Baron Samedi is the god of Saturday because Jesus was crucified on Friday and did not rise until Sunday—Baron Samedi presides over the time when there is no Savior. November 22 is his best day. It had been said that Doc had a Kennedy ouanga, a doll in which he stuck pins.

In 1971 the slave leader Boukman, a voodoo priest and revolutionary hero, had given the signal for revenge against the white masters on November 22. Baron Samedi and Papa Doc were all-powerful, it seemed, spreading their reign even to the Book Depository in Texas.

The electricity went out. The stillness over the city was like an invisible hand, stilling its heartbeat, zombifying the living. Life was temporary, a loan that can be withdrawn without notice, which is a truth we all know, but now eerie recognition of it made people whisper and hide in the dark. The few guests in the hotel—the Red Cross doctor and his wife, the Haitian coffee dealer, and I—waited for we knew not what. There was a camaraderie in the glow of our oil lamps. We talked about President Kennedy. We talked about what would happen to us. The Red Cross doctor, who had received a good beating from his wife the night before, sat with a kind and thoughtful expression on his face and his wife stroked his hand.

Toward midnight, power suddenly flashed over a section of the capital down from the rue Capois. The National Palace was blazing with light, and within the general silence we could hear sounds of festival. Papa Doc was celebrating his victory over the enemy in Washington. The party went on all night.

THE NEXT day I was taken to dinner at the house of a rich crony of Papa Doc, a Swede, or maybe a Russian, or maybe a German—no one seemed sure. His name was de Morenschildt. He was a geologist who had come to Haiti to prospect for minerals. He said he had walked across Mexico to get there. Unless he walked on water, he couldn't have hiked the whole way.

Now he lived in a luxurious hillside villa. In return for services, maybe his fruitless prospecting, more likely his ability to make the Papa Doc a partner in the enterprise, he had a monopoly on sisal export from Haiti. We ate well, we drank well, and he mused about the odd coincidences in his life. He knew Lee Harvey Oswald in Dallas. He had met Jacqueline Kennedy. He wondered how many people could make the same claim.

It turned out that he was the only one. He was questioned and his name appears in the Warren Report. In the various assassination mania books, he is a frequent member of the cast. The one time I met him, he seemed proud of his peculiar place in history.

"Didn't really know him to call him a friend," he said. "Knew Jacqueline. Befriended that little fellow Lee Harvey—turned out to be rather disturbed, didn't he?"

He offered me another rum-soda ("best thing for the heat and the bites, you forget about them") and shook his head over the many coincidences in a man's life.

Everyone remembers the moment when he or she heard of the Assassination. For me, the event was a peculiar confusion on the road from the Forêt-de-Pins, a blackout over the city of Port-au-Prince and a blazing celebration in the Palais National, an odd dinner with a suave stranger who was making his fortune in Haiti.

"I HAVE CHOSEN HIM"

The white and sparkling National Palace seemed to sit on the smoking ruin which was Haiti. François Duvalier, the country doctor, sat there with his weak eyes, his diabetes, his heart disease, and his revolving resentments. Capriciousness seemed to give him perfect control. Even his personal doctor, and former Minister of Health, suffered torture in his jail nearby.

When the doctor's medical colleagues in the States made too much threatening noise, Papa Doc relented, had him put in a hospital for treatment and fattening, and then invited him to the palace for a Coke. "My dear friend!" said Papa Doc. "Had I but known!"

Standing in front of his shop, Maison Electra, Jean Weiner said: "The principal of the high school"—incline of head in direction of the palace—"has performed an economic miracle for Haiti. Taught us to live without money, eat without food." Jean's handsome face was still marked by the battering he had received during a 'routine questioning,' but he was laughing. "Taught us to live without life."

For a visitor, the country in 1963 was a laboratory in the business of manufacturing paranoia. My friends were mostly gone, dead, or in hiding. At the Grand Hotel Oloffson a band played for me, for the Red Cross doctor and his wife, and for Aubelin Jolicoeur, the skinny, squealing, white-suited journalist who did his best to befriend all visiting writers and young women. He had an enthusiastic memory for classic literature, philosophy, and Port-au-Prince gossip, but his perpetual good cheer was being sorely tested by the general turning away from Haiti, that center of the universe. Again Haiti was misunderstood; it was inexplicable; even Descartes and Voltaire could not give Aubie sufficient reasons for the absence of fun. The Oloffson's staff of cooks, waiters, and servants labored for ghosts and shadows, but the Oloffson had more clients than the other hotels. To counter the bad repute spread by ill-wishers, the Minister of Tourism, Nevers Constant, busied himself composing and erecting neon signs with messages from the President, "I AM THE FLAG, ONE AND INDIVISIBLE" and "I HAVE NO ENEMIES BUT THE ENEMIES OF HAITI." Minister Constant also asked my approval for the phrasing of an advertisement in the *New York Times* in which he came up with the enticing slogan, "We must fight evil with evil."

Floods of tourists would come rushing in pretty soon—maybe next month—as soon as news of the happy sun over Haiti reached those chilled northern shores. How did he know? He put his fingers to his lips. State secret.

"People are worried about the situation," I said.

"*What* situation? Oh, I know what you mean. We used to be suspicious, we searched and stripped people. We were looking for weapons. People used to try to smuggle in those Graham Greene lies, so we had to be vigilant."

"Stripping tourists at the airport tends to discourage tourism, Sir."

He shook his plump jowls. "In our painstaking vigilance— Haitians, mon vieux, are renowned for their patriotism—we even looked in the Tampax at the new airport built entirely with Haitian labor and design, so that it can receive the latest jet airplanes. So now please go back to your rich country and write the truth—be sure to tell the American travel agents, you will? *We are no longer looking in the Tampax.*"

He invited me on a picnic trip to visit Duvalierville, the model city with model cock fight pit, which was the Simple Country Doctor and Torturer's gift to his loving people. Formerly Cabaret, Duvalierville was one of the President's birthplaces. We made a date, Minister Constant and the simple American country journalist.

Hurricane Flora, earlier that year, had left thousands dead, tens of thousands homeless, plantings destroyed. The silt rolled down the mountainsides, fouling the sea. Trees were planted by foreign aid missions, and cut down by farmers for firewood or to clear a patch for cultivation. I heard a broadcast proclaiming a new title for President Duvalier, presented to him by his grateful people: "Protector of the Arts and Letters."

A Haitian friend, Issa el Saieh, offered to drive me to a village to see how people were surviving. We brought money to offer the macoutes at the roadblocks. "The place feels like a lighted fuse," I said.

"The fuse isn't even lit yet. It's just rotting."

The village near Croix-des-Missions, outside Port-au-Prince, had always been poor, a place of mud huts and no sanitation, no jobs, no work, hardly any workable land. Because so many of the girls became prostitutes, the village was sometimes called Croix d'Emissions. Now people were starving. Children were lying about with the swollen bellies and frizzy reddish hair of kwashiokor, a form of protein deprivation that causes apathy, brain damage, and finally the relief of death.

We visited a voodoo priest named André Pierre, sitting in the dust outside his hounfor, painting on a wooden board. He was wearing a purple rayon robe and smoking a cigar, with a battered bowler hat on his head. After the hurricane, which had also blocked irrigation ditches, there were no seeds for new gardens. There was no strength to unblock the canals. How, I asked him, do you go on?

"At first CARE brought food."

And then?

"All gone."

How do you live now?

The houngan shrugged. "Well, we help each other."

These people were beyond begging. They did not complain. They showed little curiosity as the blanc strolled through the compound, past the heaps of refuse, the uncleared caked mud and ruined huts, the exhausted children. Expecting no help at all, they did not even extend their hands.

A voodoo priest conducts ceremonies, summoning the village to the gods and the gods to the people. He is both a mother and a father, leading his/her children through the maze of belief. His celebrations on Saturday night—and on other holidays—bring visions of heaven and hell down to Haiti where they can best be appreciated. A *houngan*, priest, is orator, entertainer, intermediary with the powers of government on earth and beyond; he can be a *docteur feuilles*, herb doctor, and a singer, dancer, master of revels. On the ground of his temple or outside it, he deposits the *vévés*, drawings, which he makes by letting flour slip between his fingers. He is rapid and skillful, or slow, if necessary, deliberate, waiting for the god to help him. He may trace charms on the walls and on the central pole that leads to and from heaven.

His role can be taken by both men and women. He is touched by the spirits and responsible to them. He is one busy person.

In the case of André Pierre, the houngan at Croix-des-Missions, he also found the time to paint his visions. He sat there studying the board propped in front of him. He explained what he was seeing, images from his dreams and his faith—Agoué, the voodoo Saint Christopher or Moses, blowing on a conch to part the waters so that he can lead the people to a promised land of food and fresh water. There would be chickens and rice in this heaven. In the painting he showed me the doors of other gods—Grande Erzulie, the goddess of love and orgasm, and Ogoun Feraille, the god of war—and he showed me the separate door which would be that of Damballa, the great snake, the most powerful. The painting was filling up with emblems of hope, symbols of plenty, earth and water, fertility. Over Agoué's wooden boat flew the tortured flag of Haiti—blue for the blacks, red for the mulattoes, and the white torn out. Mountains and seas and fish would appear in this vision.

He took me into his temple. At the altar I saw a menorah among the treasures of the hounfor. But there was no food in the village. I wondered how I could give him money for food without insulting him. Issa suggested I might buy the painting.

"You can't," Andre Pierre said. "It's not finished."

"I'll buy it now and come back for it."

"You may come back in a week," he said.

A week later, when I returned, people were cooking on their charcoal fires. He had used the money for rice and beans. And the painting was finished.

Andre Pierre has become one of the most famous painters of Haiti. He still lives in the settlement near Croix-des-Missions. He is still a voodoo priest, presiding at ceremonies, drawing the vévés in flour dropped through his fingers.

We drove back into Port-au-Prince without being stopped at any macoute roadblocks. The neon sign was lit all day: I AM THE FLAG, ONE AND INDIVISIBLE. That Sunday, an important political celebration was scheduled. The Protector of the Arts and Letters, fretting about the enemies who surrounded him, was expressing disappointment through one of his favorite art forms—a public execution near the National Palace.

The crowd gathered. A macoute chieftan in sunglasses made a speech about how "these gentlemen" were up to their tricks again. Some people wondered if this was the beginning of the "Himalaya of corpses" enthusiastically promised by the head of the Haitian Red Cross. The accused were led forward. The shots rang out. The crowd dispersed.

Later it was revealed that the executioners had fired into the air; the Protector had decided upon mercy. Teléjiol said there were reasons for the softening of justice. Apparently the macoutes objected to killing men who had previously killed for them.

In those times in Haiti there were moments of that firefight exhilaration when a person is just glad to be alive, because in a moment he won't be; a time when fruit tastes especially sweet, kisses sweeter, every breath is a moment of dreamlike flight. Men in combat sometimes recall this joy. But torture removes this wager on life. It simply breaks a person. If he lives, he seems to be weary forever.

Every embassy was deluged with applications for visas. One of the most despised officials in Haiti was the woman who had to be bribed in order to get a passport. Latin American embassies, recognizing the right of asylum, were filled. "Haitians don't need visas," said Jean Weiner. "*Haiti* needs a visa."

Jean still spoke with the peppery charm of the Port-au-Princian. He also had had human shit rubbed in his face by the bogeyman. He was very cautious about seeing me, wanting no last-minute commutations for himself. He recited the poem that said: *The Leader is Disappointed in the People. The Leader must elect a new People.*

In the preternatural hush of the once-vibrant Port-au-Prince evening, all the restaurants and bars closed, and only a few peasant women still carrying their baskets to market—filing down from the hills, sleeping in the streets at the end of the road—no automobiles, hardly any lights but the flashing tributes to Dr. François Duvalier, Leader and Guide—I stood alone in a desolate downtown park and listened to a serenade of recorded Christmas carols designed for imaginary tourists. In a typical error, the neon sign said: "Joyeux Noël 1964"—missing the target by one year.

GENERAL MAGLOIRE occasionally killed opponents and certainly didn't confuse himself with concepts of free speech or honest government, but he was too busy with his girlfriends, buddies, and fun to bother with the brutal repression which was Papa Doc's main enjoyment. In exchange for steadily vocalized anti-Communism, millions of dollars came into Haiti during the Magloire time. When I used to visit Anthony Lespès, the novel- and poetry-writing chicken farmer, he said he hoped to provide an example of scientific poultry raising. But as the only known Communist in the Republic, his chief service may have been to draw American aid. The novelist-poet-chicken farmer was one of Haiti's most valuable export commodities. The money to contain that lonely chicken farmer supported Miami-modern hillside villas, swimming pools, illuminated tennis courts, and some of it even trickled down to the poorest population in the Western hemisphere.

Under Papa Doc, Haiti advanced backwards toward being the poorest country in the entire world. Ten years ago, in 1953, boys carrying glue pots were killed in the streets by the Army because they *might* have been planning to put up an anti-Magloire poster. This occurred a short time before the General, on a state visit to Washington, lectured Congress on its duty to help him fight Communism. *Time* magazine compared the staunch Haitian hero with his colleague President Eisenhower, both of them rolling up their sleeves to solve the problems of their nations: "[Magloire] speeds through his work, reading documents and penning 'O.K. PM' on them.") When "PM" flew off to New York, after trying and failing to abort elections, he only took an estimated $15 million of Haiti's money with him.

Dr. François Duvalier levitated into office after a period of confusion, riots, a temporary president, electoral manipulation. In 1957, the whispery-voiced country doctor seemed harmless enough to the disunited elite, the conventional puppet-masters, the Army. They feared the popular black leader, Daniel Fignolé, a mathematics teacher and fiery orator with a following in the city slums and among the unions. When I met Mr. Fignolé, he expressed wistful longing for the abstract realms of higher mathematics and indignation about Haiti's poverty and social injustice. He didn't have a chance.

Dr. Duvalier, black, came in as an honest representative of the peasantry whom the mulatto elite and the Americans could honestly control. It all seemed normal enough. But the "simple country doctor," a stumbler, a mumbler, sentimental and confused, turned out to be serious. He turned out to be a master of stumbling and confusion. Although appealing to the disenfranchised and uneducated, his actual intentions were slow to become clear. Even elimination of the elite was not systematic. There was a Night of Blood in May of 1963, not long before I arrived, followed by construction of a monument near the waterfront on the boulevard Harry-Truman, a neon-lit black hand clasping a neon-lit pale hand. Explosions of violence alternated with appeals for "national reconciliation." Sometimes the tonton macoutes just enjoyed sleepy strolls in the cool of the evening, carrying their weapons loosely in the crook of an arm. It was pleasant to see how much respect a gun gave. "L'Union Fait la Force"—Union Makes Strength—was the motto on the Haitian coat of arms. An optimistic friend assured me that the macoute machine guns were no longer loaded, sometimes—my friend always looked on the bright side.

Papa Doc seemed to take special vengeance on his former profession. To replace the doctors killed or gone into exile, the once-respected medical school was cranking out semiliterate graduates. Macoute politicians gave or sold degrees. One of the professors in the medical school, who now only had the right to "recommend" a grade to the political controllers, told me that Haitian medicine had been ruined for a generation. The simple country doctor, who had done graduate work at the University of Michigan, managed things so that for a time there was not a single qualified anesthesiologist left in Haiti.

Since there were so few visitors to the country, I received special attention from my new friend Nevers Constant, Minister of Tourism. In his belt, which struggled in a losing battle to control his belly, he wore the pearl-handled revolver that was a symbol of status among macoutes. Periodically he dropped by to check on my welfare at the Oloffson. While his chauffeur lounged downstairs, flashing his own nonpearl-handled weapon for emphasis, Minister Constant offered to buy me a rum-soda while he took a poll of me about how I was enjoying his beautiful country. His nostrils flared, he looked out over the city, which through the palms and across the flowering plants of the Oloffson's garden, always brought me a flood of feeling. I had been happy and unhappy here; it was a part of my life.

He spoke of universal culture, the delicacies of the French tradition, the charms of Creole women, the perfidy of the enemies of His Excellence. "There are problems, my friend!"

He asked me why Americans are racist. He asked why the mulatto is racist. He asked why the elite class is arrogant.

"But I consider you a member of that class."

He smiled happily. "Yes and no. But the price for all this must be paid. We must bring discipline to the Patrie. No more sleeping behind desks! Doctor Duvalier's Rénovation is for justice and discipline."

He cocked his head. An idea had come during high-level conversation with an old friend of Haiti like myself. What would I think of that?

Of what?

"T-shirts," he said, "which the tourists would buy to carry home the message of the Rénovation. There would be a portrait of His Excellency and his message: *Justice et Discipline.*"

I ASKED AUBELIN Jolicoeur, who included the star-reporter role at the newspaper *Le Nouvelliste* among his duties, to define a large item in the Haitian budget: "Nonfiscal Accounts."

"This is a creative way of dealing with social needs," he explained.

"How is it spent?"

"At the discretion of Dr. Duvalier and the First Lady. For hospitals. For the poor."

"Do taxpayers mind their money going out for whatever the President wishes?"

"What taxpayers? Who pays taxes in this country?"

I paused over this analysis. "Who pays for the VSN?"—the initials for the Volontaires de la Securité Nationale, now the official name for the tontons macoutes.

"*Nobody* pays," he said. "The days are so sunny, the nights so calm, why should you bother your little head over such matters?"

THE BUREAUCRACY was preparing itself for a great celebration. Nevers Constant predicted that the crowned heads of Europe would soon be making an important state visit.

King Christophe killed thousands building the Citadelle, marched men off cliffs to demonstrate their loyalty. The Emperor Dessalines proclaimed that Haitian laws should be written in blood. Later, in a pattern reminiscent of the selection of François Duvalier, a general named Faustin Soulouque was put in charge. He was rashly thought to be malleable and senile, but senility is not always something you can count on. In 1849 he elevated himself to the throne as "Faustin I." He spent fortunes on furs, jewels, a crown, and creating a peerage. When he chose to smile, a court chamberlain commanded: "Smile, Messieurs." In addition to smiling, he killed more negligently than "Our Doc Who Art in the National Palace," as the improved Lord's Prayer read. The simple country doctor wished to join the company of his heroic predecessors. His followers discussed the question of whether he should become Emperor or merely, in keeping with his modest temperament, King François the First. Minister Constant came down firmly on the side of "on verra," time will tell.

In the end, of course, Doc settled for President-for-Life, plus the royal prerogative of passing the title on to his son.

There seemed to be no other plan coming out of the National Palace, but an idea was taking shape, a mysticism of suffering. Jean Weiner described it as zombification of the country. The idea eluded rational comprehension. Baron Samedi in the palace seemed to want to preside over a cemetery. He was no longer interested in foreign aid. American help had been suspended under President Kennedy partly because Papa Doc insisted on controlling the payrolls. He didn't fret now about the uncompleted projects, irrigation, soil conservation, reforestation, building, even training the Haitian army. He had his macoutes. He expelled foreign priests, didn't worry about his quarrel with the Church. He had his macoute priests. Didn't worry about the starvation. Didn't worry about tourism or the opinion of foreigners. "There were no tourist hotels in the time of Dessalines," he remarked.

Like the Emperor Dessalines, he cultivated isolation and purification by terror. After the celebration of high officials on the day of the assassination of President Kennedy, a colonel said to me: "The prophecy has come true." Many believed that Papa Doc had pricked his Kennedy doll 2,222 times in order to kill him on November 22. In the voodoo calendar, it happened to be a special day for black magic. The official telegram of condolences to the Kennedy family contained a typical moment of Papa Doc's irony. It began: "Comme Chef Constitutionel de la République d'Haiti . . ." President Kennedy's objection to Duvalier's rule had focused on his violations of the Haitian constitution.

The Parc des Palmistes in downtown Port-au-Prince, where the

Théâtre de Verdure used to house concerts, dance, and theater performances, was renamed the Parc de la Paix François Duvalier. But there
were no more performances there.

"They are putting out the lights," said Jean Weiner. "We have
snuffed out our own lives."

A DAY WITH THE BOGEYMEN

"You have seen our magnificent new developments for the poor?"
Minister Nevers Constant asked.

"I haven't seen anything of that description."

"As a profound and true friend of your own great country, I must
show you what even my beloved patrie can accomplish under the
proud national banner of the Leader." His lips smacked lustily together, appreciating in advance my appreciation for the achievements
of the Government of National Renovation. "For Haitians, suffering
is no handicap. I invite you to a day under his smiling sun, lunch
included."

His sun? I thought.

"Pique-nique," Minister Constant repeated.

Along the smudged edges of the city, along swampy harbor
terrains and in ravines, Port-au-Prince was growing. Where the worst
misery had been concentrated in the district called La Saline, new
settlements of packing-box shacks, huts made of random hunks of
wood or metal, salvage suburbs seemingly carved into waste were
growing every day. They had names like Brooklyn, Cité Soleil, Bel Air.
People from the country, where there was no food, no water, not
enough land, were coming barefoot, with no possessions, to the city,
where there was no work. Minister Constant would come to float his
guests in a black Buick through this unreality into the paradise of
Duvalierville, Haiti's Brasília.

"Did not your George Washington name a city, your capital, for
himself? Then why not this garden village of Duvalierville, a gift to the
nation?" he asked, patting his stomach. He stroked the pistol. I was
happy to accept his hospitality.

A T THE appointed hour, ten o'clock on a Sunday morning, the Minister's Buick drove up the curving, palm-lined driveway at the Oloffson. We were a party of six, a German diplomat, Bruno, his pretty young wife, Gretchen, a police observer, Bienvenue l'Aurore, the Minister, a young Mexican woman, and myself.

Minister Constant seemed to believe that if he could convince us, his Emissary Tourists, that Haiti is a tourist haven, our various compatriots would find their way to spend their currency under the brilliant tropical sky of Dr. François Duvalier. The Mexican, very young, very thin, with long straight hair, kept scratching the mosquito bites on her calves and complaining that no one had yet taught her English or French. I asked what she was doing in Haiti and she replied, "I am throwing myself into the diplomacy." This sounded like a peculiarly dramatic form of suicide. It turned out that she had come to study French at the Institut Lope de Vega.

The German diplomat was on a cultural mission. "Loffly pipple! Vriendchip!" His wife, a delicate Berliner, blushed. "Honeymoon! Lune de miel!" She blushed for me in English, and then turned to blush again in French. The couple was visiting nineteen countries in three months, and then would write their report.

The policeman, Bienvenue l'Aurore, had recently been detailed to the task of keeping me company. He had the habit of making verbal jabs at the government, waiting for my response with a radiant, enticing smile. I was usually able to dodge. His attention span was short.

The Minister himself, very fat, with a pendulous lower lip and a nasal voice, as if he had inherited a bad cold three generations back, had the habit of falling asleep suddenly in the middle of a sentence. He drove. When he felt himself falling asleep, he drove very slowly. Otherwise he conversed with laborious, thick-throated enthusiasm.

First we toured downtown to visit his recent achievements in reviving the tourist trade, the signs, "I AM THE FLAG, ONE AND INDIVISIBLE—FRANÇOIS DUVALIER" and "I HAVE NO ENEMIES BUT THE

ENEMIES OF HAITI—FRANÇOIS DUVALIER." Crammed by the Minister's side with his pistol pressing against my thigh, I assured him the neon worked perfectly.

"They're coming next week," he said. "Thousands of them—hordes. Beautiful schoolteachers, millionaires, artistes en retraite."

"Ah oui, Excellence," said Bruno. The German diplomat and newlywed, qualified in both Spanish and Portuguese, was still working on his French. He used initiative and improvisation to communicate the needed emotions for the Minister. When he saw something good (neon signs, a paved road, smiling faces), he cried, "Ah oui, Excellence, oui! oui!" When he saw something bad (hurricane damage, a fallen tree, starving children), he said, clicking his tongue, "Oh, Excellence, tch, tch, tch." Sometimes he would think further, turning to look and shaking his head from side to side. "Excellence! Tch! Tch! Tch!"

The thick-breathing Minister drove a route selected so that the oui's might outnumber the tch's. There was the neon sign that faced the empty harbor, empty of tour boats, empty of freighters, empty of fishing boats, empty of everything but the drainage ditch leading into the harbor. JOYEUX NOËL 1964. The sign was still a year ahead.

"Maybe they mean next year will be the happy one," said Bienvenue l'Aurore. Once again I gave proof of maturity—strong and silent.

A workman was tinkering with the glass tubes. His family stood about, watching him. The Minister blew his horn and stopped the Buick. They all came to attention; he barked out orders in French concerning neon adjustment in the cause of the Rénovation Nationale. He raised his arm; the revolver flashed in the sunlight; graciously he bid them rest. I asked why he didn't instruct them in Creole. "Creole, a joke for children," he said. "Personally I don't understand it. Haitians speak French—the French of Paris, not of Canada. Canadians speak execrable French, don't you find?"

I lowered my head, although I'm not Canadian.

"Bon travail, mon ami!" he called to the workman.

"Hokai, M'sieu Minist'."

We continued our voyage of inspection. Beautification and city planning were his ideals in life. Beginning on December 1, recordings of Christmas carols, in English and French, would also be heard at this spot, beamed especially to visitors, whom he wanted to feel entirely at home in Haiti. The police would arrest all beggars, prostitutes, peddlers, anyone without shoes or identification papers or good reasons for being where they were. All the tourist had to do with a Communist was to point him out and the authorities would take care of the rest. "Not like Cuba, eh?" he asked, nudging me with his pistol.

He then abruptly seemed to fall into narcolepsy while the Buick glided past La Saline, in which thousands of Haitians lived in houses made of rubbish and banana leaves, with no jobs, no chance to find one, waiting for epidemic, starvation, or fire to bring them to a better place. Patrolling the area were small gangs of macoutes that were now as common as pigs, dogs, or roosters on the byways of Haiti. But there couldn't have been much to confiscate around here.

"And this is the new jet airport for the tourists," said Minister Constant, abruptly alert, blowing his horn at the guard to open the barbed-wire gate. We drove up and down the landing strip.

"Ah oui, Excellence!" cried Bruno.

"Will also be airplanes?" asked Conchita, the eighteen-year-old Mexican diplomat.

Gretchen tapped me on the shoulder. "You come all this way?"

"Haiti is like home to me."

She asked: "Like the United States of America?"

"And our new Dr. François Duvalier International Jet airport?" demanded the Minister.

"I love that too," I said.

"Surely finished next year," he promised. "We are strictly following the plan."

"Excellence! Oui!"

Conchita had finished with the calves and was now scratching her thighs. Little flecks of blood appeared. I said in English with facing French, "Don't scratch, ne grattez pas." She had an independent policy; she scratched away.

"Moustiko bites, tch tch tch," said Bruno.

"No malaria!" cried the Minister. "Due to Haitian science no malaria! You take pills?"

"Oh, Excellence, oui! oui!"

The Minister was beeping the horn to awaken the guard. We had been locked onto the landing strip. Now we needed to be let out. The Buick dipped and bowed onto the road leading past Damiens toward Duvalierville, our next destination. Damiens was the agricultural school where Shimon Tal used to teach the stocking of waters with fish. The beggars and the starving turned to gaze at the black ministerial automobile throwing dust at them. I chatted with the German diplomat's wife about Haitian painting while Conchita stroked her mosquito bites. This was one answer to the problem of insect control.

In the midday heat I received probing questions from the Minister. The reputation of Haiti had suffered from recent murders, destructions, expulsions of priests. American aid was gone. The State Department advised Americans to stay away. The macoutes particularly frightened visitors. Since taxes were not collected in the usual ways, they were now collected in unusual ways. A group of macoutes would enter a businessman's office and beat him until he paid. Or they would set fire to his house. In their tattered pants and their "I AM THE FLAG" T-shirts, with their bands of ammunition and their M-1 rifles cradled loosely in their arms, they inspired a feeling of unease.

"Soon the tourist will come back to enjoy our National Renovation," said the Minister—"Soon?"

"That would make Haiti more prosperous."

"But a bad propaganda in the *New York Times,* CIA, my dear friend!"

"I know."

"Tch tch tch," said Bruno.

"We must build a new society, do we not?" demanded the Minister.

"Oh, Excellence, oui oui oui!"

"But the malcontents, the former exploiters, the pigs of the unborn."

"Oh, Excellence, tch tch tch."

"So," concluded Minister Constant, "the National Assembly has voted budget of twenty-two thousand dollars to place advertisements in *New York Times* that will tell the truth about Our Protector, our Doc."

I suggested that the chief problem lay elsewhere than in the *New York Times*. It might be more interesting to distribute twenty-two thousand dollars worth of rice and beans to those rendered homeless, their gardens destroyed by the recent hurricane: to the children with swollen bellies and retreated eyes who lay in the compounds in front of their caille-pailles.

The Minister corrected me again. "We must fight evil with evil."

Bienvenue l'Aurore was breathing tensely at my side. I fell to watching the scenery. Occasionally the car was stopped by macoutes who would cry, "Inspection!" The Minister cried out in return, "Le Ministre Constant! Le Ministre Nevers Constant!"

"Ouais. Permission."

We inched past the gasoline drums with which they barricaded the road. Instead of rolling them out of the way, they gazed at them. They sat on crates or lounged in the ditches and said, "Ouais, permission."

At last, on the road to Saint Marc, we poked our way to the new town of Duvalierville, the major monument of the regime, built on the site of Cabaret. The peasant village had been leveled by bulldozers. Now there were cement blockhouses with butterfly roofs, a cement cockfighting pit, a cement stadium, a cement police station, and a grid of streets going nowhere, frazzled off into the surrounding mud.

"Why was this town built here?" I asked.

"By the will of the people," said the Minister.

"Who will live here?"

"The deserving. They will pay no rent."

"How will they be selected?"

"By the census."

The German diplomat said oui. We drove back and forth down the streets of Duvalierville. People were slow to move out of the way. Even the doglike black pigs were in no hurry. The sun beat down on the denuded fields. Where once palm trees and banana bushes had grown, there now were cracked patches of clay and fetid ditches. "Soon electricity! Soon purified water!" cried the Minister.

Bruno was moving his lips. Gretchen was dozing.

Conchita wanted to know when the picnic began. "That is a

pig?" she remarked. In Mexico the pigs and the dogs had separate identities. The Mexican pig was fat because Mexico was an advanced industrial and agricultural power.

I asked if we could get out of the car a moment. The Minister mopped his brow and consented.

The Mexican diplomat and student had a way of standing and stretching, her skinny belly extended, as if she had surely once been a plumper person, an innocent and gawky child. Minister Constant noticed the little stain of sweat on her blouse, noticed the long strands of tan hair against the tan skin, and winked a wink at me which I could interpret either as *She's mine* or *Welcome to Haiti, dear friend.* I think she noticed. She yawned. "In English you don't say moustiko?" she asked.

Having inspected the Haitian Brasília, the Minister had a reward in mind. He urged us back into the Buick. We headed along the bay toward Ibo Beach. It was the former Île Cabrit, Goat Island, a sandy spit in the water that an enterprising engineer had fortified and developed. It could be reached by motorboat from the shore. We hurried into our model caille-pailles, typical country huts of straw and mud— peasant chic—to change into swimsuits, spearfishing uniforms, skin-diving equipment. Bruno was abruptly transformed into a submarine and disappeared to crawl across the bottom, examining coral and marine life. Occasionally, like a whale, he spouted. There was the usual aimless pattering of a day at the beach, sleeping in the sun, dips in the salt, drinking of rum and tradings of worn-out newspapers and magazines. The Minister held my hand tightly in his, tutoied me, and told me about his missions as a representative of Haiti in Washington. "Oh, Lyndon is my good friend," he said, "and Laddy-bird, too, you know? I have dine at the new President house these many time. You know his friend Marty? You know his friend Joe Quelquechose? Oh, I know him well, a friend to Haiti, my deep personal friend."

"Personally I don't know him."

"Joe, Joe, Joe—" He snapped his finger angrily. "What is Joe nom de famille? And now Lyndon is your President."

Conchita tried rubbing rum on her bites. No one else seemed to be bothered, but she was swelling and suffering. Nevers Constant suggested swallowing the rum instead. He winked at me. Although a Minister in the Government of National Renovation and Social Justice, he was a normal person who knew how to unbend.

"You don't know Lyndon?" he insisted.

I apologized. "I don't know many people."

"Tch tch tch," said the submarine, emerged from no place to set a conch to dry in the sun. He was wearing flippers and puffing. He stood in the sun and beat his chest to shake off the water.

"My husband does not prefer folkish art," said Gretchen. "He is Doctor of Economics."

"Is that so?"

"Soon I will teach him to love the folkish art of many nations."

In one of the most densely populated places in the world, privacy is rare. Dense crowds, strollers, beggars, children, peddlers, shoeshine boys, prostitutes, babies, herdsmen, travelers, farmers, philosophers, thieves, police, militia, poets, and others perform their business or their pastimes in public, on the road, wherever. If a person does something interesting or funny, someone is watching to perform the social acts of concern or laughter. But the Île Cabrit was an island off the island, with a strip of water between it and the shore. Except for the barmen, waiters, beachboys, and our hosts, we were absolutely alone; alone except for the fishermen sailing a few yards away; alone except for the folks clustered across the water on the beach, straining their eyes to try to make out what peculiar ways wealth and power invent to fill their idle hours.

In this peculiar Haitian version of isolation, the Minister confessed his philosophy of life, his hopes and dreams, and the repertory of surefire sexual techniques that he had tested on his fortunate wife and a series of lucky mistresses. He was tender and strong, but he allowed no opposition—they liked that. He was an important macoute. The pearl-handled pistol tucked into his two-piece bathing dress would not get wet. Swimming was not one of his strong areas. In his congested voice, coughing with emotion, he said: "I take you back five years. It is Carnival. She is a tourist, a schoolteacher from Chee-k'go—you know Chee-k'go in the Illinois?—and she is beautiful but soon the holidays end. Ah la pauvre Haiti, you have lost your

fairest bloom. She send me greeting card every year. *I am your Susie.*
She cannot forget. Don't scratch, please." That last remark was directed to the Mexican student/diplomat.

"Now tell me about your love," he urged, "healthy man like you.
You are a man?"

We were distracted by other picnic excitements. One of the
cooks had caught a lobster. He had earlier caught several lobsters. He
brought them forward to be inspected by the Minister. The Minister
turned them over and approved them as he might have approved the
vintage of the wine. Now lunch was being laid out al fresco for us—
avocado salad with tomatoes and cucumbers from Kenscoff, lobster
and ham, cheeses, Creole rice and beans, plenty of rum-sodas and
Cokes and charcoal-broiled steaks offered the American. I chose the
lobster. "It is lobster crayfish," said the Minister. "Soon we export to
the States because they do not know the difference. We who have the
tradition of France enjoy a more sensitive palate, which is a known
fact."

At the end of a long day in the sun, we loaded ourselves into the
motorboat to be carried back to shore. The owner of Ibo Beach looked
ready to weep; the Minister had signed for the food and drink and the
government did not pay its bills. But the rest of us were satiated with
sun, crayfish, swimming, talk, and old copies of *Match* and the *Nouvelliste.*

Driving back to Port-au-Prince, there were moments of sleepy
silence. The Buick skidded past potholes, rushed honking through
crowds, plowed through debris. Bruno tried to keep things going
("Oui! oui!"), and sometimes addressed me in English, since the
Minister also understood it. "Iss vonderbar," he declared, "iss fery
wonderbar, iss only zmiling vaces in zis country."

At that very moment the car was brought to a halt by a clot of
macoutes in the road with their weapons cocked, their eyes impenetrable behind their sunglasses. "C'est le Ministre Constant!" bawled
our host.

"Inspection."

"Le Ministre Constant!"

"In-spec-tion."

They made us stand out, they searched the car, they searched us, they kept the guns leveled. They were uninterested in the Minister's story. He was just another rich man from Port-au-Prince to these nameless ones. The Mexican girl began to weep. When she bent to scratch a bite, a macoute waved his rifle and ordered her to stand up. Her tears ran; she was afraid to scratch or wipe. The German's wife, Gretchen, pale and icy, stood silently watching while le Ministre Constant argued in Creole. He was sweating, nasal, and dismayed. They did not know him. They asked him to open the trunk of the car. They tapped the spare tire. They prodded the cushions.

At last they accepted a toll from Minister Constant and allowed us back in the automobile. But they still kept the guns on us. I asked the Minister not to drive while they pointed their weapons our way; didn't want to be shot for a misunderstanding. He agreed, shaking with rage, and asked, "Passé?"

They stared.

"M'Minist'! Capab passé?"

Finally one of them turned on his heels and strolled off. He was followed by the others. Monsieur Constant wheeled past the gasoline drums in the road, accelerated, and we sped down the road to Port-au-Prince, the capital, and the known world beyond it. After a moment of silence, Bruno spoke:

"Excellence? Excellence? Tch tch tch."

O NE MORNING a man I didn't know appeared while I was having breakfast on the terrace of the Oloffson. C'est-Dieu, the ancient, ageless waiter, brought mango, bananas, French toast, dark Haitian coffee and heated canned American milk. In Haiti the bananas you eat without cooking are called *figue-banane* to distinguish them from *platanes,* cooked as a vegetable. I was staring out over the city, the sun dreamers waked at dawn by the barking and cockcrow and the need to find a way of living through another day. I thought my only problem was to change rooms in the empty hotel, since the shouting and screaming of the Red Cross doctor and his wife kept me awake, a more piercing set of sounds than the soothing drums which resounded between the hills.

The man I didn't know waited until I looked up. He was as skinny as C'est-Dieu and, it seemed, almost as old. "Bonjour, Monsieur."

"Bonjour."

"Let pou ou." Letter for you.

I read the note. It gave me the name of a woman who owned a bookstore in town, the Caravelle. I knew her house. The unsigned note asked if I could visit her at ten o'clock that evening. The macoutes roamed the streets and normally people stayed home after dark. There was no formal curfew, but too many people out after dark disappeared forever. This tended to create a de facto curfew.

He waited until I said, "Yes, give Madame my greetings," and then he slipped away.

Booming-voiced Al Seitz came up with morning greetings. "Someone looking for you! It's nice to have friends."

He ambled down the terrace to wish a good morning to the Red Cross doctor and his wife, silent and puffy over their breakfast.

He came back to me and said, "Too bad people don't enjoy their food. Have you ever had French toast as good as this?"

"Never. Not since yesterday."

"Be careful, okay?"

I walked out that night as if taking an evening stroll. A few people stood in their doorways and murmured, "Bonsoir, Monsieur," in the courteous Haitian fashion, just as if it was normal for a *blanc* to be out walking on those eerily quiet streets during those bad days of 1963. There was a "panne d'electricité," as usual—no electric lights—but starlight and moonglow, candles, a few oil lamps made it seem as if a giant temporary encampment had moved onto the hills. When I found the house, a door opened and I entered. A half-dozen people were sitting in the darkness. They had been invited by the solemn middle-aged woman who owned a bookstore, had a Ph.D. from an American university (Harvard, I believe), and was the leader of this group.

I expected some sort of organized scheming against the regime. Instead, we sat in a circle in the dark and exchanged news. A doctor had been murdered by macoutes in the street, with his wife and children watching. An Army champion sharpshooter had been killed only because it was assumed that, if there were a revolt against Papa Doc, he might be the one to kill the dictator. The poets Morisseau-Leroy and Jean Brierre were in exile. Roussan Camille had died. A pilot was now flying for an American company abroad; his wife had just been released. My friend Jean Weiner had been beaten, and suffered head and eye injuries. A coffee dealer was beaten and spent several weeks in jail for "seditious talk." He was seventy-five years old. The newspaper editor Georges Petit's presses had been destroyed. Dr. Bastien was disappeared, presumed dead, his house burned down. Anthony Lespès, the novelist, poet, and chicken farmer, was said to have been forced to drink the urine of a macoute, and after being beaten, made to clean up the blood on the floor with his tongue. . . .

The meeting, which I had thought was some sort of political action, took the risks these people took in order to tell each other things they already knew. They hoped I would write about it and a magic solution from the United States would then save them. They also still thought that every American, even the schoolteachers who still visited Haiti during vacations in search of temporary true love, worked for the CIA. They didn't understand why the USA couldn't do the job for them.

Pauvre Haiti.

In the humid dark, they served warm soda. They speculated about Papa Doc's health. They wondered on which day of a month with two 2's—on May 22, say—he would declare himself François I, emperor or king. The coronation of the Emperor Soulouque, Faustin the First, had taken place a hundred years ago.

We held hands. This accomplished nothing but a ceremony of sharing grief. It was a useless risk for everyone. It represented only the spirit not acquiescing in defeat and expressing solidarity by touching. We drank more soda. We whispered and there were deep looks into eyes as, following the polite French fashion, we shook hands and peered into eyes when we separated. When I said goodbye to our hostess, she shrugged, recognizing that the occasion was both sad and comic, a kind of roll call of lives lost and then of muffled laughter. If I were CIA, it would be another joke on Haiti.

In the dark, risking their lives, with their friends escaped into exile or death or sometimes the horror of the jails, they were laughing about the poster we had all seen, depicting Jesus with his arm around Papa Doc and the caption: JE L'AI CHOISI.

Jesus was saying: I have chosen Him.

AVOIDING DRIVING past the macoute barricades, I took the tap-tap to Kenscoff along with a load of peasants ferociously amused by my efforts to remember Creole. I could still twist my French sufficiently to be the butt of jokes, and as the overloaded, shock-sprung painted truck careened around hairpin curves, there was much slapping of palms. *"Blanc capab palé Creole!"* Well, I was happy to be here again, since home remembered is a place of dreams. The blanc dreamed fluently in Creole, even if he spoke it badly.

The tap-tap dropped me at the Hotel de Florville. The Vichy colonel had gone to his heaven where there would be no one but the right kind of Frenchman. No new foreign pensionnaires had yet arrived. Would I like my old table for lunch? What might I desire to eat? Now I had grown a beard, but just yesterday I had been a boy novelist in Kenscoff, amid this freshness of eucalyptus and onion. I was happy.

For a reminder of humanity in a balance of solitude and tact, there was still the hoot of voices across the fields, worksongs and lovesongs, an occasional long rise of women's laughter, and the softly modulating drums of a *coumbite*, the cooperative work rite, a survival of a West African custom, in which the people of a district join to do a job while making a small festival of it. Often they will construct a caille-paille for a family in need, completing the house in a day. This time a group of neighbors was clearing rocks from a steep slope. They worked their picks in rhythm, singing, while the "officers of the coumbite," with ribbons and medals and titles like General-in-Chief and President, led the singing, beat the asson, blew the whistle, slapped and stroked the drums.

From the gallery where I sat for my lunch at the Florville I could see the mountains on one side, the Caribbean, the long bay, and the smoky blues and grays of Port-au-Prince far below. At my back I had both the Dominican Republic and an *anolis,* a lizard which came to make little spitting sounds, stick out its tongue, puff its throat, cock its slit-eyed head.

Intending to rejoin the circle of philosophers, I walked up the narrow road, filled with children who hadn't been born when I used to visit Kenscoff, many born of parents who were only children when I lived in Haiti; past Jean Weiner's house in which I had camped with typewriter and schemes; past the stalls and straw mat "supermarkets" where the Madame Saras, market women, spread out their single sticks of chewing gum, single cigarettes for sale, paper tubes of sugar and coffee and flour and rice. I stopped near the church where the Breton priest used to counsel his flock, and I used to watch the white-clad celebrants streaming in wearily for Sunday Mass after their night's session with the gods. *Jesus is good . . . . Damballa powerful.*

The circular stone porch of Judge Noh was empty except for the coffee scales and the weights. It was swept clean. There were no stray beans in the crevices. I knocked and waited. Madame Noh opened the door, said, "Oh!" and greeted me with a firm handshake, congratulations on my survival, a cup of coffee on a tray along with the can of condensed milk—she remembered I liked to buffer the powerful Haitian roast. Her husband was gone, she said, *disparu.* The doctor-lawyer was disparu. "The old, Monsieur, cannot wait forever. They disappear."

What would they be waiting for if they waited?

"I'm sorry I haven't been back," I said.

"My husband would have preferred to wait. He would have preferred to be here with you. We don't have the choice, do we?"

Although an emeritus member of the Cenacle des Philosophes, I found nothing to add on the subjects of free will and death in Haiti. Madame Noh pulled out two woven chairs and, for the first time, sat with me. We said very little. Two cannot make a circle. Before I got up to leave, thanking her for the coffee, she took my hand in her small dry brown hand and continued to say nothing. "Goodbye," I said finally.

"Politics!" she said. "Food and water. Medicine. What children my husband and all of you were!"

"I'm sorry."

"My poor husband. God disposes. Perhaps *He* knows what to do with a doctor who practices philosophy and not medicine."

"Goodbye"—this was a world of goodbyes.

"One continues," she said.

But she didn't continue. When next I returned to Kenscoff, the judge's house was closed, locked, and the Philosopher's Circle disbanded forever. Madame Noh had joined her husband. The coffee scales awaited the next occupant. Chickens picked in the yard.

CHAPTER
TEN

"Here Is the Young Leader that I Promised You"
— DR. FRANÇOIS DUVALIER,
President-for-Life of the Republic, Chef Suprème et Effectif

T HE PRESIDENT-for-life died a natural death in office in 1971. His Annointed Son, Jean-Claude, aged nineteen, was confirmed as the new President-for-Life by a unanimous act of the legislature. The Dignified Heir, as he was called in one of the first of a cascade of new titles and honors, would receive the counsel of his mother, The Inspirer, who owned a full panoply of titles of her own.

I had been banned from Haiti because of my reporting on the Duvalier regime. I was informed that I would be turned back at the Port-au-Prince airport, if lucky, and if less lucky, admitted to the country, poisoned, shot, or "disappeared." Although not many foreigners suffered these inconveniences, a few had been killed or beaten—I had seen a bloody photograph of my friend Bernard Diederich as he was hustled onto an airplane—and decided to stay away for a few years and write my novels. I remarried, was the father of three more children. I sang to them the lullabies my older daughters Ann and Judy had learned, "Fais Dodo," sleep my little one.

Not long after the death of Papa Doc and the accession of His Plumpness, the Son, I received a postcard from Aubelin Jolicoeur—a photograph of a bare-breasted Creole maiden—upon which Aubie had inscribed a kind of visa: *Herb. Please. You may come home.*

The distinguished white-suited journalist, tourist official, man-about-Haiti, and Cartesian philosopher was offering absolution for my sins. I hurried back to this peculiar home of mine.

159

The new regime had launched another lightning campaign to revive tourism. Already a few cruise ships were docking, a Club Med had opened, Carnival was lively, and the tonton macoutes were being gently reigned in. Lacking a taste for terror and torture, Jean-Claude preferred to play with his toy cars and his motorcycles. His father, who liked to be thought the incarnation of Baron Samedi, guardian of the cemetery, had put so many troublemakers there that people thought peace and foreign aid might come back. He had also stolen so much money that optimists predicted the Son would be content with his nest eggs in France, Switzerland, and the United States.

Issuing blue uniforms to the macoutes and calling them the VSN, Volontaires de la Securité Nationale, would surely make them "responsible." Indeed, the road barricades were gone and the random extortions were less random. The Affirmative Misery program was suspended. People went out at night.

At the airport I watched the unloading of crates of sporting goods stenciled CORPS DES LEOPARDS. There was a Ping-Pong table. There were soccer balls, mitts, and sneakers. Baby Doc had hired a former American Marine to train the Leopards, his own palace guard—Nikes, white socks, shorts, muscles, doubletime reviews—and they seemed more interested in boyish games than in the anarchic malevolence of the macoutes. Exiles in Africa, Canada, and the United States were urged to come home. Jacques Large, a journalist back from Africa, where he had been an aide to Dag Hammarskjöld, ironically promised me a return to the "golden age"—the amiable corruption and thievery of the Magloire regime. He liked what Jean Weiner had said: "I welcome you to the Land of Unlimited Impossibility."

Tourists drove past the billboard near the airport with the portrait of the boy President-for-Life in imperial uniform and the message: THE HOPE OF ALL THE PEOPLE. The cult of Baby Doc was part of the fun. The airport band played "Haiti Chérie," "Panama'm Tombé," and "Choucoune," friendly sounds floating up the ramps, and pale northerners left stale air-conditioning to descend into the tropical richness of this place known for exotic, for strange, for wild, for pleasure. Duvalier *fils* lacked sufficient concentration for the paranoia of Duvalier *père*. He suspended the "Son et Lumière" torture shows at Fort Dimanche. Sometimes he gave visitors Jean-Claude wristwatches with his face where Mickey's would be on a Mickey Mouse watch. Although generally unavailable for interviews, an attractive Englishwoman managed to persuade him to take presidential time away from his toy trains, cars, motorcycles, and watching the Leopards train. She asked if being President-for-Life interfered with his studies.

"Not a night goes by that I don't fall asleep, my arms wrapped around my school books," he said.

At the Oloffson, jovial Al Seitz—sometimes grumpy Al Seitz—was playing his part for visitors, storing the money on his desk and the stationery in the safe. A band serenaded diners on the gracefully decaying terrace. I marked the passage of years as the children of the band grew older, but no less enthusiastic about repeating their repertory of merengue classics. People came for Carnival, for Christmas, for birthdays, for a sexual adventure or two, and to meet friends in the fraternity of Haiti fanatics. They bought paintings, they tanned by the pool, they caught up on things since their last visit.

The hotels also filled up with Germans and Americans establishing their businesses in this place of cheapest labor—baseball sewing, dollmaking, fake Tiffany-glass gluing, electronics assembly, gluing or sewing little pieces of something to little pieces of something else. The government established a strict pay scale for workers in the foreign "transformation industries"—a dollar a day. Baby Doc's family and cronies were usually partners in these enterprises at the new Industrial Park near the airport. The Boy changed his cabinet every few months because this was the democratic way; nobody but the Family must control. At the Oloffson I met the white-suited Englishman who traveled monthly to Haiti to pick up the money that went into the Swiss bank accounts. "Le Bagman," said a Haitian journalist, proud that his little country had every modern convenience that Chicago or Las Vegas could offer. Le Bagman's taste was for women who were exceptionally round everywhere that counts.

During the worst days of Papa Doc, people were afraid even to whisper to one another, afraid to go out at night because the macoutes might think they were planning to whisper. Now, under the relaxed reign of the Maximal Son, people were no longer afraid to whisper.

Jean Weiner, who used to meet me in secret places, now lunched at a popular spot at the Rond Point on the boulevard Harry-Truman, along with government and businesspeople. "Ah Haiti, la pauvre Haiti," he said, sighing as always, but now he could stretch his long legs in public.

Electricity was on more often than off. The telephone, which used to be an objet d'art, a paperweight, or a sculpture, now sometimes rang and the sound of a voice might issue forth. The old telephone lines had been something like decayed U.S. Army field issue, and seldom worked in years when it rained. Brisk new American Embassy and international aid officials checked in for rounds of receptions, cocktails, appointments.

The mahogany and coffee trees were mostly gone, burned for firewood. Erosion had made scrub barrens out of once-fertile slopes. The population was increasing at a frightening pace, despite the chief means of control, which was infant mortality. Bobby Baker, President Johnson's friend, was raising beef in Haiti for export to the States. Later, another entrepreneur bought blood from Haitians for export. One could see undernourished people lining up to sell blood so they could feed their children. When I wrote that they were also selling bodies for use in American medical schools, a corpse crop which could be harvested every morning on the streets of Port-au-Prince, Haitian officials issued fervent denials on the order of: This is not true, a vicious calumny, and we're not doing it anymore.

An American businessman declared: "Our company is strict. It is our policy. We will not pay bribes to government officials unless absolutely necessary."

Aubelin Jolicoeur, in his white suit, his white cane, surrounded by his aura of happy giggling, cast me keen looks and cited French poetry to explain that . . . that. . . . Everything and nothing had changed. Unmarried men and women were coming to be married and divorced in Haiti. He explained that newlywed women were as apt to fall in love with him as divorcing ones, thanks to the blessed conjunction of their regret at losing the happy condition of freedom with the warmth of his welcome to an island in the sun. His look was not keenly modest. I always ended by forgiving him.

Enterprising Haitians developed part-time occupations, such as selling paintings. One officer, Captain Beaujean, whose full-time occupation was bringing happiness to visiting spinsters, also sold works of art. He would show a lady a painting, name a large price for it, receive her regretful no. But he could tell she liked the painting. Toward the end of her stay, he would sigh with love. "You must have this authentic masterpiece of my people. I give it to you."

"No, you can't."

"But I adore you, and you must have it! You have such feeling! It will make me remember you to know this work hangs in your house in Chicago."

She refused, he insisted, she found it wrapped and delivered at the airport.

A month or so later, when the painting was installed, and the lady had enjoyed the admiration of her friends for what was indeed a fine example of Haitian talent, she would receive a letter from Captain Beaujean. Oh, terrible reverses. The health of his mother. An operation essential. It destroys him utterly, but that painting represents his only savings . . . . Could she either send it back or send him a little money?

He had let her know the price. To remove it from her wall, to wrap and ship, to lose something she had come to love, and also to deprive his mother of the operation that might save her life. . . . It was so much better to buy the work.

The Captain never lost his gamble. How could one live comfortably on Lake Shore Drive with a masterpiece, a *valuable* masterpiece, knowing that a passionate third-world hero had given it away while his mother needed a few hundred dollars for medical care?

UNDER BABY Doc the good times seemed on the way back. Coffee, sisal, and sugar exports were down, but tourism, transformation industries, plus such hard-currency enterprises as blood and corpse sales, were bringing back echoes of the golden age. A Haitian doctor, familiar with the practice of buying blood drawn from the veins of the poor, said: "The plasma cows are tired most of the time. But there is no other work."

"Good times" in Haiti means something different from good times elsewhere in the world. The total economic assets of Haiti— "book value"—would fall easily within the means of a confident American billionaire. Sometimes speculators were tempted. A Texas company called Dupont Caribbean, Inc., which seemed to have no DuPonts but definitely had some well-connected Haitian partners, was making a small step toward buying the country. It had a contract to control the Île de la Tortue, also called Tortuga Island, an almost forgotten buccaneer island off the northern coast across from the town of Port-de-Paix. Dupont Caribbean, Inc., planned a combination free port, resort, retirement community, convention park, harbor town, industrial center. Jim Hobbs, the resident manager, a brisk, bright, lively young man from Dallas, smiled and shrugged when I remarked that his employers were dealing in one of the most beautiful and unspoiled spots in the world, twenty-three miles long, four miles wide, and only paying two dollars an acre—less than the total investment for a small apartment complex in, say, Eastland, Texas, which was the home office of Dupont Caribbean, Inc.

"Let me show you," he said. He was flying to the island in a small plane.

The plan was to have no taxes, this new entity Texanized into "Tortuga," a kind of sovereign nation. After Radio Havana and Radio Moscow claimed that the Texans were stealing another nation's property, the offer was sweetened to ten dollars an acre. There was, after all, a Haitian partner. So no one could say it was stolen from Haiti.

We flew in Dupont Caribbean, Inc.'s Lockheed Lodestar and landed on the new airstrip. There was a beach of impeccable sand, not a trace of plastic, paper, contemporary debris. A few thousand Haitians eked out a living from corn, goats, and fish. They would be given work in the hotels and industrial park.

We spent the day picnicking and swimming at this blazing and perfect beach, snorkeling at the edge of the coral reef, eating the food packed for us by the kitchen of the Grand Hotel Oloffson. I remembered the last time I had been in Port-de-Paix, which is several days from Port-au-Prince by jeep, through rutted streambeds. A white man was considered very strange. Crowds followed until they got used to my color. Then, when I went skinny-dipping with my Haitian friends, there everyone stood again, deeply entertained. "But by now they know I'm white," I said.

"They didn't know you were white *all over,*" my friends told me.

The idea for Dupont Caribbean, Inc.'s project also looked white all over. Venture capital had found a hidden unspoiled spot that deserved development. As the sign in Dr. François Duvalier International Airport said:

> "My Father made the political revolution.
> I, I will make the economic revolution."
>
> —Jean-Claude Duvalier
> Ninth President-for-Life

One of the lesser riddles was to try to find who filled out the ranks of the other seven Presidents-for-Life. It was one of the mysteries of life in Haiti at that time.

At the end of our day on the beach, I stood with Jim Hobbs, waiting to fly home to the Oloffson. We looked out over the still expanse, the sea steadily surging up the long expanse of sand. A few people stood silently under coca palms, watching us. "I have a dream," I said. "I have a dream of golf carts with hundreds of retired corporate officers, their caps worn rakishly backwards on their heads, speeding from the fairway back to the condominium for cocktails . . . I have a dream . . . every wife with a staff of servants to supervise. . . ."

"I'll drink to that," said Jim Hobbs.

But the plan for the mini island nation stands unfulfilled. Dupont Caribbean, Inc., had dealt with the wrong friends and family of Baby Doc, the wrong twenty-five-year-old partner. In one of the many turnovers of cabinet personnel, the project was annulled. It's not clear who ended up with the profit from this dream out of Eastland, Texas.

O N MY way with Jean Weiner up the Pétionville road, I noticed a VW being erratically but speedily driven by what looked like a cute ten-year-old girl in horn-rimmed glasses. Although she was given a wide berth by other motorists—we drove off the road to avoid her daring automotive swoops—nobody signaled, honked, or shouted at her. She was the daughter of a police colonel. Jean congratulated me on guessing her age correctly.

Jean was aging fast without his family, who had emigrated to the States. He stayed, he said, because a man in love with a country is doomed and he was doomed. He said he was stupid and could not bear to leave. He said he hoped to do something for Haiti and knew he could do nothing. "Dear friend, don't torment me by asking me to be sensible. Didn't I already say I am doomed, stupid, and old?"

"Not old, Jean."

"Mon cher, why do you have to pick up all our bad habits, such as politeness?"

He still stretched his legs in that graceful way, and laughed and shook his head in dismay over the newest Rénovation Nationale— *"Mes-z-amis!"*—and used his inhaler to help him when his laughter was interrupted by the wheezing of asthma.

We told each other lies about how well we looked, how little we had changed.

"Do you see any hope?"

A look of kindly anxiety crossed Jean's face. He wanted to be helpful. "Hope?"

"Hope."

"Dear friend, that might be rather difficult. If I find any, you will be the first to know. Drink your juice, you must hydrate in this climate."

I thought of the voodoo chant with which I reminded my grown children of their year in Haiti, or told my young ones about what to expect. *Papa Legba, ouvri porte ou.* It was a prayer and an invocation. Papa Legba, open the door.

Papa Legba, guardian of the crossroads, points the way. He knows the path.

His family scattered abroad, Jean lived in a little house on concrete blocks, crowded with the debris of equipment, a shortwave radio and inoperative telephone, photographs and piled-up magazines, bare bulbs hanging, a disconnected Zenith record player. He showed me photographs of his daughter, who now lived on West Ninety-second Street in New York, and his son, an engineering student. "There is a Riverside Drive Park," he said. "Mes-z-amis, they can dress up my grandchildren in pretty clothes and look at the Hudson River."

Naked kids, their skin grayish with dust, were playing in the compound outside. In the silences between our words, I could hear sounds like the blowing of leaves, the chirping of birds, the hammering and pounding of rocks. There were people down the slope laughing, explaining, flopping their clothes against the rocks in the stream. When they didn't have soap, as they often didn't, they found this cleaned pretty well; also thinned and bleached in the sun. They bathed, washed, scrubbed things, and drank from this narrow rush which grew deep and foaming during the sudden storms. Sometimes burros also wallowed in the water. People took care to drink a body's length from the animals. That's how far the stream needed to flow before it became pure—so they believed.

"Haiti has not yet achieved the status of an underdeveloped nation," Jean said. "It is just *un*developed. No infrastructure and no structure, either. You see plenty of limes in the market, but you couldn't get enough together to manufacture lime jelly. Can you imagine this country which grows oranges and we import marmalade? All you need is sugar and a pot—any housewife can do it—and we have sugar. A Frenchman came and set up a little marmalade plant, but it was closed by the authorities. The so-called government. It's easier to collect taxes on imported marmalade and that's what they care about. Customs receipts are more fun than checking account books."

He showed me his jar of Smucker's marmalade and grinned. "With a name like that," he said, "it's got to be good." The flesh was eroding around his mouth. My handsome old friend was very tired.

"And take these transformation industries, where they bring in the goods and the dollar-a-day labor screws or sews or welds. Or glues it together. What does that do for Haiti? It uses no local material, it develops no base. It pays a few salaries, and everyone who works there tries to feed his whole family." He shrugged. "Maybe that helps. Until the Haitian partner drives the blancs crazy because he doesn't see why he shouldn't take a hundred percent, since he knows the Baby personally—"

I remembered the widow of an Army colonel who, after his death, sued an American company for the bribe owed him and a court upheld her plea. The "commission" for electrification of an outlying district of Port-au-Prince was considered a normal business obligation.

Jean got up and lumbered to his generator-powered refrigerator. "I forgot. You like our Shadek." He poured me a glass of grapefruit juice. "I did this myself. As a retired electrical engineer, I still know how to squeeze grapefruit."

As usual, he warned me about the people I met on the terrace of the Oloffson. "I know you think I'm paranoid," he said.

"A little."

"But now, after all these years, you see I am right, yes?"

Jean Weiner had helped me find my way into Haiti, but there was no way I could help him find his way out of Haiti and the world. I sat with him in this room with its table, a cot, a couple of chairs. He was wearing a bathrobe. From the nearly empty Smucker's marmalade jar, a line of ants was carrying out the last sugared grains of orange peel. A bare bulb reflected the light on his pink scalp between the remaining tight curls of white hair. I smelled his asthma medicine, eucalyptus, charcoal smoke from the compound outside. He spoke with the hasty eagerness of an old man while his energy was up: "Tell me what you think, mon cher! Tell me everything!" (Quick, quick!)

He used to ask: "What will save us?" Now he asked: "Have you ever seen anything worse than this place?"

"You look comfortable here, Jean."

His laughter fluttered and wheezed. "I suppose I am! This country, dear friend! This poor country!"

He stood outside and waved as I started back down the road. Through the rearview mirror I could see the slump of a man who had kept up his smile, his tall posture, the brightness of his eyes for old times' sake.

EVERYONE, OF course, including Jean, warned everybody else to beware of Aubelin Jolicoeur, that elegantly white-suited, skinny, high-pitched charmer whom Graham Greene called "Petit-

pierre." He seemed not to change over the years, a survivor, sometimes a great friend of Papa Doc (he saved his life by astute information gathering during a coup attempt), a great friend of Baby
Doc, a tourist official, journalist, eager gossip, chaser of foreign
women, art dealer. He also had a classical education and, seemingly, total recall for French verse, American visitors, and female
conquests.

What saved him was that he periodically went out of favor. With
his cane, hat, bouquets of flowers, he played boulevardier in this city
without handsome boulevards. Once I drove with him (he had a
chauffeur during his times in favor) while he bought a wholesale
batch of flowers, dropping off bouquets at various hotels for various
tourists. "I love her, Herb. . . . I love her, too."

When he was out of favor, he was irate and gloomy. He wrote
open letters to Baby Doc, the prince who needed to be protected from
bad advisors. He should listen to his good advisor. But even without
his chauffeur, without money for his bar and restaurant tabs, without
any income other than the occasional sale of a painting, he was always
immaculate in his whites, spinning merrily on the point of his cane
when he arrived at the Oloffson, making his rounds to greet every
interesting or pretty visitor. Like Haiti itself, the fact of perverse
durability somehow justified Aubie.

Holding court on the terrace of the Oloffson, a tradition there
like C'est-Dieu or the art collection or the ritual rum-punch offered
the punchy folks just off their flights, Aubie assured me that a new age
was dawning. "The troublemakers are gone. Of course, those who are
still alive are welcome to come back and contribute to the Jean-
Claudiste New Order." I thanked him again for my postcard visa.
"Even Graham Greene must come back now! Please, as soon as you
see him, tell him Petitpierre longs to share his life with one of the
masters of Anglo-Saxon prose!"

He shot me the familiar we-know-the-secret-services-are-all-
linked look. That all journalists were CIA was as real in Haiti as the
bakas, loupgarous, zombies, and malign spirits that raced their cars at
night, sometimes without heads. "Tell him—" Aubie pronounced a
happy benediction—"we no longer shoot so much . . . don't hardly

poison drinks anymore. . . . This little free nation is so beautiful, such music, such art, such girls! Not even the soup of the Enemies of the State, my friend. . . ."

IN 1971 THE choice of Jean-Claude as President-for-Life was confirmed in a popular referendum, carefully supervised by VSN experts in democratic process. The vote: 2,391,916 in favor, none against.

The boy President-for-Life was not putting his adolescent shoulders to the wheel of state. The folks who attempted to work their wills behind him included: the Sainted Widow & Mother, "l'Inspiratrice"; one of the sisters, along with her husband, brought back from the exile to which Dear Departed Papa Doc had sent them; Luckner Cambronne, Minister of the Interior and of Defense and partner in many businesses; plus such "dinosaurs"—old-time Duvalierists—as General Claude Raymond and Gérard de Catalogne, a nimble fellow who suffered the disadvantage of light skin.

Under divided leadership, it seemed that no one had the privilege of capricious terror anymore. People were cautious anyway; if they could speak up, it tended to mean that they could *think* about speaking up. But Papa Doc's years seemed to have temporarily exhausted the appetite for chaos. He had promoted fear for its own sake, and used his extortions to support the macoute agents of terror. The new folks, the dinosaurettes, were moving into an appropriate modern epoch. Swiss bank accounts. Property in Miami and New York. They welcomed foreign investment and use of docile cheap labor. *Fattening* the Swiss bank accounts.

"Everybody important is coming back," said Aubie, "all the friends of our beautiful con-tree!" And he pirouetted on the point of his cane, his balding head bulging with sheer brain and nerve. "And I know them all, Herb! All the beautiful people!"

"You never change, Aubie."

"I am weathervane, yes? You do not know where the weather blows until you ask the weathervane, Bob Dylan says. I am writing letter to *Time* magazine to invite *everybody* that they may come home."

"Keep it brief, Aubie."

He shook his head sadly. Such were the limitations of life on earth. The letters column of *Time* would not honor his references to the other great writers of Rome, Athens, Paris, and Jacmel.

At this time the dark little Haitian tourist office in Rockefeller Center, New York, was staffed by sleepy men who reminded me of the lounging, heavy-lidded macoutes who hung about the bars, restaurants, and hotels of Port-au-Prince. But a tourist drive was on. Haiti Drumbeats, a p.r. handout, gave news of the film company shooting a project called "Goodbye Uncle Tom." The publicity staff was not exactly apt. Haiti Drumbeats suggested wonderful opportunities for photography fans. "Black faces make marvelous subjects—their big, warm, wonderful smiles. . . ."

Its news flashes also included "the very, very spiffy cocktail parties and black tie banquet" hosted by the new l'Atelier Galerie d'Art, "with plenty of the primitive flavor that collectors love so." It invited visitors to the International Casino, "open again, under the direction of Mike McLaney." Little balls splashed into metallic dishes. Little clicks hopped around grand devices. Little rumors about ownership flew by the telejiol. Whenever I stopped by, the International Casino d'Haiti reminded me of a funeral parlor, croupiers presiding over the death of money. Yet there were suddenly-rich Haitians and less-suddenly-rich tourists who patronized this place which resembled a pre-Castro Cuban casino, only made of toothpaste. The air-conditioning, the darkness, the "Haitian hostesses dressed in Creole costumes," the "Latin-type shows" provided an atmosphere appropriate for visitors to Haiti who didn't want to be in Haiti. It was toy Las Vegas, mini-Batista land.

In the early seventies, junkets of travel journalists were flown down, cruise companies courted. The Grace Line, the France, the Holland-America Line brought mahogany-purchasers, textile-fingerers, painting connoisseurs, and the crews carried boxes and shopping bags of booty back on board. Some snorkeled. Some merengued. Some even sightsaw into the staged voodoo ceremonies that are almost real. ("I liked Haiti. Haiti was Island Three, wasn't it, dear?") The actress Yvette Mimieux, the TV personality Mike Wallace, and a few retired doctors or adventurous millionaires bought property, spent vacations in their little colonial houses in Jacmel that could cost less than $15,000 to buy. Miss Mimieux said: "The people are dignified and proud." The travel editor of the *Miami Herald* wrote that Haiti suffered "from stories—some perhaps true, some perhaps false—that have emanated from political situations. . . . The things you've read or heard about Haiti's secret police or civilian militia may be true or they may not be true, but they have nothing to do with the tourist."

Despite such recommendations, Baby Doc's regime made progress. The country was too different, too interesting—French, African, and fun; painting, voodoo, and good accommodations. With just a hint of tranquility, the tourists returned. Nelson Rockefeller, representing President Nixon, stayed only one night at the Villa Creole, but announced that Haiti was a terrific anti-Communist little place. When Aubelin Jolicoeur heard that he was leaving the next day, he approached the governor and said, "Mr. Rockefeller, it hurt us that you stay one night. If you stay longer, I will try to get you the room free."

The "Office National du Tourisme et de la Propagande" issued a brochure summarizing the position of Baby Doc: "Haiti, a democratic country and second only to the U.S.A. as the leading independent republic of the New World, follows her destiny on the road of progress and prosperity."

Take that, Brazil, Argentina, Chile, Canada. It seemed curious to praise "progress and prosperity" in the poorest nation in the western hemisphere. It came of the same logic that said French was the language. True, some people were getting rich and some people spoke French. And it was also true that the tourist could be safely entertained.

Radio broadcasts were the chief means of communication after the telejiol. In a nation with at least 85 percent illiteracy, and where newspapers were published in French, not Creole, the haranguing voices of announcers, which often sounded like the sound trucks of the early fifties, blared out a kind of information. Sometimes one radio served several houses, plus passersby on the road, with music, advice, political commentary, and advertisements. "Anacin! Anacin! Anacin! Headaches! Colds! Flu! Anacin! Anacin! Anacin!" ran one insistent chant. Manischewitz Kosher Wine was still absolutely kosher . . . guaranteed kosher . . . many people have discovered it to be more kosher than any other . . . if you don't find it to be kosher, your money back. . . . Aphrodisiac drugs, imported from the Dominican Republic, probably contained irritants. The native aphrodisiacs, such as clairin soaked in "bois cochon"—pigwood, a gnarled root shaped like an exhausted phallus—had the defect of being too familiar. I examined a bottle of Manischewitz at the Belle Creole shop. "Is it really kosher?"

"Try it and see," said the young salesperson, averting her eyes and giggling.

In this time of détente, the radio toned down the news of political turmoil. When a "perturbation" occurred in downtown Port-au-Prince, the "speakerine" noted that "several people were injured not up to the point of being considered dead. Calm prevails."

The syntax offered clues, but to what was unclear. The local importer of sweet Manischewitz wine was more specific.

Most of the people I had gathered with in 1963, the secret plotters at that blacked-out house of the bookstore owner—plotting mainly consolation for their troubles—were now dead or in exile. I met one of them, an elderly doctor, on the rue du Centre. He was wearing a white summer suit, the kind of dark tie favored by postwar professors at the Sorbonne, a straw hat. He raised a finger to draw attention to his perfect recall, reciting like a good French schoolboy lines from an article I wrote about that brave and futile gathering. We stood in the street amid the din of man-pulled carts, vendors, honking cars, beggars, amid people sleeping on the sidewalk, children crouched along with their parents, and he shouted his litany about the regime. When he named specific malefactors, such as Jean-Claude Duvalier or his "dinosaurs," the old guard, he winked meaningfully and switched into English. He said the macoutes were still running things, though no longer on the streets as living advertisements for death. There were still abrupt disappearances. The prisons were nearly empty which—and he shrugged—meant that the prisoners had been destroyed. But: Now he could say these things to me in daylight on the rue du Centre.

I told him that my eldest daughter, Ann, had come to visit this place of her childhood and given me the news about Jean Weiner. We shared a moment of silence together amid the street jostling and uproar. We pressed hands in memory of Jean. I remembered him in his white linen suit pacing the deck of the Panama Lines vessel steaming southward toward Port-au-Prince in 1953. I remembered how he apologized for the tears of laughter that ran down his face when he contemplated my foolish gullibility, the innocence of a young man in a place where every morning seemed both new and drenched in history like the sound-drenched morning air of Port-au-Prince, various and enticing. "These are selfish tears," he had said, "because your foolishness is not my foolishness—if only I could have yours!"

I used to tell him we were probably cousins, both Ashkenazic, but he answered, *mes-z-amis,* no cousin of his, African or Jewish, could be so easily taken in.

The old doctor and I stood there on the rue du Centre, waiting to go on with our lives. It was still bewildering to me that Jean was gone. The doctor was watching my face with an attentive smile in case I wanted to say more. No, he didn't have the date of Jean's death in his carnet. It happens so often with friends, you see, that a person stops noting it down.

Probably the exact date didn't matter. But I wished I knew.

"That's natural," said the doctor. "All such procedures are natural."

I tried to understand his words. Eventually I would.

"And I trust your daughter was not disappointed in our interesting little nation?" said the doctor. "If I am still alive next time she visits, I would be honored to meet her."

When we parted, he raised his elegant long instructional finger: "As Monsieur Johnny Carson would say, 'Don't quote me.' " And he slapped his thigh with that rich Haitian laughter which means that no one is as simple as he seems, and no one as complicated, either. When he laughed, I saw the young, terrifically fun-loving Haitian medical student of the Quartier Latin within the grayish-black skin of this old man.

DRIVING ON the Bizoton road one Sunday just before Carnival, we passed a band rehearsing with their Haitian fantasy costumes and insignia—captains in the Hungarian navy, outer-space cadets, movie-star versions of Papa Legba, a man in a missionary's blue nylon safari suit with a fish as a bow tie—and the bamboo flutes, the Marine whistles, a battery of drums promenading, swarming across the road. We stopped to cheer these admirals (how quickly one promotes the captains!), movie stars, prancing missionaries, musicians. The drums with their shrill accompaniments were thrilling as they always are. Then a tap-tap, an exuberantly painted bus with the name JESU BON on the grill, careened into the crowd and knocked a paper mask flying. Beneath the mask was the head of a boy. He was bleeding from the nostrils and ears, eyes rolled up and open; no reactions, no reflexes.

"There's one who won't provide plasma," said one of my friends.

His wife was crying. He put his arms around her and muttered, "Maybe he'll make a trip to the University of Toronto Medical School."

The people were screaming at the tap-tap driver, he screamed back, his passengers waited silently for the ride they had purchased to be completed. Since nothing more could be done, the mission to celebrate Carnival went on, first the whistles, then one flute and an answering battery of drums, and then the dancers flowed forward with their intricate connections among music, the gods, and each other.

Mardi Gras brought visitors back year after year. Tourists didn't need to go out to the streets, although I liked to let myself be swept along by the throbbing, surging bands in their wild array, African, French, European, and Haitian with their peppery satire, nightmares and daymares, ecstatic invocations of all the gods of danger and love. Late that night, returning to the Oloffson, I stopped to talk with an American cabaret singer and her escort, pointing her profile into the darkness while the music and dancers, torches and banners swirled in the garden below, sometimes advancing up the stairs, grimacing, showing masks and butts, then turning back. "Why don't the devils just attack and get it over with?" she asked. "I'm ready, Bruce."

Even Bruce, who had other plans for this evening, was willing to stay awhile longer, watching. Everyone was exhilarated by the rhythms, the assons, bamboo flutes, the whistles, laughter, drums, and also by all the food, rum, and sun we had taken. But I was thinking of the boy under the mask of Papa Legba on the Bizoton road earlier that day.

HIS EXCELLENCY Jean-Claude Duvalier the Ninth, President-for-Life, the Dignified Heir, the Young Leader, "whose nobility and generosity of intention make our struggles even more sublime" (quoted from the Official Review of Foreign Affairs, as phrased by Dr. Adrien Raymond, Secretary of State for Foreign Affairs and Religion) was growing up. He was the Chief. He was the Prince. He was a rather stolid young man, or as he would be titled in the worshipfully capitalizing Haitian manner, a Rather Stolid Young Man, His Overweightness, Furniture Face. Guided first by his sister and The Inspirer, his mother, he began to refer to himself in his speeches as the Worthy Continuer.

As time went on, the Worthy Continuer made gestures of independence. He moved from toy trucks and trains to grown-up motorcycles and sports cars. Eventually he married Michelle Bennett, whom one might call The Inappropriate, in a $2 million celebration, and thereafter was guided by her lighter-skinned family with its drug-dealing son and its connections with the most corrupt elements of the old elite. After his marriage Baby Doc's own skin mysteriously began to lighten. This has not been fully explained. He also became the First Servitor.

Along with the return of tourists and cruise ships, the electrical plant was repaired and blackouts were less frequent. The Leader-Fully-Responsible named a new power plant after his Devoted Self. He read his speeches with improved fluency, the Plump Finger following the words. He wished the Pope a happy anniversary of the crowning. He congratulated President Nixon on American Independence Day, and received in reply a note of "profound satisfaction for your amiable message." This was headline news in *Le Nouvelliste.*

The Review of Foreign Affairs for August 1971, noted that the Chief of State received the credentials of an Argentine diplomat with "ease and simplicity." The President-for-Life made a speech in which he swore that Argentina and Haiti would be forever united in the struggle against "material philosophies." The extensively upholstered First Citizen evidently intended this advice for his subjects, not for himself.

I DROVE UP the road to Kenscoff, this mountain village with its rapid streams, intense cultivation of good things for the table, chatter of market women washing their vegetables, their clothes, and themselves, smell of eucalyptus overhead and onions and tomatoes below. The temperature was often twenty degrees cooler than Port-au-Prince. Sometimes I would just climb onto a tap-tap for the careening ride up the mountain.

Kenscoff still suggests the Swiss Alps with elegant little mountain chalets and roads lined with flaming bougainvillea. Some of the houses are built with steeply canted roofs, as if to let the snow slide off. In winter it is never cold enough for that, although the crisp air and mountain nights bring out cable-knit sweaters in visitors. The peasants build charcoal fires and don't wander the roads at night as they do in the sultry lowlands. On these steeply terraced slopes, people work at perpendicular farming, balanced in the fields like storks.

Years ago, when I stayed in Jean Weiner's house, I took my meals at the Florville, three dollars a day for breakfast, lunch, and dinner in a room with a mural painted by Enguerrand Gourgue, peasants and drums and stylized voodoo. At night, I could hear the ceremonies nearby or, if I chose, visit them by following the sound until I heard the chant, *Ap vini blanc, ap vini blanc.* The white man is coming, the white man is coming.

The Florville had always been too modest for the wealthy elite who drove their girlfriends to Kenscoff for a cool night of romance. They preferred the Swiss chalets. Occasionally a coffee dealer from Jacmel might appear, or a gloomy husband escaping a quarrel. My company at meals used to include the exiled Vichy colonel, marching back and forth between courses ("Culture physique! Je me défends!") and complaining that the victory of Communism in France meant that he had to "manger du chocolat" for the rest of his life. He ate chocolate, which he didn't mind, but he also had to live among these chocolate-colored people. Once the Haitian doctor-lawyer who had treated me for malaria appeared for a night. "Voyage d'études," he explained in his dandified finicky way. He was still wearing his green catskin shoes with his white suit and Panama hat, and carrying his heavy walking *cocomacaque.*

Had I ever suffered a regrettable return of malaria? he inquired.

No, thank you.

"So much the better," he said.

The nearby market, Tuesday mornings, as always, still sold rags sewn into dresses, fantasy patchwork, gloomy mahogany bowls, candlestick holders tapped out of Pet Milk cans, besides fried pork, vegetables, paper rolls of sugar, rice, and beans from sacks sprawled on the ground. I spent my time tramping the hills. I found a friend of Eugène Noh, a colleague from the Cenacle des Philosophes on the porch where peasants used to bring the coffee beans in straw baskets carried on their heads. He was a retired judge and he shook with Parkinsonism, stiffly trying to walk in front of his house.

I told him I missed Monsieur and Madame Noh.

"Yes, he's gone. He lived seventy years. I'm used to it now."

"Still, it's sad," I said.

"And there's no more coffee. The trees are gone, too."

"I've heard."

"But I could make a cup for you," he said.

Instead, I offered him a coffee at the Florville, but he said it was too far to walk. He didn't like to leave his house.

The war in Vietnam had ruined the coffee business (actually, the peasants burned the trees to make charcoal); a plan by the Americans had resulted in the closing of Le Perchoir, the lovely little restaurant

with a view of the city below and the plain all the way to the Dominican border, mountains, and bay (actually, it was the depression and
immobility of the Duvalier years which had killed Le Perchoir). The
Kenscoff Adult Academy of Paranoid Explanation had not entirely
faded away.

"There is no excuse for that war your country made in Vietnam,"
said the old judge. "Whereas we Haitians have made peace with each
other." And his frozen face lit up, broke into a grin, stumps of teeth in
that ruined landscape. As we sat outside his little house he turned his
cup upside down and let the grounds drop for the chickens. "No one
left to make war, Monsieur."

CHAPTER
ELEVEN

In Haiti,
They Run From

I HEARD OF the runner who had finished last at the Montreal Olympics. Several other Haitian runners achieved Olympic fame by finishing last in their various competitions. In the spring of 1982, I decided to pack up my Nikes for a visit to work out with the Haitian champions, just as if this were a normal place for an aerobic vacation.

It was jeopardy jogging time in Haiti. There was no Gatorade, no track, no club. The Leopards, elite guard of His Excellency, Baby Doc, studied running, but did running his bodyguards count as sport? Sociobiologically speaking, fleet feet are emergency transportation, what you do when you're hungry or afraid.

There was plenty of fear in the early eighties. The Boat People were using their leaky makeshift vessels only because they couldn't run or walk on water. The blue and white Caribbean sea was a menace composed of sharks, surf, coral reefs, barracuda, more sharks, and the Unknown Beyond. I was heading off to run in a place where all the running I had seen was *away*.

Not to worry, as it turned out.

Emmanuel St.-Hilaire ran the 1,500 in 4:23, which was twenty-four seconds slower than the next slowest man to compete at the Montreal Olympics. Dieudonné Lamothe—soon to become my running buddy—ran 18:50 for the 5,000 meter race, five minutes behind the next slowest in his heat. Olmeus Charles, who ran a forty-two-minute, 10,000 meter, was lapped seven times, delayed the Olympic scheduling, and was booed by the astonished throng.

This was my kind of running. But it turned out that there were good runners here; that Dieudonné Lamothe, with whom I ran in the Haitian mountains, was training and turning into a winning competitor, with some Caribbean championships to his credit. And the slopes of Kenscoff provide some of the most beautiful marathon trails in the world.

Once again I tucked myself into my home away from home, the Grand Hotel Oloffson, this time sending out messages by telejiol that I wished to make contact with the runners of Haiti. I whispered into the delicate, shell-like ear of Aubelin Jolicoeur. "You *what*, Herb? Have you gone mad in la Californie? But I do not judge my friends!" He pirouetted on his cane, in his white suit, all the brilliant black 120 pounds of him vibrating with hospitality. Hospitality vibrations provided all the isometric and aerobic conditioning Aubie needed. The journalist, man-about-the-tourists, famous friend of Papa Doc, now a bit estranged from the Distinguished Son, spun off the ground, his shoes seeming never to touch the floor, giggled merrily, and leaped away to join three tourist schoolteachers who were swaying to the merengue tune, "Choucoune," which had been played for thirty years by the band on the terrace.

Word got out. The telephone seemed in repair this season. Messages arrived in the briefcases of ancient delivery dignitaries in pre-World War I worsted suits. Jeeps pulled up to the Oloffson. The secret society of Haitian runners gathered its force. *Yes! We thought you'd never find us! We're here and we're running!*

Matt Cucchiara, M.A. geologist out of Fordham and N.Y.U., fanatic runner, had come to Haiti to look for copper. He found no copper, but decided to stay, manufacturing wood products, selling paintings, trying to get paid for his wood products and his paintings. He was a runner. He may have given up geology, the plan to become a millionaire, and a certain amount of his Long Island Italian Catholicism, but he knew damn well he was one of the best over-forty marathoners in the world—or would be, as soon as he turned forty. Or at least one of the best Americans. And certainly the best American living in Haiti.

Matt swung by the Oloffson one morning at six A.M. to pick me up for a little training marathon in the mountains. There was that immediate ease between us of people who share an impossible love. We were a bit late getting up the mountain, due to barricades by the police, armed with guns and whistles; the problem turned out not to be a revolution or invasion, but the funeral of the boy President-for-Life's grandmother.

Waiting on a corner in Pétionville, we picked up Dieudonné Lamothe, who had improved so much that he had entered forced retirement as the World's Slowest Olympic Runner—a skinny twenty-six-year-old security guard who believed the talent for running is a gift of the gods—and also a twenty-two-year-old retired Leopard named Desroses, a comer in the running line. We shook hands, exchanged compliments in French and Creole; and, in low gear, climbed through the village of Kenscoff and into the mountain fresh-ness leading toward Furcy and the Forest of Pines. We edged along precipice mists amid Nepal-like vistas of one of the world's longest waterfalls (its name is Long Waterfall). There was a clear, bell-like sun shimmer in the air. We were at about 7,000 feet. "Okay. *Allons*," said Matt Cucchiara.

We began to run. I planned to drop off at the bridge across a little gorge, a few miles down, and let the real runners continue on their pious nine- or eleven- or fifteen-mile rounds. I felt like a happy animal, loping and roaming and chatting with Matt, who was running easy, bare-chested and gleaming. Peasants by the roadside were shouting encouragement: "Look at the white men sweat!" (Haitian proverb: Stupidity won't kill you, but it'll make you sweat a lot.) A wizened market lady with a pipe clenched between her teeth and a basket of onions on her head muttered in Creole, "They don't look like thieves. Why are they doing this?"

Matt explained that folks were now used to runners on these mountains. Sometimes, as a joke, people ran alongside for a while. Sometimes they offered to sell an orange or a grapefruit, or a tomato, or a refreshing interlude in the grass; and of course, one of the great things was to pay a man with a machete to lop off the top of a coconut so you could drink the cool milk.

There was an American teacher named Connie from the Union

School. She ran down the mountain from Pétionville to work. She ran back up.

There was a Haitian of Syrian descent, graduate of the City College of New York, where he was a muscle athlete—wrestling, weights—who ran.

There was Jean-Claude Armand, a handsome fiftyish devil of a Haitian, tennis player and runner.

But the Captain of Running in Haiti, the Admiral, the High Priest, the Big Boss was Matt Cucchiara, proprietor of "Certainly Wood," West Indies Hardwoods. He ran the trails above Kenscoff in the cool fresh mountains; he ran a measured mile down in the industrial park near the Dr. François Duvalier International Airport. He was a coach and financial benefactor of the Haitian runners. He was fanatic about the religion, or as some call it, the sport of running.

IN TOWN, the smoky air becomes greasy with sweat and flesh, a pungency beyond the mere pellmell shedding of flower scents, charcoal burning, rot and composting, sun on flesh, fiber, goods. Armpits are a metaphor elsewhere. Here in Population Explosion City, everything seems to be God's Grease, fried vapor.

Corruption consultant or terror manager for the government was the best job a young man from the urban slums could hope for. The Duvalier family owned most of the money; the work could be done by others. A few favored ones, plus adroit foreign investors and managers, got the leavings. Out of foreign aid and cheap labor, the Family had created several hundred millionaires.

Digging a foundation hole for a house for a police chief, a man worked with sculpted muscles and an impassive heroic African face like the ones that stand in the little squares of Dakar. Walking down the road from the mountains beyond Pétionville, bathing in the trickles in the ravines, among donkeys and goats, beautiful girls put down the baskets on their heads; they seemed to be carefree, their laughter tinkling and pealing. No wonder some tourists could say "happy natives"; the tourists were partly right. The beggars with scabby stumps and wasting diseases, and the nameless dead found at morning in the streets, must have been the less happy natives.

From the newspaper *Le Nouveau Monde,* "The National and International Daily of Haiti," 14 May 1982: "The Leadership of President Jean-Claude confers a new dimension to the democratic epoch sung by him. . . . More than a Cornellian hero, the President Jean-Claude Duvalier, whom contemporary history is in the act of welcoming already as a forger of Democracy, is illuminating his trajectory as an eminent man of politics and, by the Titan-like devotion that he gives in the exercise of his profession as Chief of everything, fires without caution a defiance which belongs to every thoughtful Chief of State in the Third World: to raise Democracy, the *True* Democracy."

What this meant, only the gods who speak Délire Verbale might decipher. The Boy President's philosophy, emblazoned on billboards and through nonstop cheerleader harangues on the radio, was named "Jeanclaudism." Sometimes he climbed into a limousine and was driven about the city, his sturdy fingers extended, sprinkling coins upon the crowds—philosophy in action.

Protein was lacking. No Supply Side existed for the peasants and urban poor. This was misery like Chad, Upper Volta, and Bangladesh, but located only a short flight from Miami. We ran among Haiti's cheerful suffering, familiar misery. "Only the knife knows the pumpkin's heart," say the peasants of Kenscoff. The government was the knife here, and so was the worked-out soil, the dilapidation of the hillsides, the remorseless leap of population. When I lived in Haiti in 1953–54, the population was an antheap pile of 3½ million souls crammed into a land the size of Maryland, crumpled in God's hand, terraced and desperately tilled on the steeps. The population was now 6 million, heading toward 7—no one really counted anymore.

"Hey, gi me fi cents!" the kids cried or whispered, clutching at your hand. And then they laughed. They thought it was a good line. You didn't need to leave by the next plane just because they reached for your hand; they needed consolation, and they didn't insist if you preferred not to walk down the street holding the hand of a stranger. "Gi me fi cents! Gi me shirt! Gi me somet'ing, blanc!"

Birth control was mostly taken care of by billboards that announced: MONSIEUR ET DAMES! FAIS PLANNING! (Sirs and Madames! Plan!) Despite this Titan-like and Cornellian effort, almost every woman between the ages of thirteen and forty-five seemed to be pregnant, or had just given birth, or was about to become pregnant.

I drove around Port-au-Prince with Matt Cucchiara. Later, a visitor arrived from New York, a friend whom I had enticed with the story of running in Haiti. ("Are you crazy?" "Are you?" "Well, I'll bring my diving equipment.") But I made her look at the city before I'd take her to a beach.

The graceful crumble of Port-au-Prince was interspersed with *caille-pailles* and the occasional plaster Miami Beach payoff mansions of the rich. Frangipani, mango smells, and charcoal smoke filled the air. There were an estimated 20,000 bathrooms for 6 or 7 million people, all of whom improvised bathroom functions someplace. So there were other smells, too. After a mysterious explosion and fire, the decor of the National Palace was redone by a decorator resident in Haiti, Lawrence Peabody II of the Boston Peabodies.

The Marché au Fer, that painted cast-iron circus of thrills, haggles, craftsmanship, diseases, beggars, donkeys, meat and tin and painting, was a boiling African market in which people were born and died and found bargains going each way. Annual income in Haiti was about $250 *per year*. Per *family*. Bargains were available. A friend, visiting me in 1954, had bought a Haitian painting for $35 and I accused him of driving the price up; it should have been $25. Later, he sold the painting for about $4,000 at a Parke-Bernet auction.

"I have extended," said Baby Doc, the inventor of Jeanclaudism; "I have extended the olive branch of clemency . . ." Of course, some of those to whom he extended it were dead, maimed, disappeared. Since the Family was rich enough now, some thought Jean-Claude wanted a friendlier image in history than his father's. But he still had to satisfy his new wife's family. His brother-in-law had gone to prison in Puerto Rico because his private plane arrived with a load of illicit substances.

Except for Jean Weiner, Haitians didn't suffer "that strange melancholy which often haunts the inhabitants of democratic countries," according to de Tocqueville on America. Instead, they do their best. They keep busy. Haitians by the side of the road are always doing something, hammering tin, working leather, bathing if there is water, cooking if there is food, laughing and chatting if they are not dying. On that running excursion to Haiti, I wished Jean were still there to tell me I should have been doing something else.

If given the chance, Haitians have the character and bodies to make good sport runners. Runners, as a race or nationality, often carry a haunted style, even in America. They are not necessarily happy, but they love that piston thing they do with their legs, that explosive aerobic soma lilt that comes into heart, lungs, arteries, blood. Look at Haitians walking and you know they can run if they have to, and if the opportunity comes. Not just *from* and *away,* but also, as I saw in the hills of Pétionville and Kenscoff, for the soaring joy of it.

Many traditional Creole songs praise the sun of Haiti, the air, the sea, the sun, the sun. And true, the island is sea-washed and mountain-fresh in many places. It's also humid and hot. Intelligent people keel over and put their four paws in the air during the hours of early afternoon. At night, dancing and play; and in the early day, work, unless you are unemployed or a government bureaucrat. Nevertheless, there were also runners running in God's fistful of Caribbean island.

Even if the Haitian Olympic runners finished last in Montreal—a kind of distinction, after all—*they ran.* They continued to run. Dieudonné Lamothe was now far from the world's worst, although not yet the world's best. Running in Haiti was like the building I saw near Sidi Bou Sahid in Tunisia, with its painted sign, "The Tunisian Atomic Energy Research Institute." It's not that they did it so remarkably well. It was just remarkable that they did it at all.

Watching the runners here, teachers and businesspeople, the former Leopard, the security guard who was lapped a couple of times at Montreal, reassured me that an ancient passion for loping, roaming, and scampering, just for the joy of it, could survive even in a place that knew so much grief.

Dear Jean: I know you wouldn't approve. I did it anyway.

SOMETIMES WHEN Dieudonné Lamothe and the others went to the airport to emplane for a Caribbean marathon, the flight took off without them. No one arrived with the tickets from the government agency that said it would support them. Sometimes the official arrived, shrugged, and said, "No tickets." It was discouraging. Once Matt Cucchiara, who was not a rich man, laid out $900 for tickets. He said he couldn't see Lamothe crushed like that yet again.

Lamothe was supposed to compete in a race in Tegucigalpa, Honduras. (The *Tegucigalpa* Marathon? Yes.) He waited with his bags packed at the airport. He didn't go and was so depressed he didn't run again for two months.

A Cayman Islands meet. Same thing. He sat in the airport for two hours and the promised private plane never arrived. "No money, man," said Cucchiara. "Some generous donor."

Lamothe won the St. Kitts International Half Marathon in 1980. In 1981, as the defending champion, he was invited back to be honored and to run again. Imagine the thrill for the Haitian runner who became the butt of jokes at the Olympics. Matt Cucchiara, who was already in St. Kitts, went to the airport to pick him up. He wasn't there. Same old story. They had sworn the ticket would be issued.

"Fortunately, as an American resident, I could run for Haiti," said Cucchiara. "I suppose I might run for Haiti in the Olympics if I get to be an Honorary Citizen. But it won't make Lamothe feel any better."

Sometimes the Royal Haitian Hotel or the Prestige Bar helped to support Lamothe and Robert Desroses, about whom Cucchiara said: "He's nothing special in a ten-kilometer race—about thirty-four minutes—but I'd like to put him in a twenty-four-hour race. No one could beat him. Once we had a meet and he ran to the race, ran the race, and then afterwards ran home four miles."

Desroses was a night watchman at the Brasserie. That kind of sedentary job, a fellow likes to get a little exercise.

As the runners brought success to Haiti—a team third place in the Caribbean meet in Aruba in 1981, for example—other benefactors occasionally appeared. Baby Doc showed sudden interest in running and asked to see their trophies. They were delivered to the National Palace. Evidently he looked and looked, but found better things to do with his loose cash. He kept the trophies.

Despite the eccentric situation of runners in Haiti, Matt Cucchiara said he would live and run no place else. He struck out with his geological explorations and his first wood factory, but he was happier in Port-au-Prince than in Queens. Haiti was an addiction, like running; sometimes painful, like running. I understood his mania.

"Sometimes you run in sugar fields and it's ninety-five degrees and when you can't stand it, you jump into the ice-cold aqueduct vats and then go on. Those sugar fields, it's like running on wood chips— cane husks on the roads, a springiness." —Matt Cucchiara. And the look of a natural animal came into the B.A. (Fordham), M.A. (N.Y.U.) geologist-woodworker's eyes. The flush. The cheekbones. The nostrils. Wasn't running something that human beings took up in hostile environments, in worlds of desert hunting and forest seeking, chasing animals, preening for partners, sometimes being chased? The Haitian running team enjoyed an ancient reality. "This is runner's hell and runner's paradise," said lean, long-legged, fanatic Matt Cucchiara.

When they returned victorious from the St. Kitts half-marathon, thousands of Haitians greeted them at the airport. "Vive le Champion de Saint-Kitts!" Even the television gave up its coverage of President Baby Doc's mumblings to show the triumphant hero, Dieudonné Lamothe, lifting his arms in a victory sign.

When Lamothe made negative history at Montreal, he was running without a real training program and in a strange northern place—he had never been abroad before; without a diet and exercise program, without a job that gave him time to work at running. But he became a competitor. Dieudonné Lamothe (his first name means "Given by God") gave his firstborn son an English word for a name: "Runner." Another son was named for an English expression he frequently heard while running in Canada: "Wat Zat."

I asked how it felt to be abroad for the first time, among people who don't speak Creole, in a place so different from his own. "Flat," said Lamothe. "Good running. Good shoes."

He had just run nine miles in about fifty-four minutes, up and down the mountains of Kenscoff. Columbus described this place to the King of Spain by crumpling a wad of parchment. Now Given-by-God explored it, loping, conquering the hills with his feet.

I remembered the crates of cargo that I thought might be food for the hungry, clothing, medicine. They were marked Corps des Leopards, and it was sporting goods, Ping-Pong tables, soccer equipment, racquets, nets, gloves. "We had track meets," said Desroses, the former Leopard. For a boy from a village, life in the Leopards must have been thrilling.

"**O**KAY, HERE'S where we start."
It was another dewy, chirpy early-in-the-morning. By the side of the road, near a stand selling cigarettes one at a time, rolled papers of sugar and coffee, and warm bottles of U.S. Reject *Kancer Kola,* we piled out of Matt's car. Desroses, Lamothe, Cucchiara had that eager jumpy look of runners cooped up for a while but ready to go; I'm not sure what sort of look I wore on a face that had discussed politics, et cetera—mostly et cetera—until the middle of the night. "*Allons.*"

Again we were running one of the trails from Kenscoff to Furcy. The others planned to do about eleven miles; I planned to do a couple of miles to the swinging bridge, where I might stop and admire the view while they shot ahead. The road, rutted but dry, springy, felt good. We ran past Madame Saras with baskets on their heads, pipes in their mouths; we ran past donkeys, leaving their steaming droppings for us to avoid; we ran past a school. It was Flag Day. The kids were parading in blue uniforms, yellow ones, checked ones, green ones, each class in formation, and in the distance, a marching band played; and suddenly, as they were laughing and pointing at us, a whole class was running after the crazy runners, like the tail to a kite.

"*Blanc,* you're still sweating!"

We were, and they were running after us, screaming with pleasure. Even the teachers were running.

This time I didn't stop at the bridge. There was eucalyptus and pine up ahead. There was a mob laughing and singing behind. I was the joy of their day. So I ran, breathless with that pleasure of being in Haiti again.

ONE AFTERNOON at the Oloffson, listening to the cock-crow and dogs, the clack of shoeshine boys hitting their boxes, the screech of traffic and street banter, I decided to walk down toward the National Palace and the Place des Héros ("des Zéros"), just to take the air. Past the palm and mango trees of the Oloffson's mange of garden into the street, and then there was a special screech of brakes that seemed to be aimed at me, and my old friend Theo Duval, former Director of Tourism, newly appointed to the Embassy in London, was leaning out of his automobile to ask what the devil I was doing in Haiti. I told him.

"You came to run? Let the record show, friend, that the gods have made you crazy."

HAITI WAS free; by official notice prosperity had returned; government was now responsive to the people. The Youthful Leader was paying attention. When racing his cars or his motorcycles palled on him and his video games provided no respite, Jean-Claude Duvalier would make a sortie into the countryside for a few moments of personal frowning at the problems of water, health, education, and starvation. He threw coins at the crowds and they shouted, "Vive Bébé, Fils de Doc!"

While reporters watched his grateful subjects fighting in the dust for the strewn cash, the motors started up and the President sped off, refreshed by contact with the People. The newspapers reprinted the text of a speech that His Youthful Excellence did not bother to deliver.

In the market of Gonaives I found the special souvenir medal bearing the likeness of Dr. François Duvalier, President-for-Life, which had been given to journalists, along with a twenty-one-gun salute, during one of the previous revivals of tourism and the economy.

I was traveling with an earnest public health specialist from Pough-keepsie, who was explaining something to his Haitian counterpart in a medical survey while we watched a man scramble up a coconut palm, getting us our milk, chopping off the top of the nut. Dr. Poughkeepsie remarked admiringly to his counterpart: "What I don't understand is how you have all these fun qualities, plus you're a damn good doc."

"Thank you. What qualities?"

"Last night at the reception—"

"Yes."

"—and I know, strictly speaking, you don't have a different skeleton or more joints than I do, but when you danced, your..." He struggled to find the right word. "Your... *rhythmicity.*"

"Drink well of our coconut milk," said Dr. Bandeur.

During this period of détente and revival, the official Regime Dissenter came to the Oloffson to present his card, his beaming face, his delighted laughter. His name was Gerald Merceron and he was well connected. He was also multitalented, a lawyer, writer, jazz composer and performer. He showed me clippings of his reviews in *Downbeat.* He had invented "Caribo-jazz." "Look at me! A mulatto, member of the traditional elite, good hair, and am I persecuted? Am I in peril? No, no, a thousand times absolutely not, my dear friend!"

His visit was one of philosophy and social criticism. He shared the famous Oloffson French toast with me while, bursting with feeling, he explained the good news that he hoped to share with the rest of the world: *Jean-Claude Duvalier was not so dumb as everyone said.* He was not cruel. He was not vicious. He was a secret admirer of liberty and democracy.

This was good news indeed.

The billboards declaring, "My Father Made the Social Revolu-tion, I Am Making the Economic Revolution," expressed Baby Doc's most intimate thought. I could stake my life on it.

I thanked my new friend and co-philosopher.

For example, he himself, Gerald Merceron, at the President-for-Life's invitation, was writing an uncompromising critique of the gov-ernment, past abuses, corruption, everything that was in error. He also included everything that could, in the future, be made right.

Terrific. What a tome, I said.

He reminded me that Switzerland was once the poorest country in Europe, a small mountainous wilderness with a clever people its only resource. And now look at it. In the moment of silence, that thick cacophonous silence of Port-au-Prince, we looked.

We ate our papaya. We drank that dark Haitian roast coffee that brings logic speeding into the mind. "When will your book be finished?" I asked.

"Soon. Very soon. And as a depth thinker yourself, I know you will be overjoyed to hear the basic *optique*. I am attacking the regime from top to underside, but of course constructively, in a positively constructive sense."

"And you have no problems about that?"

"Absolutely not! Jean-Claude himself, speaking with his spirit of open generosity, assures me. Jean-Claude *commanded* me—" He half rose from the table and made a little ducking boxing gesture. " 'Pull no punches, Gerard!' He calls me 'Gerard.' "

The word "punches" made me think of a rum drink. "Your position is secure enough? The President and the . . ."

"Dinosaurs. Say it. I am not afraid." Dinosaurs was the term for Papa Doc's leftover inner circle.

"—and his entourage are willing to let you speak out?"

"How many times do I have to tell you? Herb-air, if I may call you so, the cynical past has made you mistrustful. I have his total support. 'Write, write, write,' he said to me in his own words, 'only tell the truth, my dear friend Gerard.' "

I thought of the thousands who had been murdered or tortured, the castrations, rapes, disappearances, extortions, lootings, house-burnings, the destruction of a fragile society. I thought of the Benet family and the bodies left to rot in public places. I asked for some hints about the dimensions of the Merceron critique. He described recommending that the tonton macoutes, now Volontaires de la Securité Nationale, "could become something like your American Peace Corps." If once they had been gangsters and torturers, wearing jeans, T-shirts, and sunglasses, now they were already your friendly neighborhood militia in their neat blue uniforms. Wouldn't it be even better to give them badges? with numbers on them? Perhaps even names? And U.S. Aid could provide the handsome badges.

"You know, my friend, there were abuses in the past. *You* know, *I* know, all depth thinkers know this."

"When will your book be published?"

"So I must pull no punches."

"When does it come out?"

"Oh my friend, my dear friend." His mouth formed a little regretful kiss in the air. "Such a book could never be published in Haiti."

STRANGE WAS back in business, convening the secret society of those who were unlike other tourists—the voodooists, the artists, the seekers, the black Americans celebrating this first independent black nation of modern times (some came to stay; few stayed). The black American who had opened a dry-cleaning establishment lost his business. Lavinia Williams, a dancer, still ran performances of Haitian dancers for the hotels. Katherine Dunham, the dancer and anthropologist, owned land, a small hotel, and studied voodoo. She hinted that she was also a priestess and kept a collection of snakes for ritual purposes. There were addicts, sexual seekers, remittance folks, and fugitives.

And there were the normal visitors in whom strange places bring out edges and brinkiness. One afternoon at the Oloffson pool, I heard a real estate developer's wife ask a French novelist: "So when did you write that book à la Paris?" An individual in a bathing suit with antique skirt introduced herself to a woman executive of a yarn company that had an embroidery plant in the industrial park near the airport: "I'm a free-lance lesbian mystic, who are you, darling?" A distinguished film producer confided in me: "As I enter the latter third of my life, all I really want is the bottom-line basic truth—rest and companionship in the warm, mature, slim arms of a twenty-two-year-old who really understands me."

Trouble was, he explained, they get to be twenty-three and want more than walk-on parts. They want to *speak*.

Paris and New York are loneliness towns, enthralling and challenging, monuments to achievement, projections of human intention. Port-au-Prince is a swollen village, a colonial port whose intention has been obliterated and whose achievement is represented by eroded monuments and the few thick-walled buildings that recall the lost riches of the sugar and coffee trade. Some of the heroes represented by statues in the Place des Héros were reject sculptures from various South American commissions. Despite Haitian artistic talent, when a President sought commemoration, he habitually sent the money to Colombia or Paris.

Yet I could walk about Port-au-Prince in the magic hours of nightfall or dawn and always take pleasure in the boil of life, the engorged seasons of every day. Noisy and filled with flowers, littered with ruin and rot, the town was dusty, companionable; African, Caribbean, colonial, French, and a place of instant extended family. On this trip I had brought my daughter, Nina, aged nine, in return for her promise to keep a journal and do her school homework every morning after breakfast on the Oloffson terrace. We avoided taxis or renting a car, preferring the "publique"—usually rattlers called "bogotas" because they had been rejected in Colombia. The publique, a common taxi that picked up anyone on its path, roamed the city, depositing passengers at their destinations on the potluck principle. If we wanted conversation, we just stood outside, waved down the publique, marked with its red ribbon dangling from the rearview mirror or aerial, and asked to be taken to a bookshop or an art gallery or to drop in on some acquaintance. No problem to enter the lives of our fellow passengers. The drivers, if they weren't splitting ears with music, were expert on the CIA, the FBI, the history of the universe, not including present doings in Haiti, about which they were cautious.

We were heading toward the port on the "Boulevard des Millionaires," where chickens, burros, beggars, market women, porters, crippled children, thieves, peddlers, jostlers and hustlers and madmen came swarming together. Laughter and shouts rose above this fuming, smoking disaster. I wanted Nina to understand and didn't know how to explain. She was seeing for herself. At the entrance to the street, in a guarded fort—one of those thick-walled colonial buildings—rows of half-naked artisans were gluing Tiffany lampshades together for export to shops in New York, Chicago, and San Francisco. The American owner, Larry Peabody, long a resident in Haiti, had redecorated the National Palace for the Duvaliers.

I left the Tiffany glass manufactory and walked with Nina through the Boulevard des Millionaires. She whispered, "Dad . . . Dad. . . ."

A child with bent, rachitic legs, wearing nothing but a T-shirt on which was stenciled a portrait of the President and the words JE SUIS JEAN-CLAUDISTE, stared at us with clouded eyes from the muck-filled gutter. I could not answer the questions my daughter was trying to ask. Why is this child here? How can such things be? And what joke of fate dresses a dying child in a T-shirt with the grinning face of Baby Doc?

Later, driving the crumpled hillsides, we toured the districts of Pacot, Canape-Vert, Bois Verna, Turgeau, sweet with flowers and gardens, crowded with the plaster villas of the new elite, the Bon Ton Macoutes, and the carved wooden cuckoo houses of the old elite. An enterprising family in Pacot, young sisters who started the business in their teens, made delicious ice cream. Nina tried the peanut-butter flavor. From up here, where it was cooler, looking at the steaming ruins below, the name Port-au-Prince seems paradoxically merited. We are all princes of poverty and hope here. Proud despair is the mood of everybody.

Robert Dussaint, a young "masters-of" recently returned from the graduate studies at Princeton, was an urban planner. I asked him how he envisaged solving the problems of "the métropole," as Haitians call Port-au-Prince. He smiled with the hilarious frankness of a bright young man who knows the correct answer. "First of all, we must have an earthquake. Then you will send us machinery to bulldoze the whole place into the bay. And *then*"—he hoped I enjoyed the meticulous Haitian craftsmanship of his logic—"and then we appeal to the United States and they say no and so we appeal to the United Nations and they move too slowly and so we appeal to Cuba, the Soviet Union, and China, and then suddenly the United States reconsiders." He sighed. "But I suppose that's too much to hope for. We haven't had an earthquake in centuries."

"Why does your scenario need an earthquake?"

"A volcanic eruption would do nicely, but unfortunately we are fresh out of volcanoes. We must start with a drama. Starvation, disease, kwashiokor, political . . . eccentricity—" He snapped his fingers. "Insufficient appeal to the American imagination. Idi Amin cornered the market in mass murder and crocodiles eating supreme court justices. Bokassa is a French monopoly. We Haitians are a little dilettante with our terrors, and the Boy"—he nodded toward the poster of Jean-Claude—"likes for American investors to eat their breakfast in peace on your lovely terrace of the Grand Hotel Oloffson."

My visitor had not learned at Princeton the new American habit of the protein-packed breakfast. All he wanted was black coffee. He indicated the hefty breakfasters a few tables away and said, "I see you have company again."

It was the defrocked English banker—call him Ferdinand— whom I often met here. He was in charge of transporting the Duvalier scrapings from the treasury into their American and Swiss accounts. His official job was something on the order of tourist consultant. Over the years, we became friendly—he had very little to do except pick up the money and enjoy himself. Dressed in a three-piece white suit, foulard instead of tie, slightly overweight, perhaps to keep Jean-Claude company, he usually had a lady friend from Miami arm-in-arm with him. She was kind to my daughter. Ferdinand would proceed in his limousine to the National Palace and the lady would proceed to the swimming pool with her bottles of oil and her Harlequin novels.

The Chicago word for the defrocked English banker is bagman. The tobacco tax for the entire country, plus other taxes, custom duties, and export rights, never entered fiscal accounting. Despite the elegance of his clothing, nice white and pleated linens, Ferdinand would occasionally lean over my table to take small items—napkin, extra silverware, the salt—saying, "Parm my reach." An appropriate apology, but one he should make to the people of Haiti.

Still, things were better. My friend the Official Dissenter, Gerald Merceron, pointed out that he could write freely. Others were allowed freely to, well, *whisper*. Dissent could be expressed by a rolling of the eyes, so long as one didn't make a hissing sound. Said Gerald Merceron: "I okay, you okay." The Leopards of the Son did not have the sharp eyes of the tonton macoutes of the Father.

Busy polishing his book, Gerald visited me to pass on some exciting news. To relax from the rigors of a no-punches-pulled critique of Haiti, he was taking flute lessons. Would I like to watch him play the flute? Would I like to look over the largest collection of Dinah Shore records in Haiti?

My daughter perceived that there were still a few injustices. Many of the death notices, mentioning bodies found in the street, simply said: Unknown adult . . . Unknown child . . . "That's not fair," Nina said.

The new "industrial park" near the airport used to be a *terrain vague* of mud huts, cockfight arenas, voodoo temples, dirt-scrabble farming. Now I found the Choo Choo Train, a German-owned short-order restaurant in which deliveries of sausage and hamburgers were made by toy trains to chair groupings labeled Milano, Paris, Bremen, Stuttgart, München. The owner, in his German trainmaster's cap, announced deliveries in guttural French over a loudspeaker: "One shipment of blood sausage bound for München . . . . Three cheeseburgers to Paris. . . ." The *Bahnhofmeister* was bringing fun fast food to a developing nation.

In the industrial park itself, custom furniture of palm fibers and cast iron was produced to sell for high prices in New York by workers who now received from $1.60 to $4 a day. A good job in Haiti. On the wall of Mahotières Industries was written KALITÉ PAS KANTITÉ. Quality, not quantity. The resident manager was John Burns, a Creole-speaking American whom I knew in 1953 as an eleven-year-old white voodoo kid, a barefoot ragamuffin in his jungle village, Tom Sawyer in Haiti.

Dieter von Lehsten, a German businessman, explained that Haiti's labor costs made capital investment unnecessary. Why pay for a lot of machines when human beings will do it for $1.60 a day? Textile and shirt manufacturers subcontracted here. Plastic assembly plants were moving from the Far East. The commercial section of the German embassy was busy. "Quality plus convenience plus cheap labor," said Dieter. "And I can enjoy myself, besides."

Under Baby Doc's economic revolution, Haiti was once again becoming a playground for briefcase-toting businessmen. Eventually 70,000 people worked in "transformation industries." The basic elements were shipped back and forth, transformed, and the element added was labor. Several buildings bore the same sign in English:

LARGEST SOFTBALL AND BASEBALL FACTORIES IN WORLD. In one plant, which specialized in employing recently converted Christians, the manager liked to shout, "Hallelujah!" and the line of weavers answered, "Dieu éternel!"

A fun-loving Frenchman named Olivier Coquelin developed the Habitation Leclerc for visitors committed to enjoyment. He believed in sincere erotic coddling amid a setting of extraordinary luxury, including both public and private swimming pools, a decor of genuine copies of ancient paintings and libraries of multilingual pornography, grottoes and nooks and sunken bathtubs with Jacuzzis, everything your average free spirit could imagine for his honeymoon or non-honeymoon. There were horses, two servants in constant attendance of each guest. Both riding lessons and voodoo ceremonies could be scheduled. This walled enclave was situated in the midst of a desolate industrial slum, a kind of concentration camp designed to attract Jacqueline Onassis and Oscar de la Renta, who never seemed to be there when I passed through the gates topped with broken glass and patrolled by armed guards.

At the Caravelle Bookshop, now a diminished skeleton of its former life, I met a young man who had been a member of the Etincelles Group, a Trotsky splinter party. Were there other members? "No," he said sadly, "I was the only one. And now there are none." "What happened?" "I expelled myself for undignified behavior. I was a traitor to my ideals. I got drunk."

I put my hand on his. "I forgive you, son."

Meeting this young man reminded me of the time when there had been a Haitian bohemia of drinkers, poets, late-night talkers, like the bohemias of the Left Bank in Paris or the Bodeghita del Medio in Havana. It must have been difficult for the expelled member of the one-man Trotskyite movement to keep the torch uplifted.

A quarter of a century earlier I had walked along the Pétionville road with my daughter Ann, who was then four years old, marveling along with her at the flowers, the goats, the burros, the Madame Saras swaying with their burdens on their heads. And now I was walking down the road from Kenscoff with my daughter Nina, aged nine. She was marveling at the stream in which the Madame Saras washed, at the painted trucks named "God Is Good" or "My Panama Hat Fell

Off," at the smells and chickens, the noise and the drums, and the smiles, bows, the "Bonjour, Monsieur, b'jour petite!" of the steady file of hundreds passing; the goatskins drying, the flames of bougain-villea, the grace of pipe-smoking market women, swaying with their burdens still balanced on their heads; still surviving, it seemed—unkillable Haiti.

Nina said she was happy. Her father knew he was happy to be here with her. We weren't sure anybody else could understand why.

CHAPTER
TWELVE

Minglers

MANY HAITIANS couldn't go home, but I could go back. I had heard of an American church group that responded to the news of protein starvation by sending over a shipment of high-protein shampoo. I returned to see how the tourism campaign was working out under Baby Doc's softer version of his father's regime. I wondered how AIDS was affecting the American and European lust for Strange in the eighties.

For years Americans had been visiting Haiti for duty-free sex. In his song, "Katie Went to Haiti," Cole Porter wrote:

> So Katie stuck to Haiti
> Delighted with her fatie
> 'Cause Katie still had Haiti
> And practically all Haiti had Katie

It was partly the glamour of French-speaking people of color that attracted the Katies and Kens. Often it came down to a simpler matter—they had difficult love lives at home.

Diana, whom I met one afternoon at the Centre d'Art, was a Mingler from Miami. She was glowing with the excitement of her first all-night voodoo ceremony, refreshed and impeccable in her Banana Republic safari outfit. "This wasn't one for tourists," she said, "this was the real thing. Captain Beaujean took me. The temple was all in earthtones, beige." She was excited and happy to find events that matched her clothing. "The roof was open. I wish I could have seen the spirits come down, but they slipped by me when I wasn't paying attention and the people went nutcase. It only cost forty dollars."

She thought about it some more. "I love those tin roofs they have on the ranchettes. The straw ones must get icky when it rains."

Diana was one of those who come to Haiti to go through a tropical sex crisis. When one-day divorces were the vogue, there was a rapid turnaround—still married in the morning; time for a swim and a nap; madly in love all evening; and then hiphop back to New York by American Airlines next day, bearing souvenir bottles of Rhum Barbancourt, mahogany salad equipment, a painting, and one heck of a lot of crowded memories. I tried to avoid becoming the confidant of women who came to have love affairs with handsome Haitian officers or government torturers. It wasn't disapproval so much as the repetitiousness that wore me out. The most distressing were the wives of international aid officials, diplomats, or American military men who arrived full of complaints about the "colored" everywhere they looked. After a brief retreat into the isolation of the American Club, boredom and curiosity drove them into adventures. The charm of Haitian men— those French accents! the skin-diving expeditions!—was a part of it, too. ("They *move*, you know? I learn so much every time.")

A friend imagined these heroes giving Creole lessons to lonely Americans and composed a phrase book:

They beat the man so much he did Number Two on himself.

What a happy crowd gathered to hear the Ultimate Leader and President-for-Life at the National Palace this morning.

Please give me some money and I won't touch you.

Please give me some money and I will touch you.

Diana, the unblinking young woman from Miami, was preparing to buy a selection of paintings at the Centre d'Art. She had interesting asymmetrical eyes. We began to chat, but it wasn't the right atmosphere for trading tropical life stories and philosophies. After she made her order, wrote her check, and asked to have her purchases delivered to the Villa Creole, we went to the air-conditioned restaurant at the Rond Point, opposite the Institut Français, where Haitian businessmen and bureaucrats gathered for an American-style lunch.

She was dubious. She fanned herself with a flier from the Issa Gallery. "This is kind of tacky, you know?"

"I know. But the heat of the day, it's cool."

"Do they have root-beer floats? Love the easygoing laissez-faire, miss the root-beer floats—*long* for it, you know?"

"By analogy."

"Pardon? Well, Captain Beaujean of the Haitian Air Force . . ." He wasn't present. She was musing aloud about the tradeoff against the root-beer floats in Coral Gables, where she worked as "a highly paid legal secretary."

It may have been the first time I had heard someone describe him/herself as a highly paid anything, but I respected her honesty. She was an upfront individual. She was the kind of inner-directed, upfront individual who was attracted to Haiti, when it wasn't the kind of devious, sly, secret person who found Haiti useful. "I understand from Captain Beaujean," she whispered, "he's right up there in the government—" Her asymmetrical eyes darted to the right, to the left, back to the right, and she lowered her voice. "—the conspirationists around here—"

"Pardon?"

"Conspirationists."

"Revolutionating?"

"That's it."

I put my finger to my lips. Perhaps my own asymmetrical eyes darted a little. She looked happy. Sex was more fun in Haiti than back there in Miami where evidently there wasn't enough for Diana. Here she could join the turmoil.

"What makes you come?" I asked.

"Here?"

"I meant Haiti." But if I happened to be the kind of creep who would pry into her sex life, she was ready to answer.

She watched the waiter carry things to and fro, wondering if he was getting our sandwiches. (When in Rome, one gives up the idea of root-beer floats.) She considered changing the order to have the bread toasted. She asked if I thought the bread came from the Cole Bakery, which was the bakery of choice of the foreign colony, or just from the market. I said just from the market, but it would be okay, and it was probably okay for her to ask for toast. She needed time to formulate an answer to the question every old Haiti hand asks every other old Haiti hand—I repeated the question.

And she answered: "Captain Beaujean made me come. It's his whites, sets off the skin and teeth, plus he was thoughtful, plus it's some kind of je ne sais quoi in the vibes."

She sighed. "I was there sort of thing," she said. "I got off this one time on a cruise and it happened—I mingled! So now I'm here sort of thing."

I sympathized with Diana. People arrive through one accident or another and then the country becomes part of their metabolisms. Diana developed the habit of flying to Port-au-Prince during her major holidays or vacations, maybe three or four times a year, for what she called a Mingle. "You're divorced?" she asked. "Your mistake was getting married. I know marriage used to be the trend, but I figured out a new trend for myself. Not that I don't like children. I do. I'd like to have one of my own, about six years old, clean, with a nice old-fashioned white dress."

"A girl?"

"Wouldn't have to be."

She used to mingle with any handsome Haitian she met in some okay spot, like a hotel bar, but since the AIDS trend, she confined her mingles to a few known individuals. And now she only visited Haiti on very major holidays and during her annual two-week vacation. I wasn't sure how this answered the AIDS problem—perhaps it had more to do with air ticket costs. A bright legal secretary with a well-off but not a wealthy condition, she tried to sell a few Haitian paintings in Coral Gables, thereby establishing a small art business, making the trip an expense for taxes. This was a mere IRS detail. The reason for her steadfastness was how much she loved Haiti and Haitians, the music, the romance, the diligence Haitian war heroes gave to mingling.

"Mingle," I repeated, picking at my chicken salad sandwich, practicing the word.

"That's my trend. Get yourself a mingle, not a wife. Are you a Scorpio?"

"Pisces."

"I knew it! I almost said Pisces! I can tell you're a water sign. Do you run, my dear?"

The *my dear* slipped out rather patronizingly, but pronouncing the words set off the poignancy reflex. Her eyes misted over. It had been awhile since her last real mingle. It turned out that the mingler she counted on—Captain Beaujean—had just told her he was in love with the wife of a UNESCO official. "I swim," she said. "I do my charts. I meditate. I'm having a fun time. I don't need that bastard. I can find men everywhere."

"I run a little," I said, "but laps in the hotel pool is how I wake up."

"Want to have a picnic at the Cabrite Plage, maybe if I rent a jeep?"

"Let me call you."

"The telephones don't work, Herb."

Diana and I parted after our chicken salad sandwiches, untoasted. Neither of us was what the other was still looking for in Haiti.

THIS DREAMLAND, the complications of desire, and AIDS have a peculiar connection with a novel, *Slave Trade*, published by a nongay writer from San Francisco in 1979, in that last respite before Acquired Immune Deficiency Syndrome had been diagnosed. Art imitates life, sometimes in advance.

I intended to write an entertainment about a San Francisco private eye who wandered into the business of transporting Haitian boys to boy-lovers all over the world. It's a shady commerce, destined to lead Sid Kasdan—an imaginary frazzled person—into real dilemmas. It led Sid Kasdan's begetter into a belief-taxing incident one evening. Haiti's most abundant natural resource is the taxing of belief.

My story grew out of memory and rumor. The facts were not secret. During my years in Haiti, I was friendly with a charming and cultivated American priest who educated lads for export. The image in his robes of the man I'll call Father Martin, with his company of smiling acolytes, wearing uniform white cotton shorts, serving in the garden, stayed in my mind.

Slave Trade was intended to offer a lively passing of time. Modestly I promised that the novel would be the best book ever written about the intersection of Haiti and San Francisco in the specialized commerce of homosexual concubinage. For my friends, the proprietors of the Grand Hotel Oloffson, the Habitation Leclerc, and the Relais de l'Empereur, *Slave Trade* contributed to a surprising result—a boom in gay tourism.

Overvaluing the impact of my book, as writers sometimes do, I decided to visit Haiti one last time just before it was published. I expected to be banned again.

One of my friends in Port-au-Prince, Jacques Large, had been the Official Uncloseted Haitian Homosexual during a time when there was no other. He had also worked as an assistant in Africa for Dag Hammarskjöld. I confided in Jacques; the idea of the book amused him. "But mon cher ami! Would it not be interesting for you to come down from the clouds?"

"You tell me, pal."

He offered to show me some of the factual basis of the novel I had written from hints and rumors.

Vladimir Nabokov remarked that Gogol built the firm foundations for his books after he finished them; I accepted Jacques' invitation. He would lead me on a tour of the house of Monsieur G., who was in the business of cultivating, training, and exporting comely lads. The best time for our visit, Jacques decided, was during Monsieur G.'s regular Friday evening salon. I arranged for my daughter, Nina, to spend the evening with friends. Jacques would make all the other arrangements.

I wasn't sure what to expect. "Du calme," he advised.

An evangelical group had put up a sign in English on a house: HE IS COMING AGAIN IN GREAT POWER AND MAJESTY, and as we drove by, Jacques murmured, "But I'm sure Doc is still dead." He told me his cousin in Jacmel once saw Grande Erzulie dancing on top of a commode, told her priest, and the priest berated her for superstitious backsliding. That couldn't have been Grande Erzulie, the great goddess of fertility and lust, on that commode. That must have been the great Virgin.

And then Jacques took to whistling and humming to himself,

keeping his patience while he steered around what looked like a water buffalo on the road, with the black, doggy pigs nipping at its droppings.

The house of Monsieur G., in the Martissant district of Port-au-Prince, was sealed against harbor breezes, unlike most Haitian elite dwellings, and equipped with an electrical generator, stereos, speakers, rugs, a samovar on an inlay table, paintings, extension cords, air-conditioning. In addition to sporting goods, imported fashion magazines, and terrific kitchen and bathroom equipment, there was a large family of pets. Our host, a fast-moving person in a wig, greeted me cordially, held my hand in two of his. Monsieur G. was bald. His wig, oxidized by time and weather, and perhaps by the fumes of his dream life, resembled a rusty Brillo pad.

The other early guests were middle-aged, middle-class, well-dressed, mulatto, except for one white Frenchman in twill riding clothes with puttees. There were also three or four black houseboys in white shorts, busily filling glasses with scotch and whisking away debris.

Now about that debris. Most of it came from a half-dozen un-caged monkeys, chattering and leaping from perches and furniture, sometimes timidly clinging to abutments from the ceiling, making cute snapping sounds—it sounded like flags in a wind—but nervously dropping monkey dung upon the leatherbound library, the records, the furniture, the people. This was a surprise. Monkeys are not indigenous to Haiti. The chief task of the houseboys, after filling our glasses and passing trays of fried Creole goodies, sweet and crusty morsels of pork and goat, was to lift off the monkey droppings before they could stain a room that was already sufficiently decorated in earth tones.

I had not described any of this in my novel—how could I? Like so much of Haiti, it would be difficult to imagine, were it not for the fact that it happened to be true. In any case, the salon of Monsieur G. was too peculiar for a novel that aimed to convince readers that the story it recounted really came down upon poor bedraggled Sid Kasdan, San Francisco private eye.

The Frenchman began to chat over our drinks. He complimented me on my command of the language of Proust and Cocteau and I complimented him on his. I asked how he happened to find himself in Haiti. Easy to answer. Smiling, suave, and gracious, he explained that his insomnia required two black boys each evening, two different ones every night—it was the only remedy. Otherwise sleeplessness tried his patience. In Africa, dear friend, he had tossed and turned. Haiti was the best place. The monkeys were chattering above us, making those snapping, clicking sounds.

How did my new French friend earn his living? By distributing used Pong machines in the bars of Port-au-Prince. There is room for an entrepreneur even in Calcutta and Port-au-Prince, but Calcutta, alas—he had tried the subcontinent—failed to live up to his personal requirements. The boys were not quite dark enough—"pas suffisamment foncés." Life is difficult for the specialized man.

As we spoke, a new group of guests was arriving. These were young men in tight jeans and T-shirts, often bearing witty advertising slogans, such as HIALEAH RACE TRACK, HIALEAH UNIVERSITY or "APPLY BELOW." Besides a color difference—they were darker—their French was Creolized, unlike the Parisian diction of the businessmen, broadcasters, and professional people who had arrived earlier for scotch and a few moments of quiet meditation. The monkeys grew more agitated. The houseboys did their best to keep up.

The boys were lanky and shy. The men tended toward stocky and plump. The monkeys leapt. The houseboys poured drinks and scraped monkey shit.

No matter how outlandish, a story needs to make real connections with real life below the reverie line. The writer must be convinced and so must the reader. So here is a little list of items inappropriate for my novel: this house in the waterfront Martissant district of Port-au-Prince, our Brillo-topped host, the parrot on its perch, the white-shorted houseboys, and especially—on a Caribbean island that is poor in wildlife, deprived of monkeys—*monkeys*. I aimed for verisimilitude. There could be no monkeys in my book.

I suppose I was trying to treat this evening at the salon of Monsieur G. as a normal social occasion—aimed for suave, unembarrassed, man-of-the-world. Small talk is always helpful.

Sipping scotch, the French Pong merchant and I began to discuss the German occupation of Paris. It turned out we were born the same year, and while I had been in the American Army, he had joined the blue-shirted Petainist youth militia. As we gossiped, a tall, broad-shouldered, slim-waisted young man in tight blue jeans and a T-shirt printed with the face of Baby Doc and his slogan, TRAVAIL FAMILLE PATRIE—Work, Family, Country—listened, frowning, turning first to me and then to the Pong dealer. He was trying to follow the conversation. Since he was paying such close attention, the Frenchman smiled upon him and asked his opinion about the Nazis in Paris. The lad answered with a shy stammer: "Les juifs sont des a-a-accapareurs."

Although my French is pretty good, I only understood the first part of the sentence: "The Jews are . . ."

Winsomely, shyly, with that sweet little stammer, the lad struggled to get through to the white visitors. I listened attentively as he explained that the Nazis must have had their reasons; otherwise why would they dislike the Jews? He himself was the proud possessor of a German lover in Miami Beach, where he worked as a hospital orderly, and his close German friend had explained that the Jews are a-a-a-accapareur.

I seemed puzzled by that word, so he translated into English: "Poosh-y."

Jacques Large was infuriated. Our host was busy settling people on couches, showing them albums of photographs, urging curls of goat and pork upon them, tickling a timid new arrival to make him feel welcome. The houseboys were scurrying at their labors and the monkey shit was raining about us. Jacques raised his voice at the lad in the Baby Doc T-shirt: "You are a black man who has suffered from the white! from the mulatto! You were born to this suffering! And you say Hitler must have had a reason, the Jews did something to deserve their trouble? What have you done to deserve yours, idiot?"

The Frenchman murmured to me, "Il est mignon, mais pas fort dans la politique." (Cute, but politics is not his strong point.)

"Sans-maman!" said Jacques—in Creole this means without-a-mother, therefore shameless.

While the young man's lips moved in a slow silent stammer, Jacques jabbed his finger at him. "I know! You work in a Jewish hospital in Miami, yes? And you're a lazy boy, sans-maman, and those Jewish doctors don't say you're cute, but they keep telling you to do your work, yes? And so they're pushy, yes?"

The lad was troubled. He was wearing Puma running shoes with a hole cut in one where something had fallen on his foot. He stared at his naked swollen toe. He was frowning. He was unhappy. He had made a contribution to the discussion and now people were paying undue attention. He was only trying to be sociable. This confused him. The French Pong salesman was beaming at the fun that was preceding the orgy—better than electronic games; maybe foreplay wasn't so bad when it just happened naturally. He glanced at the lad's pinkish toe, protruding from the red and white striped Puma.

I was embarrassed. I was a guest here. I told Jacques not to worry, but my daughter was asleep back at the hotel and perhaps it was time—

We left. Jacques was still fretting. Our host was sorry to see us go; many boys yet to arrive. He planned to play the complete recording of *Manon,* just in from Paris, unless I preferred "Ovair Ze Rainbow par Zudee Gar-lan." The houseboys were busy and so were the monkeys. Our kind host in his Brillo wig followed us into the sudden silence, the humid Port-au-Prince night with its insect noises, and said he would oblige the lad from Miami Beach to make special amends if I so desired; I could ask anything—whatever I liked best.

The parrot on its perch croaked: "Bon soir bon soir bon," and rattled its chain.

Jacques Large withered and died of Kaposi's sarcoma less than a year later. He left an adopted daughter—the granddaughter, he told me, of the first man who seduced him.

Aubelin Jolicoeur, representing the Haitian government, telephoned to ask if I wanted to be Honorary Consul for Haiti in San Francisco; politics and the AIDS panic had destroyed tourism. I declined.

LATER, WHEN I described the evening at Monsieur G.'s salon to Dr. Tom Waddell, an Olympic decathlon competitor and the founder of the Gay Olympics, he became intensely interested in the possibility that the monkeys were a vector for AIDS. A research team visited Haiti to examine these household pets. "They're the wrong kind of monkey," Dr. Waddell reported. "South American. Not infected."

O N O N E of my walks down toward the heat and *vacarme* of the waterfront, I found an herbal shop near the Marché Salomon that sold remedies in old bottles plugged with twigs. The sign outside the shop was painted on wood with Christian, Jewish, Islamic, and Hindu symbols; there were voodoo vévés and a sailboat escaping to a land of bountiful good health, fortune, chickens, pigs. The *docteur feuilles,* herb doctor, a thin brown man, neat and small, wearing dark glasses with the lens over his left eye poked out, smiled and bowed when I complimented him on the enseigne.

There was very little business in the tiny shop, although he was ready to cure asthma, fatigue, catarrh, tuberculosis, impotence, arthritis, and *déboires,* which could be translated as griefs or disappointments. People were too poor to take care of themselves. On a later visit I noticed that he had taken on a more current malady, Sida (AIDS), but he still seemed to be sitting on his stool alone all day, or standing in the shade at his door, smoking and meditating.

This time I brought him a customer. A medical professor from the University of Virginia was particularly interested in the aphrodisiac, that twist of root soaking in what looked like clairin, the raw white rum, now slightly pinkened by whatever it was leaching out. He bought a bottle to carry back to Richmond for analysis, since he was a scientist and my explanation—pigwood in white rum—seemed too metaphorical for a rigorous teaching physician.

"Look, the root resembles a tiny woman's hand," I said.

"That's what I mean," he said. "Just because I'm running away from a situation with my little lady back home doesn't mean I give up science. . . . You're right, it's like the cutest itty-bitty bunch of fingers, in'it?"

I had come for the sign outside the shop; I had dreamed about it back in San Francisco. Cautiously, with care for his feelings, I suggested to the herbalist that he was not only a *docteur feuilles* but also an artist and would he consider selling the *enseigne*? I needn't have worried. He immediately began to calculate the price, writing on a scrap of paper:

$8. paint
12. wood
25. labor
500. Cérémonie
$545. Total

I told him I did not require the blessing.
He said he had already performed the ceremony for the enseigne.
I asked if he could make a copy, without blessing.
He said the enseigne was no good without the blessing.
I said I would take the risk.
He said he could not be responsible. He had a family, grand-children.
I offered to accept any bad shadow the gods chose to cast.
He shrugged. He considered me part of his family.
"What if I give you two hundred dollars for a copy without ceremony?"
Continuation follow-through of previous shrug.
"Two hundred fifty?"
"*Impossible.*"
Sometimes, in silence, with no argument, if one person waits, the other person changes his mind. I could hear the hum of insects, the creak of boards underfoot. The other person did not change his mind.
"Then I can't buy it," I said.
With a courteous little incline of the head, but a delighted smile sneaking to the corners of his mouth and also visible in the eye which I could see through the glassless side of his spectacles, he murmured in impeccable professional French, without any Creole accent: "Je suis desolé, Monsieur."
He was a professional with standards, like the scientist from the medical school in Richmond, Virginia. His competitor around the corner and down the alley called Ruelle No. 6 only sold Elixir de Vie, Precious Medicine for the Curing of All Diseases, Formulated by a Doctor of the Faculty of Spain and Trinidad. This was too inclusive, it seemed to me, and the sign outside his shop lacked authority, no blended symbols of the top religions. I could find a botanica selling cure-everything herbs on Mission Street in San Francisco if that was all I required.

W HEN I first met Pouki, she was the adopted child of Terry McTeague, the retired fashion photographer who was part of the expatriate colony of Port-au-Prince during the golden age of the fifties. In succession, she was his daughter, his wife, and his widow. Now she lived in one of the gingerbread houses of Canapé-Vert on a cooler slope above the city. She was still doing okay as a madam in her own establishment, making a resigned but optimistic shrug in the general direction of the universe as she said in Creole: "Good times not paradise."

She had sagged contentedly into middle age. I complimented her on the handsome little house, filled with tropical flowers, although she may have reached too far in the direction of bourgeois chic with plastic confections from Japan—tulips, yellow roses, pink passion fruit, peeling and shredding in the heat. I picked up a wax grapefruit and she said, "Cadeau pou ou. Ce oun merveil, M'sieu."

I refused to accept the gift, took a glass of unplastic grapefruit juice instead. The brothel business was no longer prosperous with tourists, but the local demand still needed to be fulfilled. She grieved over the early days when Truman Capote came to Haiti, and then wrote *House of Flowers,* and Graham Greene visited Terry McTeague, and Pouki was Terry's precious daughter, wife, model, and hostess. She shed a tear when I said people still treasured the bare-breasted postcards he sold. It was a photograph of Pouki, high-breasted and staring off into the middle or model distance, which had been the postcard visa sent by Aubelin Jolicoeur in 1971. "I was pretty," she admitted matter-of-factly. "Now . . ." She touched herself here and there. I tried to imagine her as others did, as she saw herself, as a woman in late middle age, but I still saw the little girl.

"You've gotten intelligent. You always were."

"Necessité."

"Some people do without," I said.

"Oh, my friend! I was a happy virgin until I was nearly eleven, and a happy daughter and wife to Terry. When I sent him to jail, it was for his own good." And she grinned like the little girl called *Why?* She gazed into my eyes, shaking her head. "I think I am much less happy. And it is not entirely the fault of politics."

Bad times not purgatory.

ON MY next visit, this time with one of my sons in 1983, I heard of a discharged American Army officer drinking out his days in Kenscoff, that sweet-tempered mountain village. Like all visitors, Ethan and I took deep breaths of eucalyptus and pine as we strolled the paths among donkeys, children, chickens, and the Madame Saras swaying along with their produce on their heads.

At the same ramshackle Florville Hotel, where I had taken my meals for a time in the 1950s, and where I had met Colonel Chocolate, the French collaborator, I found the American former colonel deeply engrossed by rum. He was liverish, emaciated, and noisy on his stool at the bar. He had been an intelligence officer in Vietnam; he spoke Chinese. Soon the battered colonel and my eleven-year-old Ethan were exchanging words like "choo-choo train" in Chinese.

Then the colonel began to talk about the war. He was explaining in a mixture of Chinese, English, and French. He was slipping off his stool, he was weeping, he was leaning on the boy, and I took ourselves away. The next day the colonel was arrested for wandering in a house not his, committing "scandale publique." He sobered up in jail, then returned to Kenscoff. Here in this world of magic and nightmare, we heard an echo of Vietnam.

Not long afterwards, the colonel was found in a ravine, nosed by wild black Haitian pigs, pecked by chickens, murdered by drink, dismay, and history, which cannot be escaped no matter how far a person flees.

Years ago, some of my expatriate companions in Haiti were runaways, the obsessed, losers changing their luck, winners who had grown tired of winning. In recent times I find AIDS, spiritual mutilation cases, and a few castaways still washing up on the beaches. Yeats said, "When the mouth dies, what is there?" He was maddened by desire and dreams. Given a choice, the castaways will go for the dreaming every chance we get.

CHAPTER THIRTEEN

The Perfect Dear

"Tomorrow I go to Hayti. They say the President is a *Perfect Dear!*"

—Ronald Firbank, on a postcard to Osbert Sitwell

JEAN-CLAUDE JUST didn't have the blood lust of his daddy. He played with his toys, tossed coins to the rabble. He married the lovely Michelle Bennett. He spent millions on celebrations of weddings and birthdays.

Baby Doc's Michelle, the straight-haired, chain-smoking, the very bored, air-conditioned the National Palace to a deep chill so that the plucky First Lady and her entourage could display their new fur coats at parties. Her father, Ernest Bennett, became very rich. Thanks to his daughter's advantageous new marriage (she had two children by her previous husband), he achieved an airline and other profit centers. Michelle's brother, impatient for his own profit center, was convicted of flying drugs into the United States and did hard time in a Puerto Rican prison. Michelle herself liked jewels, dresses, dances, travel, and expressed a desire to escape the onerous duties of a First Lady in favor of the simple honest life of a high-fashion model. Alas, this was not to be.

An American reporter accompanied Madame la Présidente on a tour of the new hospital named in her honor. In a room with oxygen tanks, a frightened doctor approached, whispering, "Your Excellence, your cigarette . . . . We will explode." She handed the lit cigarette to an aide to hold for her. Along with her health activities, she competed with Imelda Marcos in the World Shopping Olympics, and when questioned, said, "After all, I'm the First Lady." She shared the wealth among her decorator and other friends, including Cartier's and

Tiffany in Paris and New York. She wrote checks against "discretionary funds" from the Treasury.

Light-skinned, the Bennett family was not considered elite. They were nouveau elite, and very greedy—Bon Ton Macoutes.

A LITTLE PROBLEM OF LEOPARDS

Baby Doc's Leopards, a favored faction in the network of competing armed forces, emphasized sporting goods rather than battle—Ping-Pong, soccer, military consignments of athletic uniforms. The Praetorian guard served the President-for-Life's pleasure.

Olivier Coquelin, the high-spirited Frenchman who had developed l'Habitation Leclerc for a clientele of movie stars, fashionable travelers, Chicago politicians, and happy honeymoon couples, saw his dream of the world-class "erotic hotel" sink toward bankruptcy. Thieves scaled the walls spiked with shards of broken glass. Silt drifted into the swimming pools. The land—supposedly owned by Katharine Dunham, the anthropologist-dancer, supposedly once the property of Napoléon's Empress Joséphine—was reclaimed by the normal ruination of Haiti.

Undeterred, Olivier built another, smaller luxury hotel, Le Relais de l'Empereur, in the town of Petit Goâve a couple of hours drive from Port-au-Prince. Lonely without any visitors or tourists, he imported two baby leopards as pets. In time these get to be big cats.

One day at the Oloffson, a pretty young woman from Berkeley showed up in a jeep to bring me to the Relais de l'Empereur. She worked for Olivier and he had sent her to negotiate the difficult road. Of course I could spare the time to visit Petit Goâve and Olivier Coquelin—one comes to Haiti to let anything at all happen. This qualified. As we drove through the rough edges of Baby Doc's paradise—children with kwashiokor, the disease of protein starvation I had seen in Biafra; people with yaws, that leprosylike rotting which had made a comeback in Haiti—the young woman from Berkeley spoke of her nostalgia for California. Her name was Cindy. She was an astrologer; she wanted to know what my sign was; she came to

Haiti because voodoo unlocked the secrets of life and also because she had met Olivier Coquelin. It was meant to be.

"Haiti is just like everyplace else," Cindy summed up, "except it's Haiti."

"Does that make a difference?"

She fell silent, and then gave me a shot of her high beams—blue-green eyes people must have remarked on—as she steered the jeep. "Hey! What you said! I'd have to think about that."

When we arrived, she fumbled with her keys to the imperial front door of the inn. I could hear a violent shrieking and snarling as the gates swung grandly open. A leopard was tearing out the throat of a dog.

The astrologer from Berkeley darted a look of consternation at me: "You must have bad karma."

Although Olivier promised to keep the leopards tethered during my visit, he loved them too much to prevent their wandering about. While not an expert in hotel administration, I suggested that leopards tend to roam and stalk—they were big cats, getting bigger—and maybe that's why I was the only guest. Despite my adverse karma, one slinky beast seemed to enjoy strolling back and forth between my legs, pressing me ardently against her coat. (She might have been a he; I never looked.) When I complained, Olivier gave me a shirt with the coconut patch of the Imperial Cocoyer Yacht Club of Petit Goâve on the sleeve. I gave him a Levi shirt from San Francisco. We were pals.

The inn owned a small island in the bay for swimming, picnicking, and tropical reveling. We chugged out in a motorized canoe, flagship of the Olivier Coquelin/Imperial Cocoyer Navy. Nervously a seasick leopard swung back and forth, shoving its lithe but massive body against my more fragile one. I asked if they were dangerous. Olivier assured me they were his favorite animals—not quite an answer to the question.

I kept thinking of the poor dog. With one moment of karma crisis, the leopard could have altered me forever.

Even during these last years of Baby Doc's reign, a few foreigners clung to their condition of privilege in a place where some could do anything and many could do nothing. As our canoe chugged forward, a fisherman in his own dugout paddled furiously toward us, holding up a fish for sale. The fisherman had great staring eyes, unforgettable because below his eyes, above his mouth, there was no nose—a great gaping hole in his face where yaws had eaten out his flesh.

A few weeks later, one of the leopards attacked a small boy in Petit Goâve, putting him in the hospital. There was outrage in the village and word got back all the way to the National Palace. The President-for-Life telephoned the police chief of Petit Goâve, who promised to look into the matter. Jean-Claude didn't approve of his Ping-Pong–playing Leopards acting up without authority in the provinces, biting small children.

The police chief launched into his investigative mode. He telephoned back to report: "Your Excellency, this Leopard is a leopard!"

"I want him arrested!" cried the Maximum Leader in his squeaky voice.

"But Your Excellency, this leopard is an *animal.*"

"That goes without saying!" shouted Baby Doc. "To prison with him!"

When the confusion cleared, Olivier's pet was forgiven, paroled in the custody of its master. Olivier promised it wouldn't happen again.

ALTHOUGH I dream of Haiti every night, I don't expect a Haitian presence in daily life in San Francisco. One morning I received a call from Aubelin Jolicoeur at the Mark Hopkins Hotel. His voice was high and happy. Through all the difficulties and vicissitudes of Haitian politics, he had survived his way into one of the ultimate goals of Third-World journalism—a press junket under the auspices of the U.S. State Department. I invited him to meet me for lunch on the terrace of Enrico's Coffee House in North Beach.

He arrived before I did. By the time I got there, he was friends with everyone, a startling narrow-waisted apparition in his white suit, spinning on his cane and graciously introducing me to my fellow San Franciscans. People were not used to his eloquently accented, enthusiastic, Paris–Jacmel brand of English. "I am Aubelin Jolicoeur! You have read *The Comedians?* You have seen the movie? The actor he play me was black genius track star at Yale, Mister Roscoe Lee Browne! I am Aubelin Jolicoeur, the Herb Caen of my beautiful country of Haiti! You may call me Aubie!"

A few months later, I received a telephone call from Aubie, back at the lazy Susan serving table of the regime. He was calling from Port-au-Prince in an official capacity. Again the powers at the top were considering me for supreme awards. He had the privilege of bearing these glad tidings. Would I accept appointment as Honorary Consul for the Republic of Haiti in San Francisco?

No, thanks.

Well, then, 'erb, would I do him the personal favor of asking Madame X, the wife of a prominent attorney, if she would enjoy this job? She had political ambitions, she was wealthy, she circulated in Washington, she knew many important people, such as Bianca Jagger.

I telephoned Ms. X. I explained the offer. Haiti particularly needed representation at this time because of the AIDS scare that was inhibiting tourism. The advantages of the job were: Special license plate, so you can park in red and yellow zones. Everyone on the highway will see you're a Consul. You will get invited to the consular parties. You can print special stationery with the Haitian coat of arms. You can fly the Haitian flag. You can put a bronze plaque over your door. When you visit Haiti, you might be given a jeep and driver. You will be invited to the Palais National. You might even meet Baby Doc and his lovely Michelle.

Those were the advantages. Also you would not have to do much work. The title was *Honorary* Consul.

"Oui," she said.

Wait. Now for the disadvantages. You will be representing a brutal and corrupt dictatorship that oppresses its people and steals most of the national product. Someday there may be a bloody revolution and you will have been the Duvalier apologist in San Francisco. "It's a little like being Honorary Consul for Nazi Germany, Fascist Italy, or Idi Amin's Uganda."

There was a moment of silence. The humming sound over the

wire was the sound of thought. "Well, Herb," she said, "before I accept, I think I should consult my constituency among the gay leadership."

"You really want to do this?"

"I'm not sure yet."

"You're thinking about that special license plate?"

"Well, also the political considerations. The gays don't want to accept the onus of AIDS alone, you know. . . . I think the word is 'onus,' isn't it?"

THE LITTLE band of Haiti addicts who kept returning to the Oloffson enjoyed their continual remeetings, year after year. Some came on anniversaries, some to avoid Christmas at home, some for Carnival and Rara. They accused each other of working for the Haitian CIA, keeping tabs on each other, although "Haitian Security" is an oxymoron. Nothing was ever that organized, even the repression.

There was a black American performer with his French lover, organizing their epic film about the Haitian revolution, scouting locations, doing research, *planning* to do research. They haven't yet gotten around to producing the film, but the trips were a business expense for tax purposes.

There was the ponytailed English millionaire—I'll call him Lord Stout—who spent his life in a heroic steadiness of purpose. He always arrived with a beautiful half-Indian model, and filled the hotel with joyful revelry and occasional episodes of jealous battling. Lord Stout kept to his chosen path—forever the beautiful Eurasian, but a different one each year. He had won his bet with the magi and popped sari-clad ladies out of a bottle as the last of his three wishes.

There was always a new crop of hustlers, hoping to work some scam with the government; the missionaries; the homosexuals; the minglers fascinated by French-speaking black men who thought they were young, beautiful, and rich because they were white; the journalists; the Peace Corps, AID, UNESCO, and CARE people, the do-gooders and bureaucrats; the variety pack of restless seekers for whom adventure is essential to the deal in the corners of history.

Hans-Christoph Buch, a German writer, came to look for his Haitian relatives. He had black cousins and Nazi ones. Ferdinand, bagman to the Family, was in a category all his own. A sallow defrocked English banker, with skin that looked as if he had a permanent liver condition, thin straight black hair water-pasted against his scalp, he spoke with an accent that peculiarly mixed Cockney and Oxford. "Top of the morning, Sir!" he would cry out on the terrace over his French toast à la Oloffson. "Had a good flight, did you?"

With his bag and his broom, Ferdinand arrived every few weeks to sweep the contents of the Haitian treasury into the numbered Swiss bank accounts. For this duty to Jean-Claude and Michelle he was paid by the Haitian government for "public relations services." He was a man of many secrets, among them how he managed to keep his hair so lankly polished and wet. His companion, later his wife, a plump lady from Miami, large, ample, pick your adjectives, was always smiling, happy, fully perfumed. Her nature was generous, her dresses flowered, her joy complete. When I visited Haiti with my children, she paid attention, was kind and cajoling, motherly, chatting with my son or daughter and giving off little pops of powdered makeup, explosions of heat from her cheeks, forehead, and mountainous shoulders. She towered over Ferdinand.

Only once did she express a darker sentiment. When I wrote a description of a rat dashing across the terrace of the hotel, she was offended. I tried to explain that this was merely a fact, part of the scene. "Facts," she said, "can be rude sometimes."

"I guess this was one of those times, Estelle."

She gazed at me with concentrated irate motherliness. "So don't do it again."

I understood her loyalty to the Oloffson. It was difficult for me to understand the ethical problem. Ferdinand's profitable abetting of the Duvalier kleptocracy posed no moral problem, it seemed; a sentence about a pointy-muzzled rat was a violation of her code. Because she was kind to my children, I grieved—for five minutes—about offending her, making the little powder bubbles explode along with her emotions as the sweat broke through.

Ferdinand was a calmer operator. He smiled, smiled, and did his job. Mornings he would dress in his elegant colonial whites, slick down his hair, head off in the limousine to the Palais National for his appointments with Baby Doc, Baby Doc's colonels, and the treasury officials. After a few days, he would fly away to Miami or Geneva. He accumulated lots of frequent-flier credits.

He loved Haiti for reasons different from mine, but he was always interested in my wanderings. One morning, hearing that I was driving up the mountain to Kenscoff and the Forêt-des-Pins, he had a personal request. "You're heading up, old chap? Tell you what, be so good . . . There's a pharmacy on the road, more like a grocery, nice market lady there—get me a bottle or two of sellé-bridée . . . sort of a health-giving aperitif, old chap. . . ."

"What's it good for?"

"For the climate, dear fellow. I find jet lag enervates a person, don't you know? Be so good, would you? I may not be pronouncing it correctly, but she'll understand."

He gazed speculatively into my face. "Maybe pick up a bottle for yourself, too, I'd advise. Good fellow, you will?"

He hadn't intended for Estelle to hear this conversation, but she was graceful in the way of some overweight people and had swum up silently behind him as we stood on the terrace after breakfast. "It's good for people who have emotional problems," she said. "Ferdie's right. Pick up a bottle for yourself."

"Maybe two," said Ferdinand.

My spirits always rose with the climb from the heat of town into the cool fastness of mountain forest and streams. It was good to be alone; it was good to be among Haitians. When I stopped at the roadside stand, I saw a poster depicting the *cochon noir* with the legend in Creole, HAITIAN PIG—OUR FLAG. I found the "sellé-bridée," a milky liquid sold in reused Barbancourt rum bottles. It looked like the remedy the medical researcher from Virginia had bought from the *docteur feuilles* in the little shop near the Marché Salomon, but he had neglected to send me his analysis of the formula. There was a black root visible at the bottom of the bottle. I brought two bottles back and Ferdinand asked if I wanted to share a toast with Estelle and him. I asked C'est-Dieu, the ninety-year-old waiter, what the root was, fermenting in milky clairin, and he giggled, showing his several teeth. "Bois-cochon, M'sieu," he said—pigwood.

Henry Kissinger and others have said that power and money are a wonderful stimulus for sexual desire, but evidently they weren't enough for the man who had the honor of carting off the Haitian treasury for the benefit of Jean-Claude.

JEAN WEINER used to assure me, stretching out his long legs and sniffing from his Benzedrex inhaler, "We have a two-party system, mon cher. One in the palace and the other in the cemetery."

But for a while violence seemed to disappear, a little on the model of the French traveler elsewhere who reported: "Cannibalism has been eliminated since the last ones were eaten by the authorities."

At the café La Palette, on the rue de Seine in Paris, I enjoyed a happy reunion with an old friend from Haiti. A businessman, he was wealthy enough to travel, and although he occasionally spent a few nights in jail, and had scars to show for it, he was still opposed to the regime. In fact, he said, the overthrow of Baby Doc was coming soon. There had been a number of ineffectual attempts; a small band from Florida was quickly exterminated. Perhaps a hundred well-armed and determined men could do it, arousing the people and scaring off the Duvalier henchers, but in the past they came in with only a dozen or two. The various oppositions couldn't seem to get organized except to publish their newspapers in New York, Paris, Montreal, Miami.

This time would be different.

In the past, the armed opposition was overwhelmed, once because they sent out for cigarettes and let Papa Doc know how few they were. Or they were found in hiding and their bodies left to rot at the airport. Or they were picked off or just disappeared.

This time the invasion would be brisk and effective. My friend (call him Lucien) assured me victory over oppression was imminent. "I have close relations with the military commander of the Haitian Revolutionary Force. He doesn't see a change until November 23, 1986. And then it might be a bloodbath or a peaceful evolution after Baby Doc."

"Why, Lucien, that date in particular?"

We sat amid students from the Ecole des Beaux-Arts, footsore

tourists, gawkers, lovely green-skinned unhealthy Left Bank bohemians, and Lucien said: "He just doesn't see it. The Military Commander's half-brother is the intellectual guide of the revolution. He's
the best numerologist in Haiti."

I think I groaned. "You're letting astrology plan your revolution?"

"Of course not. That would be ignorant superstition. *Numerology* is scientific."

I stared into my cup. November 22 had been the day Papa Doc
arranged for the murder of John F. Kennedy, an important date for
Baron Samedi.

Lucien took pity and gently explained, "That's not the total
planning, Herb. We have confirmed the modus operandi with a Hindu
seer from Trinidad, a great lover of Haiti who gave us his advice with
no charge at all." They cross-checked the numerologist with the
Hindu.

The Revolutionary Command used modern mathematics; Lucien supplied a complete collection of his Omnis. He was working
now on Quantum Numerology to predict the results of the next
century. "The future will send messages to the past, my friend, this is a
little-known fact. At this very moment we're working on the linkup."

"They better be well-armed. You better get some people who
don't send out for cigarettes in the middle of the fight."

"Herb, the linkup was wrong that time. Don't keep harping on
the past."

Nearly two years later, in 1985, the riots began. The Americans
said to Baby Doc, "Hey fella, time to go check personally on your
banking arrangements." The Boy President, now thirty-five—
inevitably a nineteen-year-old President-for-Life ripens if he hangs
out long enough—sped around Port-au-Prince in his BMW, everyone
cheering, and went on television to say in his thin, high-pitched voice
that no, he wasn't going, he was "strong as a monkey's tail."

Nevertheless, after a few more days, on February 6, 1986, he
again drove through Port-au-Prince at top speed in his BMW, the
grim, chain-smoking First Steno at his side, along with their children
and a few retainers. This time he headed for the airport. He left on a
plane provided by the United States. It was riots in Gonaives, general

strikes, a failure of nerve, a sufficiency of hidden cash, and American pressure that sent him to his luxurious exile in the south of France.

I congratulated my friend Lucien, the opposition leader. "You see, I predicted it," he said.

"But it wasn't really an armed uprising. It didn't happen on the date it was supposed to. Your numerologist isn't much of a prophet, pal."

"Those are mere details," he said.

O N A last visit shortly before the uprooting, Ferdinand's broom had swept the treasury clean, leaving hardly a glint of cash. I wonder what the bagman is doing these days, retired from a hard career of consultancy in a hot climate. Without sellé-bridée, the pig-wood brew, a chap must need a little help to get through the lonely nights.

CHAPTER
FOURTEEN

The Uprooting: 1986

BABY DOC retired to the south of France, in the spring of 1986 a junta was in charge, led by Henri Namphy, lately a colonel, then a general, rising through the ranks during the Duvalier days. The Americans and some Haitians thought the Army could run things, control the "dinosaurs," suppress the macoutes, keep order, prepare for a new constitution, punish the brutes, collect the Duvalier booty, organize an election. With the dreamy optimism of the early days of revolution, people thought the solemn career soldier would work the necessary miracles. He liked his drink, he liked to hang out with his military buddies, he was not known as a torturer. Since he said so little, and could hardly be understood when he did speak, maybe he was thinking deep democratic thoughts.

Flying back, I looked at Haiti from the air and saw a shape roughly like a human heart—a heart with lumps and growths attached to it. It's a combination of geography and memory which created that illusion as my flight lazily circled the island, the late afternoon mists rising from the sea. Time in Haiti, for Haitians and for me, is computed in regimes, in failures, in perverse hope. The towns of Jacmel, Jérémie, and Cap Haitien used to seem nearer to Paris—one could go by ship—than overland to Port-au-Prince. Now there are roads, but these provincial capitals—what a grand naming of villages!—seem closer to Africa than to the Americas. Haiti is a throbbing, not a nation.

At the airport a little girl in carefully braided pigtails, tied with red ribbons, suddenly burst into passionate screams and tears. There was a dog burning, racing like a live torch while people shouted and a few laughed and others just watched. The macoutes were sending another signal. The friend who came to meet me stared at the swift path the dog had taken and said: "You are American. You can help Haiti. You can find it in your heart to do this?"

UNTIL THREE days before this visit, I had planned to bring my fifteen-year-old son, Ari, to a place I had previously visited with his sisters and his brother. It was his turn; he was especially interested in taping voodoo ceremonies and Haitian percussion. Other members of the family stringently opposed the trip, but his desires and mine seemed to prevail. Then this headline appeared in the *San Francisco Chronicle:*

MACHETE-WIELDING PROTESTERS
RUN WILD IN HAITI'S CAPITAL

... crowds demanded the ouster of three ministers and denounced alleged U.S. pressures ... barricades, burned tires, smashed cars ... machete-wielding gangs smashing cars in residential areas of Port-au-Prince and demanding money from people in the streets ... (AP, June 5, 1986)

At this point I cashed in his ticket. I would be looking into Haiti after Baby Doc without Ari.

On the day of my arrival, a general strike was called by a loose alliance of street democrats. All work was supposed to stop. Everything would shut down. The People, that People with the capital P, would make known its anger. But what happens when you give a general strike and nobody doesn't come? Well, of course the strikers, such as the Reverend Sylvio Claude, describe it as a great, great, *great* success. "We have made known the Will of the People."

Capital *W* for Will, too.

But of course it also means that genuine grievances are not

answered, the police come out in the streets with their Uzis, and the "ruling council" (junta) is emboldened.

Elections were promised, but there were a few difficulties. How can there be an election in a country that has never had a real one, where 85 percent of the people are illiterate, and where Baby Doc claimed the last referendum with a cozy vote of 99.9 percent? The candidates had their work cut out for them.

With rage in his voice, a cab driver informed me that two people had been killed last night by a thief up the hill from the Oloffson near the Hotel Castelhaiti. "Liberty, yes," he shouted, spewing saliva, "I believe in liberty, but that is *democracy!*" Like almost all chauffeurs, he was probably a former macoute.

In their joy at the departure of the oppressors, civil volunteers had cleaned the streets. Also, hundreds of macoutes were killed by civic volunteers. The long dismay was not over. Violence would disappear because the peaceful folks would slaughter the violent ones.

We drove to see the emplacement near the port where the statue of the first colonialist had been uprooted, shattered, and thrown into the sea. Christopher Columbus landed on this island many years ago. "*Dechoukaj*, Monsieur," said the cab driver, "they dechouked this imported exploiter."

Dechoukaj, a Creole word that comes from an old French term for the uprooting of stumps, came to be a refrain of the revolution. Haitians hoped to dig up the rot in the soil of their lives.

"INSIDE EVERY Haitian there is a sleeping President."
And outside the candidate there is someone who wants either to hench for him or to kill him.

Felix Morisseau-Leroy arrived home from exile, met by radio and television crews and a crowd of well-wishers. He stood in the airport and made a proud announcement. "I have a proclamation for you!" His aureole of white hair blew about his head and he raised his arms in a statesmanlike gesture. "I AM NOT A CANDIDATE FOR THE PRESIDENCY! At least there must be one who is not!"

Later he moved to Miami to write his books and finish his days among his family. And so now perhaps there was nobody in Haiti who was not a President.

Besides the normal 6 million shy and secret candidates, there were about 200 announced nominees. I cut this figure to 199 when one was arrested for reckless driving in Connecticut. I'm not sure why he was campaigning at high speed near Westport—normally not a major Haitian campaign stop—but this relieved the burden of trying to keep track. Now there were only 199 Saviors of the Nation who wanted to be addressed as Your Terrifickness, Your Wondrosity. For example, Colonel Williams Regala, a member of the ruling gang—it would be called a junta in a Spanish-speaking country—proclaimed: "I seek to do nothing but serve the People. History will judge me."

When a colonel speaks of History, let's run to the church of our choice and pray.

I visited three of the most interesting figures—the Reverend Sylvio Claude, a popular Protestant pastor; René Theodore, a communist trained in Moscow and Paris; and Marc Bazin, a distinguished economist who left his brief appointment as Finance Minister under Baby Doc because he couldn't clean up the mess. Sylvio Claude had gotten demonstrators out into the streets. René Theodore enjoyed success as the first open communist activist in many years. Marc Bazin, probably the most qualified, was supported by a group of earnest reformers and technocrats.

Issa el Saieh, the art dealer, sorted out the three types of presidential candidates. There are those who are capable and won't steal. That's Marc Bazin, "Monsieur Clean plus brains." There are those who steal but don't want to get caught. "Brains but not clean." And there are those who don't care if they're caught. "No brains, no clean."

I made an appointment to see Marc Bazin at six A.M. I drove to Belvedere, high in the mountains behind Port-au-Prince, where he met me in a jeep and escorted me to the terrace of a large stone house. He is a tall, sturdy, well-fleshed man who looks much too tough and happy for an economist at the World Bank, which was his job in exile from Haiti. He was recently married for the first time. Issa said it was better to make many women happy than to make one woman unhappy.

We spoke of the need to recapture some of the treasure stolen by the Duvalier family. Papa Doc spent much of the money on his security system. He wanted power in Haiti, and planned to remain until his evil spirit was laid to rest. Baby Doc used the security machinery—the macoutes, the torture—to capitalize the family for his eventual retirement. They should be able to survive on the five or six or seven or eight hundred million he has stashed away. "Perhaps, with diplomatic pressure, we can get some of it back," Marc Bazin said.

This laborious people groaned under 65 percent unemployment. They needed food, they needed work, roads, a water supply, health care. Any investment that involved labor would produce a ripple effect on the economy.

That this intelligent and forceful man wanted to take hold was in itself a hopeful sign. Bazin had made a comfortable career at the World Bank. If he was willing to work for Haiti in Haiti, perhaps other talented Haitians would be willing to work for their country—even to learn, against all the tradition of Haitian genius, to consent to paying their taxes.

Driving among the splendid hillside houses of Pétionville, La-Boule, and Kenscoff—iron gates, swimming pools, floodlit tennis courts—I saw unashamed symbols of the life-styles of the several hundred millionaires in this poorest of nations. The man in the Rolls-Royce finds tax evasion an even more engaging sport than tennis.

WHAT FOLLOWS is the tragedy of the black Haitian pig. When I arrived thirty-seven years ago, I first thought they were exceptionally quick, agile, intelligent, and curious little black dogs darting around the ditches, gardens, garbage holes, and feet. They didn't bark, they didn't look at the sky. They kept to business.

The *cochon noir* was the peasant's pride and joy, his pet, his love, his bank account, his insurance policy. It was the vacuum cleaner that got rid of waste. It ate lizards, rubbish, even insects. Perhaps it lived on fantasy, too, like everyone else. It showed a touch of fanaticism about its continual rooting. Eventually it provided the essential ingredient of *griots*, the Haitian staple meat, tight-fried little curls of piglet served with rice and beans—charcoal-smoked protein. And just as important, certain voodoo ceremonies demanded a sacrifice of the *cochon planche*, the little bugger.

One theory is that Baby Doc was brought down by the pig tragedy. The CIA did it. The Iowa farmers working through the CIA did it. The Americans came in and said the pigs were infected with an African pig virus. Every single one had to go. Amid weeping, grief, and stubborn anger among the peasants and priests, the Americans, with the cooperation of Baby Doc—how could he? how *could* he have?—swept through the country, pignapping, mad with piglust. They gave money for each pig. They would eventually replace the Haitian pigs with huge pink and white American porkers. But that wasn't the point. The American pigs, clumsy and stumbly, couldn't be led to market on a string. They weren't cute, they weren't voodoo-effective, they weren't the pig of myth and dream. And they required corn to thrive—corn imported from Iowa, corn that nobody could afford, corn that made the peasants dependent in still another way on the American dole.

It was a scandal beyond the comprehension of the American experts.

The pink and white, sometimes ridiculously spotted American pig, as giant and helpless as a cruise-ship tourist, munched with its little tail extended like a tea-drinker's pinkie. Its meat is bland. Its soul is empty—bred for troughs and pens. The gods reject it on Saturday night. Only a President-for-Life, capable of betraying his people by marrying a divorcée from a family in the cocaine trade, would allow such a disaster. He even looked like a porker himself.

During the pig pogrom, a few clever farmers, influential politicians, and idealistic voodoo priests managed to hide their heroic fugitives. They began to emerge later. You still see the Ugly American Pigs. In the marketplace of Kenscoff, a Haitian friend pointed to the roasted pink American meat. "No taste," he said, "no good for griots, I spit on it." The Madame Sara said, "Wait. Move back before you spit."

The new government declared an amnesty for the condemned. The survivors came out of hiding. They root in public like free black pigs in a happy pigworld. Let the Americans deal with virus if they don't like it. The gods require *cochon planche.*

Pig worry was part of the problem of nourishment. Scholars and aid officials were twisting and turning through new analyses of the traditional food aid programs. The price of food goes down, thanks to gifts from abroad. But this drives farmers off their land, because they produce so little and barely survive by selling some of it in the cities. They come to Port-au-Prince, seeking work, and don't find it—they look for CARE food, Catholic food, Protestant food, missionary food, U.S. Government food. The infrastructure of growers disappears. Government control of the distribution of aid corrupts the process; the Duvaliers made fortunes by selling sacks of grain marked as U.S. Government aid. But if foreigners control distribution—hard to manage in Haiti when the rulers forbid aid to the starving that does not pass through their fingers—then the cycle of passivity and dependence is perpetuated.

On the one side, the lineup for handouts. On the other, the babies with swollen bellies and crinkly reddish hair—kwashiokor—which produces mental retardation when it doesn't kill. During recent years, one of the chief forms of harvest has been raids on the food warehouses.

The insignia of the Haitian flag includes palm trees, cannon, and drums, arranged in a formal motif, reflecting the history of fertility, hard-won freedom, and an African art connected with religion, cooperative work rites, and the pleasures of dance and celebration. A revised insignia should also show the sacks of swag perpetually shipped out by Haiti's rulers.

Shortly after Baby Doc flew off, a new flag—back to the old colors—was unveiled at the palace. It hung limp and the people murmured. Baby Doc was still there; *magie noire* had stopped the wind. They must storm the palace to kill him, take control of the wind. But before they climbed the fences, a breeze came up, the flag fluttered, and the palace was saved. Instead, groups of "réfractaires"— aginners—invaded the presidential houses and hideaway, marveling over the stocks of cocaine and the porn library Baby Doc and Michelle had left behind.

Drums of victory resounded through the countryside, songs of freedom rose in the air, it's the old story of the first days of revolution. There was a Carnival joy and hope of renewal. The island seemed to be sinking into the sea under the weight of all the video and electronic equipment brought in by journalists to document the uprooting.

Like prisoners suddenly released, people didn't know the rules anymore. The police had little discipline; the army was subservient to leftover Duvalierists and macoutes; everybody was expecting griots in the sky right now. On the streets, that Caribbean male habit of stroking the pants consolingly—or enticingly in the presence of visitors—now seemed a bit ominous. The adjustments seemed to be more than heat-induced comfort moves. The suggestion was of something out of control in these idle young men; the suggestiveness was no longer comical.

In the slide toward anarchy, factories were going bankrupt. For a while nothing could be shipped in or out because the customs employees were on strike. The acting head of state, General Henri Namphy, took to his bed with fatigue. (Later he decided he really liked to run things, and began a clumsy, alcohol-fueled imitation of Duvalier statesmanship.) Offers of foreign aid could not be accepted because there was no one around to sign the letters. In 1986 the heart of Haiti was gripped by hunger, manic hope, the reality of uninterrupted suffering.

After the turmoil of the brief "Port-au-Prince spring" of *deshoukaj*, when the smiling drunk, Colonel-General Henri Namphy, played host to his pals in the National Palace, the nation quickly fell back into exhaustion. Only the graves looked fresh. The streets were garbaged with bodies—we saw them every morning—and an official explained that they were carted away on trucks without any attempt at identification because: "This is a civilized country. We can't just let bodies lie around."

At a press conference, crowded with foreign journalists, General Namphy took position in front of the bank of microphones, seemed ready to begin to speak, and then decided to move to another side of the room, where there were no microphones. The pack of journalists jostled and shoved into new positions; the mikes were reinstalled. He opened his mouth. He changed his mind. He moved to still another side of the room, moving his lips inaudibly. It was like a performance by Professor Irwin Corey. Charming and funny, wasn't it? Except that he was the leader presiding over new random and nonrandom shootings, beheadings, disappearances. The macoutes had regrouped, many protected by Army uniforms; "integrated into the social structure."

An entry-level macoute, just good for standing and glowering, stood and glowered at me. He reminded me of William S. Burroughs, famous novelist and heroin addict, who was asked by Allen Ginsberg to confirm that what every man wants most deeply is to be loved. "You want to be loved, don't you, Bill?" Burroughs said: "Not really."

Some want to be feared. Some want nothing but to pass the time. The macoutes merely hoped to survive as their leaders fled abroad or disappeared into the protection of their loot. But after a few hundred of them had been squashed, they appeared once more in Army dress, given a second life, as to prove Baron Samedi's conviction that there is no justice in the world, justice is not necessary or relevant.

The fingers of the young macoute were clenching. I reminded myself not to look him in the eye.

An occasional spokesman, appearing to be military or political or both or neither, was quoted during periods when General Namphy retreated from the strains of six or seven days of leadership. The spokesman's name was Rockefeller Guerre. I tried to imagine what his parents had in mind. Rockefeller and the fantastic wealth of America. Guerre, which means War.

Try to imagine answering to the name Rockefeller War.

The common Haitian expression, "Pas faute moin"—it's not my fault—is usually accompanied by a gesture of fingertips dusting together, washing hands of the subject. When Baby Doc fled, people took to confronting any problem—a dog in the road, a fallen tree, an overcooked slice of meat—with a more specific explanation: "C'est faute Duvalier." Duvalier's fault. It was what carnies call kidding on the square.

Each time I arrived at the Hotel Oloffson for a new visit, the ancient waiter C'est-Dieu came to greet me. "How old are you now?"

I would ask—by now he was well into his nineties—and he would always answer: "Ampile, ampile, ampile!" Much, much, much. "C'est faute Duvalier."

JEAN-BERNARD Diederich, a half-Haitian photographer, showed me his photographs of a roasting man—actually, pieces of a man—in Gonaives. He was present during the killing. The people who did it explained that it was not a man but a loupgarou. Besides the werewolf, several others died, including a werewoman and werechild. In the photograph, alongside the burned limbs, there were feathers, goat parts, and the werewolf's *jacoute*—sack—spilling its charms, potions, and leaves. A mob of about a hundred people danced and officiated over the execution, energized by *clairin*. In the distance a trumpet sounded. The people were wearing red headbands, some in full ceremonial dress. Jean-Bernard smelled the pleasant scent of weed, which was relatively new to Haiti. Yesterday I too had been offered a toke in the Protestant missionary restaurant in Kenscoff.

The reason the body needed to be cut into small pieces before being burnt was that otherwise the loupgarou might put itself back together and return to avenge the insult of being beaten and chopped with machetes.

We drove to Gonaives with Caleb Joseph, a young voodoo expert from the ethnology department of the Université d'Haiti. He wished to make sure we understood that this was not voodoo but an act of personal pillage, revenge on an unpopular figure. I studied the graffiti on walls as we headed out of Port-au-Prince. DUVALIER NOT HERE! MISERY FINISHED! "The euphoria," said Caleb, the twenty-three-year-old ethnology scholar. We spoke of the continued unemployment and the shortages of everything, including law and order. The prisons had been emptied, because who now was guilty? Former macoutes were being killed. Catholics were attacking voodoo priests. "We others, we students, knew things would be difficult," said Caleb.

At the roadside we studied the ashes of the loupgarou. We poked about the cinders. Jean-Bernard took pictures. We talked to a bright young fellow in a blue U.S. Navy surplus shirt with the name Roisentenkovsky stenciled on it. He explained that the loupgarou deserved to die. We went to see the burnt-out house. His animals had been distributed, his corn was harvested. He had had thirty-three children by his several wives. We met one of the widows, we met his father, we expressed sympathy.

Then we headed up a rutted road and a police jeep, scattering clots of mud, skidded to a stop. Four men and an officer greeted us, admired our tape recorders and cameras, and began questioning people about the killings. Out of the *caille-pailles* various explainers gathered. Six men were rounded up, each one questioned by the officer while another soldier took notes. One man, with the inflamed conjunctiva of a drunk, was shoved away. Jean-Bernard whispered to me that they had all been in the killing mob. And so were most of the others here, except for the wife and the old father. Suddenly a woman began shouting, "He's the one! He started the killing!"

"Don't know nothing," said the sullen-eyed barefoot man.

"You're under arrest."

Two of the soldiers were horsing around, pretending to duel with their clubs. They were also carrying old U.S. Army M-1 rifles. Instead of getting into the jeep, the suspect broke and began to run toward the cornfield. "You may kill him!" the officer shouted. The soldiers began firing. The woman who had denounced him shouted, "Don't shoot! Don't shoot!" Five or six shots rang out and the man didn't stop. He wasn't hit. The soldiers chased after him, followed by Jean-Bernard, who turned to yell back to me, "Watch the car!"

In the high corn, where everyone was invisible, volleys of shots resounded. I assumed they were revenging themselves on the body.

A child, about ten years old, began to leap about, screaming. People told her to shut up. The woman who had denounced the fleeing man was still sobbing, "Don't! Oh don't!" The child ripped away her sleeve. There was a deep wound with exposed veins and striations of flesh rapidly oozing blood. I began shouting, "Jay-bee! Jay-bee!" If a wild bullet had hit this child, I wondered what else could happen in the cornfield. It turned out that the man had escaped—"He knows every hole," said one of the soldiers—and they were shooting into the air to let each other know where they were.

The officer decided to put the child in the jeep and take her to a clinic. Her mother was brought up screaming, dragged to join her daughter. She was afraid of the police. She thought she was being arrested. During the Duvalier days, many of those arrested never returned.

Hysterical, she fell and knocked her head against a rock. She was loaded, stunned, into the jeep along with her daughter.

The officer began sounding his horn in imperative steady honks to summon the troops. They crowded into the jeep along with the child and her mother.

"This wasn't an affair of voodoo," the ethnologist explained. "This was an affair of pillage." I knew what came next: Haiti is 60 percent Catholic, 40 percent Protestant, and 100 percent voodoo. "That is our basis of philosophy and hope," said Caleb Joseph.

I thought of the cock's feathers left by the charred remains of the murdered—executed—man.

WE DECIDED to drive down the back roads from Carrefour Poteau, where these events took place, to Carrefour Lexis, where lives Simon Herard, one of the great houngans of Haiti, a leader of the Gonaives district with a reputation as a wise man. During the early days of the Duvalier empire, he supported Papa Doc because of the voodoo connection. The Haitian version of Black Pride, the rivalry between black and mulatto, was also a factor. Simon Herard was linked with the tontons macoutes. Later he made alliances with those who understood that the boy President-for-Life, with his greedy mulatto bride, had to go.

Perhaps to confuse ill-wishers, he runs his name both ways, Simon Herard or Herard Simon. He greeted me with the graciousness of a king or warlord in the cool shade of vines growing in thick tangles against a scaffolding, a kind of arbor outside his temple. Monsieur Herard is a thick stocky man with an African chief's belly, a deep, resonant, raspy, cigarette-and-rum voice, an impressive authority and affability. He had thrived under the Duvaliers, when he was called a macoute priest; and he had also thrived in the discontent that led to the fall of Baby Doc; and he was still thriving. He was smiling broadly and patiently. He is a person who will always thrive.

One of his wives, a mambo or priestess herself, and a number of his sons hovered about us as we chatted in this space in front of the *hounfor*, temple. We sat at a large table under a bottle of Piper-Heidsieck champagne suspended from the boughs above his head. This outbuilding on his plantation was also a place for *bamboche*.

I felt like an emissary presenting credentials. We had a "free and frank discussion," as it's called among diplomats for major powers, fueled by excellent coffee (I risked loss of face by refusing rum), ranging from the subject of zombies—he had been depicted in a sensational American book—to the subject of family planning. About zombies, he chuckled. About family planning—he believed in it.

The crowd of auditors at this impromptu seminar gathered close. They were his sons. I asked how many children he had.

"Fifty-four. But all of them *planned.*"

His sons nodded agreement. The logic of his position was that he was rich enough to give them a decent life. Wives and children are both the symbol and the expression of achievement. Everywhere he turned he saw grateful faces. "You can appreciate my point of view, I hope."

One of his sons began to giggle. He stared at him, the young man stopped, and then Monsieur Herard told me a story about an American project to distribute prophylactics in Haiti. "Use one of these every time you make love," advised the American white rabbit with the plastic suit. And the Haitian bear answered: "I'm sorry, I've tried rum, water, everything, I just can't swallow it."

I discovered unknown resources of diplomacy in myself. I laughed as if I had never heard this story. Now I hoped it was time to hear his version of the events that Jean-Bernard Diederich, Caleb Joseph, and I had come upon today. I asked about the incident at Carrefour Poteau.

"Nothing to do with voodoo," he said. "This *dechoukaj* is an excuse for revenge and disorder."

Caleb looked happy. He was rapidly nodding his head up and down. Voodoo is peaceful, voodoo is philosophy, voodoo is ethnology, people don't understand.

Jean-Bernard suggested I show him the photo of the roasting pieces of man. I handed it to him. "Oh-oh," said Monsieur Herard, with a deep chuckle. His wife and sons gathered to gaze over his shoulder. There was silence.

Jean-Bernard, whose mother is Haitian, asked: "Why the cock, why the feathers, why were they wearing red headbands, why did the trumpet sound, why the chanting? Why are there goat parts and his *jacoute* filled with—what?"

"You must understand," said Monsieur Herard. "All Haitians are werewolves"—he chuckled happily—"if you want to burn them or steal from them or only to kill them." He fixed my eyes with a stare. I resolved to agree with everything he said, at least until I returned to Port-au-Prince. "It was organized thieving, that's all. Organized with rum and disorder. Thank you very much for the visit."

Somehow the Army officer figured out where we were—telejiol seemed to transmit as quickly as fax machines—and as we were leaving, drove up in his jeep to give us the news. The injured child was being taken care of. Her mother had a headache. They would surely find the criminal tomorrow. Or maybe the next day.

He saluted smartly.

A FEW MINUTES from the Hotel Oloffson in Port-au-Prince, on the day when we had driven to Gonaives, a man was burnt in the street for being a werewolf. This time the crowd found a lost child in a pit in his house. There was a pot boiling with meat that looked suspiciously like a long pig. A neighborhood mother cut off the head of the loupgarou. A free-lance television cameraman showed me his film of the event. The crowd cavorted and danced before the camera, holding lemons to their noses because of the smell of roasting werewolf.

How did they know he was a loupgarou? A sick child had cried when passing his hut. Obviously the loupgarou drank blood. The people had long suspected it, but the loupgarou was protected under the Duvalier government. This time he had no protection. They found the lost child, they found the pot, they saw the bones.

No police came to the party. It had been a man who lived alone.

He must have been a loupgarou. In any case, he was dead, roasting, an affront to the noses blocked with lemons.

Later that evening, unable to sleep, I drove into the slum near the harbor where an artist, in the exhilaration of freedom at last, was still painting heroic murals on the walls of block after block of the rue du Magasin de l'Etat. Again, he was happy to share his thoughts with me. He was only, he said, a poor man telling his feelings. His neighbors contributed to buying the paints. They wanted their district of shacks and blank walls to shout aloud the happiness of this time in history.

The artist was mild and gentle and had found his vocation. Life had revealed his talent. His hand was guided by the gods; others were also inspired to paint the story of Haiti on block after block of forbidding stone and cement.

Because the only public toilet in Port-au-Prince is on this street, he included the tiled urinal as one of the panels of his mural. It was an ideal vision of sparkling tiles, modern plumbing. It was clean, it was bright, it gleamed, it was a blessing. It was imaginary.

He left instructions against overcrowding the facilities, painting PIPI ONE. PIPI DEUX.

"I stay on the street, I never go," he said. "Please come back to share our joy."

I STOOD ONE night outside my room, looking over the balcony at the fuming city of Port-au-Prince. I remembered the American embassy official who used to drink with me in 1954 on the wooden ramp leading to what is called the maternity ward at the Grand Hotel Oloffson. "This country destroyed my marriage," he said, "destroyed my health, destroyed my life, and I love it more than any place on earth."

The friend who had met me at the airport came unexpectedly to visit in the dark of the nearly deserted hotel. "Herb, I hate to tell you this," he said. "I think you should go home tomorrow."

"Why?"

"Because there is no way you can go home tonight. I pray for you. You must pray for us."

CHAPTER
FIFTEEN

*After the Dawn
Came Another Night*

PERSUADED THE *San Francisco Chronicle* and the *Los Angeles Times* to send me back to report on Haiti. Arriving a week before the elections scheduled for January 17, 1988, I stopped on my way from the airport to visit an old friend. "Oh-oh, you're here," he said, as if I had been missing a few minutes in a game of hide-and-go-seek. "Oh-oh, mon cher!"

I invited him to meet me for dinner in downtown Port-au-Prince.

He stared a moment, registering my American innocence, and then broke into that rolling Haitian laughter that charmed me when I first met him in 1954. "You don't understand yet? We don't go out at night. It seems like the old days—"

And wiped the tears of laughter from his eyes, just as if he had told a good joke.

"—the old days of cozy chatting around a candle, waiting for the macoutes to come in to shoot our dogs, our children, ourselves."

I had also visited him in 1963, during the worst days of Papa Doc, when the capital was blacked out on the night when President John F. Kennedy was killed; blacked out except for the National Palace, blazing with light, where Papa Doc was celebrating his voodoo success.

Later, my friend and I had enjoyed the surreal comedy of Baby Doc, his bride Michelle, and her dope-dealing family. Once, standing on the rue du Centre, we watched the car with its armored escort, the fat fingers extended, covered with rings; the scatter of coins to the rabble. The crowd fought for Baby Doc's largess.

Ernest Bennett, the First Lady's father, gave interviews explaining that money was not the important factor in his life. Like all Haitians, he was motivated by purest metaphysics. "People have hungry days, yet are they unhappy? No! But I, with my millions, I want to be Voltaire. I'll never be happy!"

Now Baby Doc was learning to ski in southern France, Michelle was complaining that she was bored and might take up a post-First Lady career as a fashion model, and Voltaire was silent. It had been agreed with the Americans that General Henri Namphy, a Duvalier officer but a relatively unobtrusive one, a heavy-drinking, stammering old army man, would shepherd the country toward its first legitimate election in thirty years. His speech defect helped make him seem strong, silent, and virtuous. When he refused to act against army-sponsored abuses, people blamed Colonel Williams Regala, another member of the junta. When the two civilian members resigned, there was still hope that the elections scheduled for November 1987, would take place. They did not. Random murders began; the macoutes were riding again, many of them given American khaki Army uniforms. It turned out that a speech defect and a comfortable belly were not perfect guarantees of democratic intention.

A news story in a government-sponsored paper stated:

> The election campaign proceeds calmly. General Namphy summoned to his side the various candidates. These last, however, complained about the machine-gunning of one of their houses where the leaders of the parties of opposition were gathered. They safely threw themselves out of the windows.

So what were they complaining about? The windows weren't that high. And only a few presidential candidates were killed during the campaign.

Haitian government was still following the rule enunciated by Professor Irwin Corey: It fluctuates. Sometimes it flucks down and sometimes it flucks up.

When I told my old friend I was returning for the new, revised, improved election, he said, "It's harder to dodge the bullets now, Herb. Soldiers shoot straight." These were the bad old days come back, the ones that caused my friend to wipe the tears of laughter from his eyes. After world outrage about the canceled election, the junta scheduled a new one with soldiers examining the ballots. The four leading democratic candidates were boycotting the charade. General Namphy declared it was illegal not to vote, and the Army would round up voters. Familiar faces from the Duvalier regime were now candidates, some less implicated than others.

It reminded Haitians of the times when 99.9 percent of Haitians voted OUI for Baby Doc and nobody dared laugh in public. A few days before the election, observers saw two possibilities:

New riots and strikes, leading to another cancellation or civil war.

A successful cosmetic election, leading to an uneasy truce until the next stage, probably new disorders.

The third possibility, intervention by the United States, the United Nations, or a consortium of Caribbean nations, intending to enforce the peace and guarantee an honest election, had been foreclosed. No one wanted to handle the mess.

Louis Dejoie 2d, one of the legitimate candidates in the election aborted in November, was abroad, campaigning for a multinational force to supervise honest voting. The United Nations, the organization of Caribbean states, and the United States did not want this unpleasant task. Other candidates were underground, calling for boycott or strike or protest in whatever form it might take. The riots, killings, and vagueness at the National Palace were ending the optimism of deshoukaj. Potentially this could lead to a leftist takeover, if any leftists wanted poor Haiti. The Communist party was a tiny grouplet. Its leader, René Theodore, was a convincing, plausible, and tireless campaigner, but the abject situation of the country, this prefeudal, anarchic state, didn't really tempt the Cubans or the Russians.

In the past, the Duvaliers occasionally used "Communism" to attack its enemies and to get aid from the United States. General Namphy echoed this rhetoric, although so far the United States was not buying it. "We need a good Communist party to scare the Americans and get massive aid," said my friend from the Caravelle bookstore days. "We need a fright doll for the Americans."

He used the word *ouanga*, the voodoo bad news charm.

"We *need* René Theodore. I love him! But are we clever enough, my friend, to rattle him around and do our native dances?"

If the cosmetic election could be brought off, General Namphy and Colonel Regala would be the puppetmasters. The United States, the World Bank, France, Canada, and the various international aid organizations might decide that this was the best temporary solution for Haiti—as they decided and dithered at various times in the past for Papa Doc, Baby Doc, and General Namphy in his first incarnation as Cosmic Caretaker. The familiar spiral downward could continue.

Having so little in the way of natural resources, Haitians mine their talents for whimsy and imagination. They also see devils because, in fact, in their experience, there *are* devils. For years bogeymen had been the basic authorities. A middle-class woman in Port-au-Prince, hearing a noise upstairs at night, cried out, "Who's there?" A timid, polite, and obedient voice answered: "It's the thief, Madam."

Amid the desolation arrived a wry tourist from Saint Croix, which is an American possession. "I feel safer here in Port-au-Prince," she said. "Isn't that weird?"

It was.

Journalists and minglers were staying at the plastic, sub-Miami Beach Holiday Inn, near the National Palace, because they hoped it would be safer. In November, a reporter was killed and others wounded. I arrived with a photographer, Brant Ward, who began by figuring out escape routes, explaining quite reasonably that he hoped to be a living father soon. I hoped things would be calm enough so that we could take our meals on the terrace of the Grand Hotel Oloffson.

People tried to figure out what General Namphy had in mind. He was a jive prince, not a rapping demagogue—a blunt, stumbly mouthed drillmaster who occasionally came on television to bark orders at his people. "The goat drops pellets, therefore thinks he's a pharmacist." He was coming to think he was the doctor. Power consoles; now he was trying for charisma. Sometimes he would wear a helmet, hold a gun, glower; sometimes he would stutter in French, sometimes in Creole. Sometimes he practiced enigmatic retreats from public view.

Early on, he was the repository of hope. People said he would prefer to drink and cavort with his soldier buddies, but it seemed that he liked high office. The macoutes and Duvalier extortionists cowering behind him knew that a democratic regime would bring prosecutions for atrocities, serious efforts to recover the loot.

No doubt they had a better solution: Cry Communism; cry anarchy; put up some sort of civilian front man—in the Haitian tradition of making nice for the foreigners. Get back American and international aid. Continue looting for themselves. Since most of Haiti's income now came from foreign aid, mainly from the United States, what difference did it make? Michelle used it for fur coats, jewels, partying in Paris and New York; otherwise it would just have gone to the hungry. The Duvalierists-without-Duvalier hoped to inherit the store from Baby Doc, who couldn't properly manage things.

Bertholt Brecht noted that when the leaders are unhappy with the people, they must elect a new people. The election scheduled for January 17 was that sort of event. And that was why my friend slapped his side and laughed when I asked him to meet me for dinner. Once again it was too dark in Haiti to venture out at night.

MARC BAZIN, probably Haiti's best chance for democracy, sat out the campaign at home, surrounded by walls, gates, and guards. Outside his door someone had glued a poster for Rockefeller Guerre.

Besides Bazin, the three other democratic candidates—who together would have received 80 percent of the vote—were urging a boycott of the stage-managed polling. "Nevertheless there will be ballots in the boxes," he acknowledged during our visit. "But who will put them there?"

"Zombies?"

"They are not a party." With an ironic smile, he asked: "And are you finding much local color these days?"

He was wearing a Tyrolean sweater against the chill here in this cool and secluded road above Pétionville. There was a dense garden, trees, bougainvillea flowering against the walls where Rockefeller Guerre also lay pasted. Bazin, an elegant, classically educated economist, for years an official of the World Bank, would be an anomaly anywhere. "Mister Clean" had served briefly in Baby Doc's cabinet as the condition for a loan, but when he couldn't rein in the thievery, resigned and returned to New York. When Baby Doc fled, he came home.

He was running for the presidency when I first met him during the days of hope a year and a half earlier. He was still running, but he was not on the list for this new, revised balloting. "I *knew* Namphy didn't want independent elections," he told me. "He did nothing to prepare them." Nevertheless, he seemed surprised that the general allowed the Army and the former macoutes to collaborate in the killings, including the shooting of stubborn Haitians lined up at the polls on November 29, 1987. He thought perhaps General Namphy was no longer in control.

I wondered why Bazin was risking his life, ending a successful career with the World Bank, living well on the East Side of Manhattan, in order to try to serve as President of a country that hasn't had a successful presidency in generations. "If you get a chance to jump over a volcano," he said, "you have to do it. Of course, if you don't make it, you don't get another jump."

"But you're jumping again."

He shrugged. Perhaps good sense wasn't what led a man home to Haiti.

We sat on a veranda in this splendid house in the cool suburb of Pétionville, served coffee while security guards strolled about. Other visitors, carefully screened, waited. Bazin had the disadvantage of urbanity and a career made in exile. "Mister Clean," a graduate student at the Université d'Haiti insisted, "is an American citizen. Not many people know this. He keeps it a secret."

This rumor, a symptom of the normal paranoia of the powerless, could be fatal to Mark Bazin. His gracefulness was as I remembered it, but the year had aged him. "Are you afraid?"

"One has to make difficult choices in life. I have an ambition for this country, my country. I knew there was a minimum cost. The experience of November showed the cost was higher than I thought. Since I want something badly, I am willing to go for the higher cost."

"And?"

"If they decide to get rough, how rough can they get? You can only die once. You have to be ready in this kind of work."

He was no longer using volcano metaphors. This was not the Philosopher's Circle in Kenscoff.

Bazin and the other candidates were calling for a general strike on Thursday, a boycott of the polls on Sunday. "You'll see trucks bringing people. Each section chief has the assignment of getting a thousand in place. There'll be a lady telling you she likes voting, but she'll only vote seven times on Sunday because the truck broke down."

His lightly French-accented English was excellent; his humor was Haitian. Although he was known as "the American candidate" because he had lived abroad so long, people were getting used to him as he went about the country. He was not under house arrest—"not yet," he said. "Even if I had been naive enough to enter this new charade, they wouldn't let me win. This stand puts me closer to the people. I was perceived as a mere technocrat. Now I think the new dechoukaj will come soon, more forcefully. Building on the same old people won't work."

What could the United States do? Not active intervention, he said, but an embargo of oil and a strong statement from the President. "In their hearts Americans wish democracy in Haiti—maybe. They want order, but not at the cost of tolerating drug smuggling."

Haiti is known as a way station for cocaine headed north. Most things, including landing rights for smugglers, have traditionally been for sale.

"If the U.S. embargoed oil, that would tell the regime: *Stop!* It would tell the Army to stop. It would say what the U.S. really wanted. Intervention would bring back bad memories, but a strong statement about democracy in Haiti . . . not 'sources in the White House,' but President Reagan himself. Someone should tell him not to do a John Wayne and send in the Marines, but just speak firmly, please, and clearly. No puppet president and no puppetmasters in Haiti."

That could do it?

"Words are effective in Haiti. So would be an oil embargo. And America is important to us."

People made the optimistic mistake—"So did I," he said—of thinking that the departure of Baby Doc meant they could finish with Duvalierism. Thirty years of it meant that the sucker roots went deep and the uprooting could not be achieved merely by enthusiasm. "We have the mandate of the people. So far that isn't enough."

Bazin considered himself the candidate with credibility. Sylvio Claude, another of the popular candidates joining the boycott, was a passionate Baptist minister with little administrative experience. About Louis Dejoie 2d, a wealthy light-skinned businessman, Bazin said he was "a right-wing populist" who could manage if he had more talent . . . "and if I weren't around." Gérard Gourgue was a lawyer and civil rights advocate who stayed in Haiti throughout the Duvalier regime and survived. "We meet nearly every day. We get along," said Bazin. "They all said things about me during the campaign, but we have a common interest in the good of the country."

He paused to take a little shot at one of these colleagues. "Dejoie should stop running around the world calling for intervention. It wouldn't work and it won't happen."

I understood how patriotism, hope, and ambition might bring Marc Bazin back during the glorious early days of *dechoukaj*. The thought of leading a nation is a powerful enticement. But now the situation had turned dangerous. Political life is most often not a good friend to ambition. I asked again why a man with a good job and perks, a comfortable and secure life in the United States, would leave it to risk himself and his family in the chaotic turmoil of this lost little nation isolated on a Caribbean island. I expected another patriotic statement about his conscience as a Haitian, his duty, his love of country and his responsibility. Or the technocrat's jargon about the need for "preemptive reform" to save the country from a new tyranny. Instead, he said: "In New York I lived at Thirtieth and Madison—just at the border of civilization and noncivilization."

And the economist technocrat's face creased in a jolly Haitian smile. Haitians seem to survive by mining their irony, the one natural resource that doesn't rust in the disaster of their history.

WHAT IF you gave a hunger strike and nobody noticed? When a group of the followers of Père Jean-Bertrand Aristide lay in front of the altar of the cathedral in Port-au-Prince, protesting his transfer to a remote parish, people gathered to murmur in awe at the idea of not eating *on purpose*. Everywhere in this country you can find people not eating. Not eating is a national pastime.

When Haitians eat, they eat rice and beans, sometimes bananas, mangoes, tropical fruit, very occasionally chicken or, on a great holiday, pork. In the markets I used to see the African tilapia that Shimon Tal had scattered in the waterways. But now even the tilapia seem mostly disappeared.

Haitians cook whatever they have on outdoor fires. They often take water from open ditches. The Madame Saras sleep overnight in the streets near the Iron Market. They don't eat very well.

A few Haitians eat very well indeed. They gather at the cafés of the Rond Point near the harbor of Port-au-Prince. They dine on fine French cuisine at Chez Gérard (quail, salmon, oysters), Le Belvedere, La Lanterne, La Belle Époque, Côte Jardin, which can be translated as By the Side of the Garden. Or they sample high-fashion gourmet versions of rice-and-beans (with added mushrooms) or *griots* as a patriotic and sentimental tribute to their origins among "the people." Often they sit high above the turbulent and smoky city, looking at the harbor from the cool hills or smiling into the eyes of a good companion. *"Isn't it really just like Switzerland up here?"*

One estimate is that 2 percent of the people control 45 percent of the wealth, but in fact, a good portion of the population has no income at all, living off food brought in by a jostling mob of relief organizations. In and around Pétionville, the Mill Valley-Shaker Heights-Scarsdale of Port-au-Prince, the millionaires dramatize their power with imaginative mansions and castles, fortresses against mortality, expressing instant old money, like the dukes and duchesses of Marmalade created by the Emperor Soulouque. Twenty servants in a house are not rare. A hotel owner drove two air-conditioned Rolls-Royces, keeping a spare in case the other needed washing.

The old elite, often educated and worldly, was sometimes even idealistic and generous. The early appeal of Papa Doc had come from his mobilization around the idea of "negritude." He assaulted the light-skinned, although not consistently. He arranged for his family, his managers, some of his tontons macoutes to become millionaires. Many of the traditional elite went into exile. Haitian doctors, lawyers, engineers, teachers work in Quebec, in West Africa, in France. There is a Haitian cardiac surgeon practicing down the peninsula from San Francisco—but what do you suppose happens to cardiac cases in Haiti?

Later, after Baby Doc decided the talent drain had gone too far, some of the elite, both black and mulatto, came back from Africa. They may have brought AIDS with them. Jacques Large, that clever and lively journalist, had been the secretary to Dag Hammarskjöld, Secretary General of the United Nations.

The rich employed some of the poor. On that flood-lit tennis court we used to have two ballboys on each side. If you don't have to chase the balls, tennis can be a restful sport, even in the tropics. One of my partners never carried his own racket to the court. His "timoune"—little one—had that job. Previously he had the job of carrying my friend's books to school.

Haitian racism was always inconsistent. "A rich black is a mulatto, a poor mulatto is a black." Even after the fall of a dictatorship inaugurated by blacks, continued by mulattoes, and abetted by white foreigners, candidates for the presidency were described as representatives of the light-skinned or the dark-skinned or the medium-skinned. But nowadays most people carry their own tennis rackets.

My friend Dr. Gérard Frederique, an ophthalmologist trained in Pittsburgh, remains at his clinic from morning till night, examining patients with glaucoma, cataracts, all the miseries of the eyes. Lines of people wait for him. "Why don't you work abroad?" I asked him. "You could make a buck. You could be more comfortable."

He stared at me with astonishment. "I'm a Haitian."

USUALLY THERE was only one. But now, with the election coming on Sunday, the level was stepped up—two mutilated bodies, the trademark evidence of macoute political campaigning, were again found in the street near the Holiday Inn. Gangs blocked the roads and searched cars. And then the streets were unblocked and our cars were not searched. Reporters hurried to get press passes, although it wasn't clear what good they were. After telling people that I wouldn't do it, I ended by standing in line myself, paying a few dollars; it would be a souvenir, anyway.

Brant Ward, intrepid photographer, had informed me that he was planning to photograph nothing but beautiful Haitian models on a beach. Now people were throwing rocks at him. He dodged an automobile heading straight at him. Some of the newspeople attending the latest cosmetic election had been here for the massacres of November and were wearing bulletproof vests. Slipping into their jackets, they grabbed croissants and rushed out of the Holiday Inn to view the latest corpses. The relevant fact was not two more bodies in the street. It was the gesture that counted. It was the leaving the bodies there for five, six, seven hours and making sure no one picked them up. *We're watching you.*

Yet there had been little violent crime against visitors and foreign residents. A foreign woman was still safer walking at midnight in the slums of Port-au-Prince than in the downtown of any great American city. The man coming toward her would smile, incline his head, and say, "Bonsoir, Madame."

At least that was the tradition. The breakdown of civility was rapid in recent years. The precedent of political murders and rapes seemed to lead to nonpolitical ones. Many foreigners now employed bodyguards for their children. I could adjust to the political turmoil, the random killings, the bodies in the street. I could understand it as the turmoil of revolution amid the snakelike death-throe thrusts of the Duvalier thugs. More saddening was the angry stare of children who used to tease and laugh. Despair and the blaming of foreigners was inevitable as nothing came of nothing.

And in this anarchy, anything seemed to come of anything, so long as it was cruel. Grief and fatigue made the heat more oppressive, as did the endless grinding of sun-drenched days in a place where hope and high spirits had been the chief gifts from the gods. The gods were busy taking back the few blessings they had given. Fires darkened the air. I wanted to preserve the dream of Haiti along with the vividness of every passing moment on this crumpled patch of island. I was no longer confident of the dream. Haiti seemed to be doing its best to murder its own hope, turn its sun into darkness, its 180-year-long dream into nightmare.

A young man with a multicolored knit cap pulled like a tea cosy over his Trinidadian-styled dreadlocks pulled out the corners of his mouth to show me teeth made for biting. There was an evil stoned glaze over his eyes. Yet when I said in my approximate Creole, "Ou requin"—you're a shark—the nasty look dissolved into giggling.

"Why are you sweating, blanc?" And those same eyes now seemed wide and shining with amusement.

Thursday, three days before the scheduled election, we were still waiting to hear if Clovis Desinor, a "dinosaur," close associate of both Baby and Papa Doc, would win his appeal to be allowed to run for President. The city was turning peculiarly desolate and quiet. People were going to the country in order to avoid being forced to vote. In November they wanted to vote and were shot at the polls. Now, with the popular candidates boycotting the election, the Army was insisting that they vote and soldiers would examine the ballots to make sure. *Let me see your secret ballot.*

A free-lance cameraman working for NBC invited me to his hotel room to watch footage he was sure NBC would not use, although it depicted carnival gaiety in downtown Port-au-Prince. A triumphant crowd was dancing and waving to the camera, but there was an odd detail in this festival. The celebrants all had a piece of lemon thrust into their nostrils. There was a smell they didn't like. Again they were roasting pieces of the neighborhood loupgarou.

The cameraman was still wearing his flak jacket in his hotel room. "Look at this, man," he said, and punched the buttons of the VCR. "Hey man, they got respect for themselves. Look at this again. They dance, but they don't like the smell."

That night I drove down to the Episcopal cathedral for a performance of the Haiti Philharmonic. Chaos in the city, and a crowd of music-lovers listening to a concert of Vivaldi, Hindemith, and Oswald Durand, a Haitian composer. I sat behind two pretty little girls, primly perched on folding chairs alongside their parents, pink and yellow ribbons entwined in their pigtails.

THE EERIE antiholiday calm was deepening as election Sunday approached. Buses were filled with people fleeing to the countryside to escape the forced voting. Businesses shut down, with hasty signs on the grilles: CLOSED FOR VACATION. CLOSED FOR ILLNESS. CLOSED UNTIL MAYBE NEXT WEEK. Within this calm, new bodies appeared on the streets near the Holiday Inn every morning. *Okay, okay, we've got the message.*

Again the boycotting candidates called for a general strike, but people had to go to the market, people still thought they had the right to eat. Trucks with armed soldiers were cruising everywhere and we didn't know what the rules were. Sometimes the soldiers stopped to search individuals or cars; sometimes they didn't. Both bodies and rumors were scattered about.

Haitians were learning to organize themselves within the context of anarchy and violence. There was a kind of normal life, persistent and moving, a stubborn inertia of survival. I kept seeing parents hugging their children, and children hugging their pets, as I remembered my daughters, Ann and Judy, in 1954, hugging their chickens, their dogs, their cats.

What follows is a gallery of coping.

MEESTER HAITI

Aubelin Jolicoeur, a survivor, had held important jobs in the ministries of tourism and information during the times of both Papa Doc and Baby Doc. At times his star shown less brightly. Women tourists complained that the Minister knocked on their doors at inconvenient times of the night. At one period he was defiantly proud of saving the life of Papa Doc during a coup attempt. (The revolutionaries sent out for cigarettes when they occupied a palace building; the nicotine emissary told Aubie they were only a few; Papa Doc annulled his emergency escape plans and had the unlucky smokers killed.) "Doc was my good friend!" Aubie explained.

Doc disappointed him in the end. He lost his governmental jobs and published a series of Open Letters to Jean-Claude Duvalier, pointing out how His Youthful Excellency could do things so much better with the help of the classically educated, internationally popular philosopher from Jacmel.

Aubie knew everyone. As the years went by, he was still the model for the character of Petitpierre in *The Comedians*. When he grew excited, his savvy English reverted to an earlier stage of fluency. The showings of the long-banned film reminded everyone that he was a movie star. "I am call Walter Winchell, Walter Lippmann of Haiti, I am call Meester Haiti! As Graham Greene say of me, I have a rare satirical courage, smiling before the firing squad!" (I'm not sure Graham Greene said this of him.) "All kind of thing, I tell them yes! I am clown! Because it take talent to make clown, but then, yes! Then I go home after the show and cry."

He paused to give me time to imagine this blend of Walter Lippmann, Walter Winchell, and *Pagliacci*. "Without bloodshed, I create public relation for my dear Haiti."

Aubie agreed that the massacre of the black Haitian pigs had finally dissolved Baby Doc's credibility. "General Namphy will bring back cochons noirs and everybody will be happy!"

He grinned. "And then we show the Americans our René Theodore and they send us money. We will have vacuum cleaners and Communist doll for the Americans, I love them, they are all my friend—especially you, dear Air-bair."

During these difficult periods of no government or too much government, macoute control or Army control, rigged election, panic and random violence that was not really random, Mister Haiti dressed up in his white suit, twirled his cane, dandled his newborn son—he had many children, many wives. He wrote for *Le Nouvelliste*. At sixty-three, he was lithe and blithe, entertained and an entertainer. No need to rush for a new job just now. Wait till things settle down.

"I have a habitation and a name," he declared as he alighted for another moment of intimacy at my table during his now self-appointed rounds of the Oloffson terrace, introducing himself and everyone to everyone and himself. " 'A habitation and a name,' my friend—do you know that your Shakespeare said this? Thus I am Aubelin Jolicoeur, philosopher from Jacmel, Haiti."

"That's pretty fine, Aubie."

But a graduate of the Lycée Pinchinat could not leave it at that. Shakespeare was only a beginning for this citizen of the Haitian asteroid. "I am also journalist, lover—*cela va sans dire*—art collector, former tourist official."

Did Molière say that?

Would I offer him a rum punch?

C'est-Dieu hobbled off to tell the bartender that Monsieur Jolicoeur was ready for his drink and it was to go on the American's tab.

Aubie survived partly off the earnings of his Claire's Gallery, named for his Canadian wife or maybe his half-Canadian daughter, who were back in Canada. He didn't really like selling his paintings. He liked giving them away to beautiful souls who would then, in gestures of cross-cultural unity and friendship, offer him gifts in return. He honored all beautiful souls; he honored checks made out to New York banks.

As a social commentator of great visibility, agitator, amuser, and wearer of white suits, he could be considered the Haitian Tom Wolfe. But since he was Haitian, he lived a little more on the brink. Laugh, clown, but don't forget the tragic double face.

Since a new management had come in at the Grand Hotel Oloffson, Aubie was no longer King of the Terrace. Many of the minglers of old were staying home in Miami, Chicago, and New York because they had heard rumors of troubles. But on the brink, Aubie still lived for the day, lecturing whatever visitors he found. "When you go back to San Francisco," he commanded me, "you will take a message to some of my deep close personal friends. To Lia and Mel. To Laura. To Sharon. To Debbie. To . . . I will give you list. You will tell them our beautiful Haiti awaits them."

"I'll tell them."

"And then tell them Mister Haiti loves them all."

"I'll be sure."

And he pirouetted on his cane. I'm certain there were times

when Aubelin Jolicoeur felt grief. He had even given me this news scoop. But Mister Haiti wasn't in the business of letting anyone peer deeply into his heart.

AN ENTREPRENEUR IN THE SECURITY BUSINESS

Apart from the fact that it put his life at risk, Manno el Saieh had found a terrific career in a modern growth industry—a security service. It was the happening business these days.

Manno was at the Holiday Inn when it was trashed by panicking journalists diving for cover on November 29, 1987. They had reason to panic. A few yards away, the headquarters of Sylvio Claude, presidential candidate, had just been shot up and the macoutes were headed toward the hotel. Later, when a journalist was killed and several wounded, Manno helped evacuate the survivors. "Actually," he explained, "my contract had expired, but I felt I should finish the job."

His father is my old friend Issa, the art dealer. When I first knew Issa, he was the lead singer in a merengue band. I used to send books from the States to young Manno at hotel school in Switzerland, when his father wondered if he would ever amount to anything. He thought books might give the boy some ideas.

Returning to Haiti, Manno organized the first "bisexual"—he meant coed—sports club in Port-au-Prince, racquetball, swimming, and aerobics. He owned property. He taught bodybuilding. He was waiting for his father to build the luxury hotel he was trained to manage. His father was waiting for Haiti to become a tourist mecca again, and optimistically had begun construction.

Manno was a member of the vivid and restless privileged class, although not the traditional elite. His father, born in Petit Goave of Syrian parents, married a Haitian woman of part-German family. Manno's wife is an Israeli whose father, an Indian Jew, was a pilot hero of the 1948 war. They have four children so far. Perhaps only in Haiti is it unremarkable to find children with mixed African, Syrian, Jewish, German, and Indian grandparents. When I asked Issa how it happened that an American Jew and a Syrian Haitian were such good friends, he shrugged and said, "Well, you know Issa means Isaac."

BEST NIGHTMARE ON EARTH

"You like security work?" I asked Manno.

"Luxury hotels are more my style," he said. "I'm waiting for Dad to finish construction. And for this politics to end, also."

THE PAINTER

André Normil's paintings hang in museums worldwide. By Haitian standards he was a rich man. He was not a member of the elite; merely a great talent. He would be richer if he didn't have twenty-two children, but they are a kind of wealth, too.

He worked in a studio away from his house. The kids made a bit of noise, and so did his creditors. He liked to buy things, automobiles especially. It was better to seclude himself from children and creditors. They tend to interrupt the dreaming.

He painted fantastic jungles, flowers, animals, and mythological creatures. There are no jungles in Haiti, and not many wild animals, but there are plenty of mythological creatures. Normil has happily resided in the realms of his imagination since the mid-fifties—he was now fifty-five years old—and showed no sign of burning out like many primitive artists. He has strong thick arms and shoulders. Greeting me, he offered me a wrist to shake so I wouldn't get paint on myself.

In his secluded studio, a new wife watched him work. Haitians sometimes have several wives; the extra ones are called "placées," placed ones. The radio played the merengue, calypso, political harangues, Baptist or Catholic prayers, whatever. He was secure in the privacy of his easel. A Miss January from an old *Playboy* was pinned to the wall—to Normil, another mythological creature.

I asked if he would like to travel.

He traveled every day. From his house to his studio. That's enough.

He was a working man. Occasionally he was a loving and celebrating man at a bamboche, a gathering of family and friends, the sort of thing people should do every weekend to remind themselves of Carnival time.

These days one didn't bamboche very much.

But one could continue painting.

THE PETER-PAUL POPULATION

A friend in San Francisco had met a marvelous driver named Peter-Paul, and in these times especially, it wasn't prudent for visitors to chauffeur themselves. Sometimes people threw themselves or their children at automobiles so that the millionaire with a car would have to pay hospital costs. Fortuné Bogat used to advise me to back up over anyone I hit, since funeral costs were less onerous than hospital expenses. In these times, a good Peter-Paul would be helpful to speak in my favor at roadblocks.

I asked how to find Peter-Paul. In the efficient way of the telejiol, Peter-Paul appeared. He said he was Peter-Paul. But he didn't actually have an automobile, so he hired one for me. His personal chauffeur drove Peter-Paul, Brant Ward, the photographer, and me, and he was full of good cheer and knowledgeable about finding what we wanted. He decided he should be a guide rather than a mere driver.

Peter-Paul turned out to be Peter-Paul the First or The False Peter-Paul. He was probably a macoute; here were a few extra bucks to be made.

One morning at breakfast a beaming, good-natured, deep-voiced, burly man headed straight for us. "I'm Peter-Paul," he said. "How's my friend in San Francisco, Tony Lehman?"

This was Peter-Paul the Second, the True Peter-Paul.

Both Peter-Pauls did a good job. Sometimes they subcontracted us to their brothers or cousins or best friends. When people in need come looking for a Peter-Paul, Haitians are capable of creating them upon demand.

"Just call me Pete-Paul for short," said the false Peter-Paul, with warm compassion. (His real name was Mack.)

One morning I had an appointment for a visit to René Theodore, the sleek communist leader. Peter-Paul was waiting. "Is it 8:15?" I asked.

"No, it's 8:25."

"My watch is wrong."

"You better change it," he advised me.

I tried to reset the time. He observed with his usual patient concern as I struggled through the digital code of a new cheap watch. He nodded encouragingly. Although I had bought the watch on my own, he bore no grudges.

When I finished, he said: "Now you're just like me—ten minutes ahead of everybody else."

ON SUNDAY, election day, I would drive myself up the mountain to Kenscoff to watch the polling, hoping to avoid the Army-controlled official tours of polling places in Port-au-Prince. Our entire inventory of Peter-Pauls was unavailable, having urgent business with their families anywhere else.

THE CAMPAIGN had some of the vanity and elegance of a French political ritual. Amid random killings, starvation, epidemic AIDS, hepatitis, and tuberculosis, candidates talked of the lack of a "science of government." Aubelin Jolicoeur thought the problem was to do away with "zombie checks," treasury payoffs to journalists, especially now that he was not getting any. A radio report about another call for another general strike was followed by a singing commercial for an analgesic "better than aspirin, better than aspirin, *better.*" General Namphy came up with an insight: "L'Armée Nationale a pour devoir de servir et non de tuer." ("The National Army has the duty of serving, not killing.") An editorial in *Haiti Liberée* compared General Namphy to Charles de Gaulle, but added the Haitian touch: "May our *loas*"—gods—"protect him." At the headquarters of the Democratic Christian Party, led by the Sylvio Claude, who asked to be called either Reverend or Pastor, I saw business as usual despite his boycotting of the election. A poster of Reverend-Pastor Claude borrowed a caption from another leader: "I Have a Dream." Before going into hiding, Sylvio Claude spoke to reporters under a blue silk umbrella. "I have the largest party . . . I wait with a certain confidence."

Some activists still supported General Namphy because they feared a "dramatic event." Yves Volel remarked, "A just government in Haiti would go about setting bombs against itself." Another pundit, optimistic, justified the brutal setup election as "the Politics of the Little Step." In other words, at least now the chaos and the killings were out in the open. A day later, the same observer, in his pessimistic mode, noted that under Henry Namphy "the Duvalier machinery is still in place. The machinery is still the machinery."

I asked a prominent career diplomat why he supported one of the Duvalier torturers in a run for the Presidency. "But I must, mon vieux," he said. "He's my daughter's godfather."

Haiti is a small country where people know each other. This same diplomat, a devoted optimist, looked on the positive side of the violence, killings, and corrupt elections. "Now people don't talk only about AIDS in Haiti."

Hugo Noel, the candidate from the Party of Jesus, was approved by the military. He ran against Satan, not the Army. He proposed raising a special flag of Jesus above the National Palace, thereby exorcising the building and establishing Love, Peace, and Union. The Army band would play his favorite hymn, "Saved, Blessed Lord, Our Dear Haiti."

The chief rival to the Jesus Party candidate was one nominated by the Virgin Mary in a bit of intrafamily rivalry. Issa el Saieh pointed his finger at me. "Well, you have your Harold Stassen and Lyndon Larouche, don't you? And your Moral Majority?"

Posters for Rockfeller Guerre appeared all over town. Modestly and secularly, he was only running for the Senate. He seemed to have changed the spelling of his first name to remove the American taint.

Two days before the election, the debate continued in the supreme court concerning the appeal of the Duvalierist candidates to be reinstated. While people fled the city and tanks rumbled down the streets, mysterious fires broke out and cars were stopped to be searched. The court debated questions about the difference in meaning between the French words "durant" and "pendant," striving for distinctions between "during" and "in the time of" the Duvalier dictatorship. There was a sense of masquerade in the deliberations of these robed judges and lawyers. (Fashion note: black robes; black mushroom-shaped hats curled over the legal heads; tasteful gold bands on the mushroom hats; beads of sweat.)

Some of the Duvalierists, including Clovis Desinor, the most prominent, were excluded. Three were admitted. This was described as "the wisdom of Solomon," although these days there was no Solomon on the court. Still, the baby was divided. The decision, taken without an actual trial, turned on the question of "zeal"—how zealous had they been as followers of the Docs, Papa and Baby?

The largely illiterate electorate prepared its secret ballots by choosing a slip of paper with the name and picture of their preferred candidate. They folded and showed the ballots to soldiers regulating the voting. The names were clearly visible through the paper.

Le Matin, a morning daily, concluded its lead story about the election with the words: "The game is already decided. We await this new episode."

Another newspaper divided its front page between news of killings and arrests of those urging boycott of the election, and an article quoting American doctors who recommend popcorn as a healthful food, providing needed fiber for tense and nervous moviegoers.

At a meeting space in the shantytown called Le Soleil, René Theodore set out posters of Carlos Marx and Che Guevara. A handsome, self-assured man, he had spent years in Moscow and Paris, but still spoke the right kind of peppery Creole. "The Nation needs technique and spirit. The Nation needs control." When he used the word "control," I wasn't sure if he meant to control or to be controlled.

After the meeting, as I made my way out, I saw a man being beaten by what seemed like an entire family, husband, wife, and children. He shouted, "I'm not a macoute, I'm just a thief! Don't kill me!"

Saturday evening Brant Ward and I drove through the uncannily dark and empty streets of downtown Port-au-Prince. No lights, no cars, a postnuclear stillness in a portside area normally filled day and night with thousands of people, buses, sleepers, hagglers, the ceaseless life. Now it had ceased. A few dogs loped through the ghostly boulevard Dessalines, the rue des Miracles, the rue Bonne-Foi. The general strike, plus abstention from voting and the pressure of the army—translate this as fear—simply closed things down.

At dawn on election day fires broke out on the rue des Miracles in downtown Port-au-Prince, smoke smudging the sky. A coffee factory, then a tailor shop, then a small hotel, stores, with people living upstairs. No fire engines. A crowd stood by, murmuring, while screaming women watched their possessions destroyed. A thick acrid smoke billowed from the roofs. Men were trying to evacuate sacks of food, furniture, and throwing clothes from windows.

Finally trucks with armed soldiers rolled by. Still no fire trucks.

The fire jumped from building to building, taking wooden structures and stone colonial walls near the famous Iron Market.

The polling area on the rue des Cesars, guarded by soldiers, was not open at seven A.M., an hour after the supposed beginning of voting. A woman carrying a Bible stood nearby, waiting.

Finally, two hours after the fires started, fire trucks arrived.

I asked an old man what causes the fires. "It's the electricity," he said. "It comes from the sky, most often at election time. *Electricité-election.*"

The fire trucks pulled their hoses and headed away, sirens screaming, while flames were still shooting out the windows and debris crackled in the street. Evidently they had another call. It was a bewildering early-morning sight—fire trucks rushing *away* from the fire.

At five-thirty Brant Ward and I headed out toward Kenscoff with the aim of finding how the rural population was treating the election. Last November they tried to vote and were shot down by uniformed soldiers. This time the men in khaki were regulating the election and people were trying *not* to vote. It was like the fire engines running away from the fires. The exercise of a freedom today was the privilege of not casting a ballot.

The paid voters voted. Groups rounded up by district chiefs lined up at polling places with sheepish or ironic smiles on their faces.

In Pétionville I approached the soldiers at an empty polling place and asked ("Bonjour!") if I could have a ballot and vote. "Of course!" I took two ballots from the selection offered me, one for Hubert de Ronceray and one for Leslie Manigat, but I didn't put them in the box.

At La Boule we saw professional voters with handfuls of ballots. In some places they inked the fingers. Outside at the fountain people scrubbed the voting finger before voting again; in some places they used lemons. The road was littered with lemons. At some booths they didn't bother to ink.

I was offered decks of ballots and could have voted a hundred times for my favorite. In Kenscoff attractive young women were peddling ballots, holding them between their fingers like bar waitresses holding paper money.

Brant Ward took a photograph of me holding a ballot over a box while a hospitable official invited the American visitor to make his choice. "Vote, please vote, Monsieur, you see it's a free election."

The procedure did not rise to the level of voter fraud. It was voter farce.

AFTER ALL the anticipation of massive killings and macoute disruption, the presidential election of January 17, 1988, passed with only a bit of killing, a few fires, an eerie calm as people left town, a lot of Army control, an undercurrent of macoute participation. The boycotting candidates had called for a general strike on Saturday, normally the busiest market day. The strike was effective, an emptiness in the streets. A few buses circulated. Plenty of soldiers rolled by on their trucks.

In overwhelming numbers, Haitians did not go to the polls, despite the junta's threats and demands for everyone to present their ballots. Many of those who did vote voted in traditional Chicago fashion, early and often. It would be a few days before the verdict was announced, but obviously Leslie Manigat had been selected by Namphy and the junta. No one, except perhaps Leslie Manigat, expected this election to solve anything.

Interviewed by reporters, President-Select Manigat was asked about the murders, the fires, the boycotts, the strike, the peculiar counting of ballots, the people who voted so often. Smiling and affable, plump, high-voiced despite his bulk, he answered in English: "Democracy is a *bay*-bee. If the baby is not perfect, do you strangle the baby?" (Makes strangling gestures with hands.) "Do you tear the baby bit from bit?" (Makes tearing bit from bit gestures.) "Do you? No! NO! You *rock* the baby." (Makes baby-rocking gesture.) "You *help* the baby." (Is stuck for a gesture; makes uplifted beseeching smile.) "Next question?"

FEW HAITIANS expected the Army's designer election to be the last word on the subject. "The Army is firmly in control" is a popular phrase in history, except that here one needed to remove the word "firmly." People expected an exhausted quiet for a time, and then a new dechoukaj.

Paranoia is a result of continuing powerlessness and frustration. Haitians have always suffered a bit of that; it goes with their history. The popular rumor was that the United States took its ambiguous stand on the anointing of Manigat for a reason. Small nations often believe that the United States has a policy of intelligent self-interest, despite the evidence of the past. The election of November 29, 1988, supposed to be honest, was aborted by killings credited to the Army and the macoutes. This new election did not include the most popular candidates; yet the United States seemed ready to recognize the result. Why?

The U.S. wanted a bit of order around here.

Haitians believed the junta had made a deal. It would cede or lease the Môle St.-Nicholas, a Haitian island, to the Americans for use as a naval base when the Cubans take back Guantánamo. Was this true? The Haitian rumor factory, the *telejiol*, runs day and night.

"I GO AROUND THE WORLD PEDDLING MY ASH"

Business was still being done. There was still money to be made. One night I met an American who informed me that I was about to be blown up because the Army didn't like all the stupid journalists hanging about. He, on the other hand, a businessman glowing in the dark, was helping to build up Haiti, literally—providing landfill in the form of garbage incinerator ash from Philadelphia. "I'm bringing it to these needy people, making islands in the sun, man."

"Is it radioactive?"

"I'm on a barge with it. I'm giving it to the metropolis of Gonaives.

"Is it radioactive?" I asked.

"I got this good friend who's a colonel there, we love each other like a brother. I gave him a whole mobile home, 22 feet, man."

"Hi," I said. "Is it radioactive?"

"It just impacts like cement," he said, "it just impacts soooo hard, and then after five years max it breaks up and you can grow garden vegetables on it. I just love these people and they're doing something for me, my barge, and the sister city of Philly. Now I found someplace I can peddle my ash."

THE COMMANDER of Fort Dimanche, Isidore Pognon, blamed the recent violence on "false journalists with cameras around their necks and sacks of stones on their backs," and also on "false boat people fleeing from Cuba to Haiti with arms hidden in sacks of rice."

Several burly men loitered at a table near the swimming pool of the Holiday Inn during the week before the election. It wasn't always the same men, but there was usually a little squad of them, sleepily watchful. They were not macoutes, of course, because the tonton macoutes were disbanded when the revolution came. But they looked like macoutes, they slouched like macoutes, they stared at the guests of the hotel like macoutes.

But they couldn't be macoutes. Macoutes wore sunglasses.

They wore sunglasses.

JEFF LITE, information officer at the U.S. Embassy, was especially popular these days. He had driven an armored car up an alley to rescue the photographer J.-B. Diederich when he was pinned down by gunfire during the killings of November 29. Young Diederich, banned from Haiti, asked me to thank Jeff Lite. It wasn't really much of an armored car.

"For you I'll put a sign on it," he said. "*Armored Car. Please Do Not Shoot.*"

Lite was one of those who stayed long enough in Haiti to become a defender of this attractive people. "They're killing more people in Jamaica," he pointed out. "In the Philippines they're going like flies." He was right. But there was 1 percent occupancy of the hotels. Most of the minglers stayed away. I found an old poster with a photo of Furniture Face and the slogan: GREAT PROTECTOR OF THE ARTS & LETTERS.

My watch had stopped working again and I considered borrowing a clock from one of the macoutes in the courtyard of the hotel. But then I thought it might be better to do without the time.

DEMOCRACY WALL

After dechoukaj, on block after block of the grimy rue du Magasin de l'Etat, a running wall mural celebrated the overthrow of tyranny. It had been a spontaneous outburst of artistic energy. Now the paintings of voodoo gods, Jesus, John F. Kennedy, Martin Luther King, of the heroes of Haitian history, and the slogans and poems, the depictions of retribution against the macoutes, of the wrath and hope of the people, were fading and chipping. The painted trompe l'oeil urinal captioned PIPI ONE and PIPI TWO was still used by people to relieve themselves.

After the painter started the project, others joined in. The people in the neighborhood contributed to buy the materials. Few painted images of freedom these days. "Do you have democracy now?" I asked an old man.

"Democracy, what's that? I just came on earth along with these other people. I just came along to help the gentlemen."

Cocks crowed, dogs barked all night, as if the dawn might come any moment now. Leslie Manigat seemed to think he was actually the elected president, but nobody took him as seriously as he did. A Haitian architect said: "We are unwilling to be a society without an echo. We have never let that happen. We are not ready for that."

WILL THE LAST TOURIST
PLEASE TURN OUT THE LIGHT?

In the bar of the Holiday Inn, drinking and smiling, a German visitor in shorts and flowered shirt, a soft blond mustache, appeared to be looking for something. He seemed to be the only tourist left over from the times when Haiti was a magic kingdom for gay explorers, then for gay loveboat expeditions. He was several inches over six feet tall, but hunched, never stopped smiling, and dressed like a boy at the beach with a toy bucket and shovel for digging in the sand.

The smiling German had come back to the fun, but perhaps for the sake of safe nonsex, he spent his days and nights in unsafe drinking, beaming over the political maneuvering and the journalists exchanging their rumors. When the talk turned to the time when a security officer frightened a journalist and the place was trashed with overturned tables and broken glass as my colleagues dived through windows, his smile grew as happy as a child's at Christmas. (The security officer shrugged at the havoc he had caused merely by raising a weapon, and strolled out.)

I asked the tall German if it felt lonely, being the only tourist in Haiti these days. "Oh no," he said. "I have been informed there is a sweetheart of a Belgian up at the El Rancho."

AT LAST A DEVOTED VOTER

I had asked people everywhere if they planned to vote. People said no, or they laughed, or they were going to the country, or just that they weren't going to be rounded up by the trucks and told where to vote, whom to vote for. Finally, however, I shared a taxi with a young woman who said she looked forward to going to the polls. "For which candidate?" I asked.

"How should I know? I don't know who they are."

"Then how can you vote?"

"I can't. I'm only seventeen, Messieur. But some day I sincerely plan to vote, *absolument.*"

AND A FEW MORE DEVOTED CANDIDATES

Among his qualifications, Hubert de Ronceray listed "Honorary Citizen of Tucson, Arizona, USA."

Another modest would-be president stated: "I don't pretend to be an expert on Haitian politics, but still and all, there's nobody in the world who knows as much as anybody else."

Asked at a press conference what he thought about the current situation, Philippe Auguste made a ringing declaration: "I am a politician! I refuse to think!"

President-Select Manigat began to seem like a prophet in his own time. "Democracy is a *bay*-bee."

THE BRIEF REIGN OF LESLIE MANIGAT

Like a good parent, President-Select Manigat wished to spend quality time with his new baby democracy. His handshake meaty, his metaphors proliferating, he emitted an aura of satisfaction at office. He had been an early supporter of Papa Doc, then a dissident in exile, a teacher, lecturer, and frequent writer of pamphlets. He was an ample man. When he felt well-fed, he seemed to believe Haiti was also happy and belching. When the junta awarded him the prize, he decided he had actually been elected.

He began to suffer delusions of presidentiality. He tried to reorganize the Army in the direction of his personal control. He ordered the transfer of colonels. He tried to limit their participation in drug smuggling. He tried to be *President!*

General Namphy soon packed him off to a hotel in Santo Domingo, where he slept in what came to be known as "the Presidential Suite" because so many Haitian leaders stopped there on the way to nowhere.

Then Colonel Prosper Avril sent General Namphy to the Presidential Suite, where it was said he wet the towels with his tears. Haiti had not appreciated his efforts.

Colonel Jean-Claude Paul, indicted in Miami as a drug smuggler but powerful in the Army, was an obstacle to American aid. To pack him off would be difficult; how to control his battalion? Conveniently, he happened to be eating his favorite pumpkin soup, laced with beef, carrots, cabbage, and other good things, watched by his wife and a friend, when he went into convulsions and died. Problem solved. An autopsy was scheduled, but I could never find publication of the results.

Two matters rapidly receding from view during the various governmental shifts had been the effort to regain some of Haiti's treasure, hidden abroad by the Duvalier bankers, and prosecution of the Duvalier torturers. The money would help. The photographs of Jean-Claude Duvalier, grinning on a French ski slope, did not help. The satisfactions of justice would help to bring pride in the uprooting of ugliness. The covert freeing of convicted Duvalier sadists brought dismay to those with energy left for indignation. Times does not heal these wounds; time festers them.

Sometimes Papa Doc referred to himself as "the Immaterial Being." In earlier periods of Haitian history there have frequently been brief reigns of what were called "ephemeral presidents" like those leaders who followed the uprooting of the Duvalier kleptocracy. Yet beneath the pattern of chaos, something tough, resilient, ironic, and brave seemed to persist—that Creole wit, that grace under suffering, a rich artistic energy, a poignant religious expressiveness in voodoo, a nervous edge of continual risk-taking. The soul of Haiti was still captivating. Others who have done their time in Haiti understand this passion. It is very like love.

When things turn so bad, so disastrous, so worn-out and fierce and dangerous with a lover, wise folks say it is time to yield, it is time to give up. If Haiti were a person, it might be a correct procedure to give up and go on to happier devotions. But this unique people, which has fascinated the world since 1804, when slave heroes defeated Napoléon at the height of his power, is not a mere charmer who has let me down. Haiti may seem to be a galaxy away, but her island is in our neighborhood, and for me, it is still the magic island.

I N THE winter of 1990, feeling homesick, I went back for the beginning of the new decade.

CHAPTER
SIXTEEN

Wonder of the World

T WAS WEEKS until Carnival 1990, and political activists and journalists were being shot up by the current "military democratic" government, but the bands were already out in the streets, getting ready for the festivals. Downtown, near the Salomon market, my car was blocked by a mob whirling and dancing around the musicians. A barefooted man jumped onto the hood in one theatrical leap. "Get off, you'll be hurt," I yelled, but he was laughing and shaking his head. *You're not moving—how could I get hurt?* He was right. I waited there while the singers and dancers played and sang. A girl, about ten or twelve, reached in to touch my arm and giggled as if stung because my skin not only looked white, it felt white.

I wasn't in a hurry. After all, I had chosen to come to Haiti and therefore it was right that I should be here, trapped in the maelstrom of a carnival band. I may have been late to meet my friends, late for dinner, but in fact I was exactly where I was supposed to be. I turned off the motor.

The song, repeated and repeated as Carnival anthems tend to be, began to sound like a Creole version of "(I Can't Get No) Satisfaction," and the man straddling the hood of the car watched with amazement as I jotted down the words, which said we were sad and poor, we suffer too much, we will all end in death, we will surely die before our suffering is rewarded, there is no reason for people to go hungry, no reason for children to die, no reason even for young and

285

happy lovers to die, not even good reason for old ones to die when so many love them, but the sun of Haiti is beautiful and Carnival has come again and aren't the gods good?

After the song had gone several times through the cycle, the cluster of dancers and musicians began to shiver and whirl in larger spaces, like an organism preparing to divide, and I knew I could start the motor again. The interested party still perched on the hood had already enjoyed the spectacle of the *blanc* scribbling in his notebook; he now prepared to enjoy the open air, riding in triumph with the *blanc* as his chauffeur. I wasn't sure if he would just stick until I stopped or if he had an idea of how far he wanted to travel. Every little while he glanced back to see if I was okay. I didn't feel it was my job to reassure him that it was no trouble at all to peer around him, making my way toward the Champ de Mars and then the rue Capois, heading up toward the slope where the Oloffson perched.

I drove very slowly. At the angle of the rue Roy he held up his hand and I stopped as he jumped off, saluted, and pretended to offer me a gourde as tip. "Merci, Monsieur!"

"Pas de quoi."

And he bowed again, just as if we were exchanging politesses and enjoying a quiet postprandial discourse and, in addition, just as if this was not the day and night when most of the civilian democratic leaders were being picked up for prison, beatings, or expulsion.

I had intended to see this Haiti of my thirty-seven years there without the careening, out-of-control erosion and avalanche of its deadly politics. I wanted to find the magic dreamland of my first smoky vision of the Bay of La Gonâve from that Panama Lines vessel, the memory of my long friendship with Jean Weiner, the spirit that somehow endured, and hoped not to find grief, though old loves often provide it unasked. I wanted to join the feast of Haiti's fantasy, comedy, and bravery once more, although the feast is served on Haiti's tragedy.

In this ragged period of increasing fear of General Prosper Avril, the handsome, firm-jawed, law-educated officer who had helped run fiscal accounts for Baby Doc, the feeling of oppression was becoming an old companion, even for foreigners. General Avril was not a simpleton, like Baby Doc. He was wily and self-contained, like Papa

Doc. He had taken power as the other seekers, Namphy, Manigat, and rival officers, failed and fell. Initially he was clever enough to make the right noises about narcotics interdiction and elections, consoling the Americans and cajoling the international community. Many Haitians hoped he might control the brutes and dinosaurs—they wanted to think he was not one. And if he pleased the foreigners, maybe aid money would come back. He appealed to the hunger for order, relief, a pause in the killing. He had a stern profile and an enigmatic manner.

Foreign residents, diplomats, and the diminishing number of businesspeople were nourishing one of the few Haitian growth industries—personal protection. Rape and bold burglaries tend to dilute the *douceur de vie*. Bodyguards for children were as popular as car phones and VCRs in the States. The luxury hotels sat empty on their hillsides. Even the Grand Hotel Oloffson, my dear home away from home for so many years, was having to make do with international bureaucrats, art miners, and occasional clots of journalists rushing in for the latest crisis, rather than the happy, money-strewing tourists. The flowered rum punches of welcome that greeted new arrivals from the airport were greeting less carefree visitors.

Sometimes, defying history, an old friend appeared—Olivier Coquelin's Berkeley aide, Cindy, the young woman who had escorted me among the leopards and accused my karma of causing the death of a dog. She didn't keep up with the news; she wasn't worried; she walked on the blithe side. Now, a few years older, she was a New Age fundamentalist in the business of buying art to sell for the benefit of an organization that bought art for the benefit of Haitian children. It seemed complicated, but at least the enterprise did good for the artists.

"I don't come from Berkeley anymore," she explained, "that was another decade, Herb. Now I'm a native of D.C., where policy for the nineties is made. Fairfax, actually."

She advised Haitians. She bought art. She sold it up north and back east. There may have been a little problem of 100 percent of the proceeds going to overhead and expenses, but the rest went to benefit Haitian children, "eyes, education, and like that."

Cindy didn't speak French or Creole or like that, but she was in touch with the goddess within, which didn't help her communication with the people without. She stared at a woman feeding a child rice and beans and asked me to translate her question: "Don't you think you're overdoing it on the carbo-loading?" There was incomprehension, so she repeated in an emphatic raised voice: "Excess of carbohydrates?"

I explained about hunger and this exceptionally nourishing breakfast.

"Well, beans have some protein and niacin, I guess. And these people, they're really good at recycling. But would you ask if the husband ever does any of the cooking, gives the mom a day off now and then?"

Cindy was a second-generation New Ager. Her mother had stayed at Milbrook with Tim Leary. Her father had been unnecessary, a drone. She had only met him in an earlier life, when she was a princess and he was a court bard. "In my living today self I prove a person doesn't need a father to be straight. I'm straight, only I'm bi?"

"Bye?"

"Bisexual," she said, "only I'm more tri?"

"Try?"

"I like women, I like men, I like black persons?"

She was another mingler. Neither revolution nor reality stopped the minglers on their appointed rounds. But her way of ending statements with questions may have meant that, despite the grounding of all her past lives, judgment was seeping through. The odd thing is that I felt the lady from D.C. (Fairfax) was obscurely moved by what she dimly came to perceive as she traveled about the countryside in her rented jeep. On this visit she didn't mingle or find her white-uniformed mingler, perhaps because the Army was too busy holding the regime together while fighting with other elements of the Army. The Air Force seemed to be grounded for lack of places to fly and people to fly there. We reminisced about the good old days of the Habitation Leclerc, the floods of tourists, the less good old days of the Relais de l'Empereur and Olivier Coquelin's leopards, the political confusions of their sharp teeth. "Isn't it terrific," she asked, "how these people just keep on painting, keep on carving, keep on trucking, with the diet they get?"

"Plus the danger. Plus the killings."

"I hear you. Plus everything, a really humid climate sometimes, don't I know that?" She stared at the woman busily wiping the mouth of the child, rattling her utensils, casting sidelong looks at the giant Americans standing nearby and jabbering in their language. The lady from D.C., Fairfax, and the distant galaxy of Aquarius smiled benignly, bent, and petted the squirming kid: "Translate for this mother how I think she's got a really cute little bambino here, only try not to do so much carbo-loading."

Gritty sandlike dust was blowing into our faces, making our eyes itch. There had been a long dry spell recently. The woman wiped this grayish dust off her child's head and brushed with her fingers around the ears as the child squirmed. This was the soil in which the rice and beans they were eating might have grown; it was being blown away, eventually silting into the Caribbean. More likely the rice and beans they were eating had arrived in sacks labeled CARE or WORLD COUNCIL OF CHURCHES or something like "U.S. Surplus Grain Program, Not for Resale."

AFTER NIGHTFALL on January 15, 1990, General Prosper Avril, the temporary permanent President-Self-Selected of Haiti, returned from his historic trip to the Republic of China, where he had gone with an entourage that prudently included most of his possible usurpers, in search of some good dim sum and some good money. Security would be tight. But Jorgen Leth, a Danish film director, and I decided we would try to greet the Maximum Leader at the Port-au-Prince airport.

The streets were filled with sirening police vans plowing through the dancing, prancing bands practicing for Rara, the voodoo carnival that follows Mardi Gras. I saw no one killed, either by the vans or the men on flattop trucks with mounted machine guns. A banner at the Place des Héros (often pronounced "Place des Zéros") said:

An Absence Noticed
A Presence Noticeable
Joyeux Retour President

On the airport road, colored lights made an improvised Arc de Triomphe. Groups stood with their placards in Creole: AVRIL FOR FIVE YEARS, VOMIT THE CANDIDATES, VIVE AVRIL! The most famous local band, DP Express, was swinging from a platform. We had parked our car far away, walking with the mob toward the arrival gate.

The nearer we got, the more soldiers, blue-suited guards, and plainclothesmen with bulging shirts. The plainclothesmen did without holsters. Some of them were dancing to the sounds of the Rara groups, trumpets, drums, whistles, and *assons*, bamboo flutes. One soldier had draped his submachine gun around his girlfriend's neck so he could dance more limberly, adding percussion with a club against a glass hotel ashtray. A Haitian friend had warned us not to try to attend this welcoming ceremony, since a kamikaze could blow us up along with General Avril.

I don't believe in Haitian kamikazes.

Inside the airport, a mob of dignitaries in dark suits, the women in pink or purple or sea-green chiffon and buckles and high heels, clamored to get through locked doors. There was a strong scent of perfume, cologne, and ambition. These middle level Bon Ton Macoutes were blocked by soldiers. I also was barred by an officer who said I needed a press pass. I turned around and wrote JOURNALIST in block letters on my visa and the officer puzzled over the words with his index finger, then said, "Okay, passez," and I pulled Jorgen along with me, saying, "Assistant! Assistant!"

As we stood under the metal detector, Jorgen muttered, "It's a miracle. Fantastic. I could never have a budget to reproduce this."

Inside, Haitian television and the table for the Vin d'Honneur were set up, and generals, cabinet officials, and selected Avril-for-Five-Years demonstrators milled about. There were wives, children, and a variety of armor. When General Avril marched down the Pan Am ladder, a military band struck up, a merengue band also began to play, and cannons boomed. At least twenty-one heavy thumps.

Jorgen tapped me to notice a plainclothesman with a gold-plated revolver. A sergeant was handing Chiclets to two very pretty girls, one in ribboned pigtails, the elder one with cornrowed hair. The man next to me, standing at attention, saluting, suddenly reached for his pistol. A civilian near the President had begun to shake and babble, possessed of a god I couldn't identify, but the crowd laughed and applauded—it was a god friendly to Avril, demanding Avril for Life— and none of the clubs, rifles, revolvers, or submachine guns inter- rupted this brief manifestation from the voodoo pantheon. The man next to me returned to his saluting chores.

I admired Madame Marie Ange Nazon Avril, First Lady and First Nurse of the Republic ("Première Dame et Première Infirmière de la République"). She was not hefty like so many others here.

A group of high officers, with as much fruit salad on their caps as General MacArthur used to like to wear, surrounded the podium. General Fritz Romulus, an Avril faithful who had been left in charge of the store while the President trundled friends and rivals off to Taipei, began to speak: "We have given one of the most beautiful examples to the civilization of the entire world in our morality, disci- pline, and political maturity during the voyage of the President..."

These were what the newspaper *L'Union* later described as his vibrating words, "ses vibrantes paroles." More ominously, the news- paper reported that General Avril knows the names of the "desta- bilizers" who sent a telegram to President Lee Teng-hui, asking him not to give money to Haiti.

I stopped translating General Romulus's discourse and tried to calculate how much the baskets of flowers cost this country where people who used to go hungry are now starving and showing symp- toms of kwashiokor. When I lived in Haiti, this didn't exist, nor did yaws. The Duvaliers and their legacy have brought them both.

At last the henchmen speeches ended. General Avril, a former money-handler for Baby Doc, always described as "clever, cleverer than the rest, he's got a law degree," stepped forward. The fruit salad on the cap of the general standing next to him seemed to be burning under television lights. General Avril opened his mouth and out of it came, amplified and echoing throughout the hall... a woman's voice: "Pan Am Flight Number (whatever) is about to leave. All passengers will please board."

As a few nervous weapons were leveled, Jorgen whispered to me, "Perhaps we should leave now to avoid the crush. I want to see the voodoo show tonight at the Oloffson. It's going to be part of my film, if we ever get out of here alive."

T HE NEXT night, shots rang out and we looked up from our dinner, stopped our storytelling, and waited. Jorgen said, "Trouble is, we'll never know what that was about." The strongest description in the newspapers would be "perturbations pendant la nuit." So we went on drinking our rum or papaya juice, and then there were more shots, this time closer. We stopped talking. I heard shouts and a woman screaming. Then there was silence.

"Well, the lights are still on."

And since the incident wouldn't be discussed tomorrow, its resonance was limited. What seems like chaos in Haiti has its own symmetry and logic. Things work like some crafty piece of furniture, with secret slidings and drawers, death hidden and forgotten. The thing still stands there. People offer theories for what is going on, but the thing stands anyway. The best course was to poke and pry, open the drawers, slide the parts that slide, and know that you won't be able to explain the shots in the night or the laughter of the people gathered over companionable iced drinks on the terrace of the Grand Hotel Oloffson.

Jorgen and I continued to gossip about our marriages, the film he intended to make, the book I hoped to finish, as calm and relaxed and entertained as tropical diners and old buddies can be. I told him about my meals on this terrace with Roland Devauges, thirty-seven years ago, his sociometric study of Port-au-Prince, his love affair with the "belle doctoresse," the two hundred dollars he lent me for my trip home. Jorgen talked about the film he shot here, starring his former wife, about a Dane obsessed with Haiti. We both remembered the band of children playing Haitian songs for the diners from the steps leading to the Oloffson terrace, those kids who grew up year by year and then, when their leader died, disappeared.

In the morning we both reported that we had slept very well, thanks. Jorgen said he took a pill against his memories. I neglected to tell him about my dream that my daughter Ann, aged five again, was walking with her hand in mine on the rue Capois when the electricity went out, the oil lamps and candles were snuffed, the sky was black, and she was asking if we would be able to find our way home.

Jorgen asked if I had heard the new round of shots, very late, maybe near dawn.

"Is that what they were?"

WHEN MORNING came, the clack of construction, the honk of traffic on the rue Capois, the almost literal flood of sunlight washed away our night thoughts. Chicken sounds make it difficult for me to keep my pessimism intact, and Oloffson French toast makes it impossible, dissolving bad dreams and wasteful nostalgia in honey and crispness.

The Grand Hotel Oloffson was a survivor, recently dressed up with telephones that worked even when it rained and a new harvest of Haitian art. When I marveled that Richard Morse, an heir to the property, a half-Haitian Princeton graduate and former East Village rock band leader, was following in the eccentric footsteps of his predecessors—keeping the stationery in the safe, the money on the desk; quickly delivering laundry to whoever wanted it most rather than whoever happened to have put it out—he said that the Oloffson doesn't attract crazy proprietors. The Oloffson spirits make proprietors crazy.

Armand, a retired cop from Coral Gables, was here because he remembered the wonderful turtle cannery in Key West. He loved working there as a kid, slitting the turtles' throats—"they were about the size of four-year-olds, I figured that out when I had a couple." But now sea turtles were an endangered species and Americans couldn't eat what our forefathers came to America to eat. He pronounced the words "endangered species" with patriotic scorn. "In Mexico you can. Turtle steak and a Dos Equis, the greatest. In Costa Rica, okay. But I figure in Haiti, I'll get me a Haitian partner, I can raise the meat pretty good."

"You think you'll be allowed to sell it in the States?"

"I'll call it real mock turtle, man. Once I got the cannery going, giving work to a lot of these fellas they got down here got no work, who is going to say you can't give Haitian fellas work?"

"I see what you mean."

He dreamed happily. "Big as four-year-olds, tangiest meat you ever did taste. Get the right partner, I'll check with my good buddy Aubelin. Maybe he might could be the right partner, too."

A diehard little group of fanatic castaways was still gazing out over the city from the terrace of the Oloffson, that grand tropical memory bank, riding immortal on the backs of its termites. In the old days, various cads, scallawags, runaways, and remittance folks found their way here to answer all the conditions for happiness, i.e., satisfying their whims while avoiding the law. Repression and AIDS had ended the beachcombing paradise period. Now art miners were using Haitian talent, wit, creativity, and low wages for fun and profit. Haiti makes "native crafts," salad bowls and forks, plaques, authentic souvenirs marked "Jamaica," "Martinique," "St. Bart," to be sold in bazaars throughout the Caribbean. Apprentice sculptors fashion napkin rings for the Virgin Islands. An enterprising young American from Florida supports her free spirit by importing straw, weaving, voodoo equipment, metal sculpture, and carvings for hotel shops in Key West, Tampa, Miami. ("Aren't these little doggies the cutest? Plus I'm learning French, besides.") A German drives Haitian crafts across the border into Santo Domingo. "Is it sold as Dominican?" I asked.

"Let us putt it zis way. It does not say 'Haiti,' my friend."

In 1990, if any vacationer asked about Haiti, travel agents said the same thing: "Why do you want to go *there?*" My own travel agent, Tony Lehman, the Haiti fanatic who had made me the ambiguous gift of the Peter-Paul driver combine, used to look for adventurous travelers, but by now had given up, because mostly they asked, "Why would I want to go *there,* Tony?"

Yet a few castaways still floated onto the terrace of the Grand Hotel Oloffson, meeting each other with or without the help of Aubelin Jolicoeur, forever spinning in his white suit, using his cane as point for the gyroscope. He seemed to bounce off the wicker and mahogany, so light on his feet that a gust from the Casablanca ceiling fans might blow him into your lap. He was for the ages, he was forever; whatever he had been and would be, he was still a marker in the history of Haiti.

"I am major in Paradoxe at Lycée Pinchinat, *meilleur lycée* in Jacmel! City of Poets and Philosophers, Village of Charm and Grace! I am prepare for life in my beautiful contree, and also Paris, Cannes Film Festival, New York, even your San Francisco, 'O Cool Gray City of Love.' "

"You're sure prepared, Aubie."

"My father bit me if I am not First. Even in drawing! Donc I am first in all things, Mister Haiti, Ambassador-at-Large!"

"A good job you've appointed yourself to, Aubie."

He giggled and spun. He spotted a prospective mingler and I heard him introducing himself: "You have read *The Comedians,* my dear lady? Petitpierre it is I, Aubelin Jolicoeur! And what fortunate city is your birthplace?"

Despite the politics of Haiti and the disappearance of cruise ships and travel agents, there were still some diplomatic openings for the ambassador-at-large on the terrace of the Oloffson. I met a karate student from Long Island, about a hundred pounds overweight, who assured me he could break a brick with the side of his hand, tear the Nyack telephone directory in two before I could say, "Yellow Pages." Everything was big but his mustache and his sentences. His T-shirt said DOWNTOWN DOJO, L.I.C. He carried a silver ice bucket around with him, a quart bottle of Pepsi cooling as he copiously sweated— even carried the bucket into the Men's off the bar.

He came by his suspicion of Pepsi thieves vocationally. It turned out that he was a private investigator come to look into suspected insurance fraud, a resident of New York who claimed to have died but maybe was living in Port-au-Prince.

There was a Christian dentist on leave from the Radisson Hotel health plan, here to help in rural clinics. "They just love gettin' their teeth pulled—some of 'em calcified, you understand that term of science? In my spirit I get to do active good in the bush two weeks a year, that's not even 10 percent but all I can afford. Got my boy eleven, my girl nine to educate. They line 'em up, I can pull two-three hundred teeth a day. Course then there's burnout, just like a fighter pilot or missionary for the Lord."

The white South African rebel, more Oxbridge than any English aristocrat, stammered when he remembered to, wore a cotton boating sweater in the heat, spoke through perfect dentures that strangely resembled the teeth of a Malibu teenager rather than a fifty-year-old battler for justice. "Ah, I went on the telly to debate one of those meliorists, ah, go slow, all in good time, ah, I call them racists. The *Telegraph* reported there was blood all over the floor. Blood, *blood* all over the studio floor."

He gave me a shot of teeth. When he grinned, I could see the gold anchors all the way at the back of his mouth. "Wasn't my, ah, blood," he said.

Tight of teeth and loose of toupee, he had come to find allies among Haitian co-battlers for justice. And also a boy to carry back to London for an AIDS test and an enduring relationship. He gave me a Xeroxed copy of his curriculum vitae, including a list of Open Letters. We didn't speak much again because he was busy auditioning co-battlers.

There turned out to be a couple of indomitable minglers, hoping to speak French or French accent with Haitian heroes, but most of the young women this year were serious art miners, enterprising and businesslike. The immortal waiter, C'est-Dieu, whom I had known for thirty-five years, was gone. The ghosts of old friends haunted the Oloffson. "How old was he?" I asked Ducée, one of the new ancient, immortal waiters.

"Oh! Peut-être plus!"

By which I think he meant: Maybe more than anyone. And as I passed the mirror, on my way to receive a copy of his latest article in *Le Nouvelliste* from the hands of Aubelin, I saw myself, frazzled, gray-bearded, *peut-être plus.*

The famous Oloffson French toast was still served by friendly trembling hands. After breakfast I drove to see a radio station that had been recently shot up. On one side it said RADIO-INTER, spattered with jagged bullet markings. In parallel, where a voodoo design protected the broadcasters, there were no bullet holes. Sometimes even macoute killers show respect for authority.

That night, as I sat with Jorgen Leth, we saw one of the minglers abandon her dream of the Haitian hero and disappear toward the Marlon Brando cottage with the three-hundred-pound Long Island karate star and private eye, dragging his ice bucket with him. The bats dipped low over the swimming pool. Aubie spun on the point of his cane.

THESE DAYS Theo Duval had plenty of time to visit with me. Under Baby Doc, he had been a cabinet minister and the Ambassador to England, but it was said—with awe—that he had neglected to enrich himself. Even during the worst times of Papa Doc—or of Hitler or Stalin—there were people who found good reasons to survive, to do their jobs with dignity and hope for better times when they could do better. We don't call them heroes; we can call them human. Theo Duval is one of those Haitians, graceful, widely cultured, seeming to know everything—he even used to know whenever I was in the country, skidding to a stop and hailing me on the rue des Martyrs—who defines the unique charm of the elite. Now he was out of a job, and over lunch at the Oloffson I asked why.

"I don't know. Maybe they want me to study television."

He had put on a little weight, a little more cynicism (he always had some), a little gloom.

"Is that how you spend your days?"

He shrugged. "I have fourteen channels. I go"—and he mimed punching a button—"and I get movies, concerts, news."

"Theo, you're sad."

"Oh not so much. Yesterday I heard the astronaut from the Columbia satellite saying they were sailing over Haiti and the weather was nice. So you see we still have our place on the globe."

I suggested to another friend that the country needed Theo's talent to present Haiti's best face to the world. He answered, "When he was Minister of Tourism, everyone had to stand up when he arrived in the morning and say, 'Bonjour, Monsieur le Ministre,' " and I said I didn't believe it, and he said he didn't either but that explained why he wasn't a minister or an ambassador. As good an explanation you get. Theo needs a friend in power and probably will either find one or go abroad, to Paris, New York, or Montreal. His children live in Paris. The former Ambassador to England could probably find work in the hotel business or travel industry.

By the third week of January 1990, the Rara bands were accelerating their practice for the voodoo carnival that follows the Mardi Gras celebrations, serious fun after the Christian fun. The political mood was in its usual state of gloomy panic—no crisis—and business was rotten. Something relatively new was the black market in gourdes, the unit of currency traditionally tied to the dollar. Now anyone with dollars could get a 50 percent premium in gourdes. This drove the art miners and the few tourists into a feeding frenzy. People wanted to get their money out of the country.

The city showed no sign of the popular revolutionary sprucing up that immediately followed the flight of Baby Doc. I could recognize union headquarters and political meeting places by the addition of bullet holes. The joyous murals on the walls of the rue du Magasin de l'Etat, celebrating *dechoukaj,* rehearsing the triumphs and pains of history, a continuing story of Haiti's dreams stretching over blocks of the street and centuries of memory, had badly faded. The paint didn't survive the weather. Garbage was piled against the walls. I couldn't find the painter who had started this project, but obviously he hadn't been able to buy strong enough colors and fixatives.

The people of the neighborhood had taken up his cause and their work was dying. This saddened me more than I needed to be saddened. But every night more Rara bands blocked the streets, every night playing better, wilder, with more drums, more bamboo flutes, more dancers. "Blanc! Vini dansé!" More laughter. So I danced, too, with a girl in pink micromini and a San Francisco Port Commission T-shirt. I had given her the T-shirt because my beard was too gray to wiggle and jump opposite a girl wearing only a brassiere and a ball-point pen over her breasts.

E ARLY ONE Tuesday morning I rode a tap-tap up the mountain to Kenscoff. I didn't expect to find Jean Weiner, Monsieur Noh, and the other philosophers, Colonel Chocolat marching past the tables of the Hotel de Florville, the Chinese-speaking American colonel from Vietnam, but I was surprised to find the grove of eucalyptus trees mostly gone. Another tree was freshly felled. The strong scent of eucalyptus was now only a faint tang in the mountain air.

At lunch at the Florville, I asked about the Gourgue mural in the dining room. The waiter didn't remember it, but thought someone else might.

The skating rink built under Papa Doc—about as logical as building a voodoo temple in Darien, Conn.—had sunk into the hillside. But the stream still dashed among the rocks; people were bathing and preparing the produce for market, watercress, lettuce, even delicious little fraises du bois, strawberries, ripe and sweet, with grains that melted in the mouth. The laughter of the woman who sold me a handful was also ripe and sweet. I remembered my children here, and Matt Cucchiara, and Dieudonné Lamothe, the champion runner, and the friend I had persuaded to fly down from New York to meet me, who said, "Okay, I see what you mean." I took deep breaths, and there was still eucalyptus.

I looked for the Belgian priest who had threatened to excommunicate one of the local *houngans*. The houngan protested that they couldn't because he wasn't even Catholic. The man of the Church thought a moment and said, "Well, I'll get a dispensation from the Pope."

On the painted tap-tap that precariously rushed a heavy load down the highway back toward Port-au-Prince, an exalted old man began to shout, "I made the sky. Me, I made the moon and the stars."

A woman giggled, bent over her basket of Kenscoff strawberries. "He's crazy!"

The man pointed his finger at her and demanded: "Crazy? Crazy? Listen, if I were crazy, would I have been able to make the sky, the moon, and the stars so beautiful?"

And they were laughing together. In Haiti all the important things are beautiful; only reality needs a bit of improvement.

ONE MORNING I was walking up the rue Henri-Christophe, past the house where I first lived thirty-seven years ago, when Jean Weiner used to drop by every afternoon to see if life was in order, and then down the rue Roy, past the Centre d'Art on a street lined with school kids studying in the shade of stone walls, and then down the rue Capois toward the Musée d'Art Haitien (the *M* had fallen off, so it was now the *usée d'Art Haitien*), when an unusually pesty street zazou began to follow me with an invitation to a day at the seashore. "I take you to sunny bitch," he said.

I hadn't come to work on my tan.

"What else you wanna?" he asked. "You look for girlfriend?"

"No."

"Boyfriend? I know you look for something. I am Haitian friend, tell me."

"How about the secret of a happy life?"

He threw up his arms. "Ah! What good fortune! How well you have fallen! I am Haitian—"

"*Sans doute.*"

"—thus I can give lessons to teach you laugh at misère like me."

And there on the wide expanse of the Champs de Mars in front of the blank, blazing white National Palace, folks were staring at the American graybeard and the skinny zazou giving each other high fives in front of a statue that might have been Pétion, may have been Christophe, may only have been the old daddy of some Italian artisan, dressed up for opera bouffe.

I've seen a city that seemed to grow with greater random, frantic, fungoid, pitiless desolation than Port-au-Prince—Guayaquil in Ecuador. Perhaps if I knew Guayaquil better, I would also know the corners and gardens, the well-worn moments of grace and human consolation, the memories that haunt Port-au-Prince and make a few wayfarers recall it with a jolt of nostalgia. Its traders struggle to redeem everything from pieces of wire to pieces of history, scraps clutched for sale in the hands of Madame Sara, the agglomeration of goods heaped in the Marché au Fer. The grand wooden fantasy houses are relics of a dream of elegance. Standing in the morning amid the human tidal wave of the boulevard des Millionaires, staring at thick-walled colonial structures with their iron grills and armory of shutters, I could see this as a place careening out of time and history— until I saw a man struggling to carry his lap-top computer and brief-case through the mob of hawkers, the stalled carts, the people stretched out and groaning on the road. A few blocks away, students at the Université d'Haiti lounged on verandas of buildings constructed like tropical hospitals. They stood about gossiping, flirting, or studying like students anywhere, in the midst of a continual smoldering war between the succession of regimes and the people. History bears down like the tropical sun, even more dire in a place rendered so defenseless by bad fortune.

One night I visited friends who live in Pacot, a district of the traditional middle class—sweet-smelling gardens, walls with climbing plants, comfortable houses. I used to like to wander in Pacot at night, taking the cool evening air, chatting with the people having a cigarette and gossiping with their neighbors, watching their dogs, strolling with their children. It's not far from the Hotel Oloffson. As the evening came to an end, I said I would just walk back down the hill. "Are you crazy?" my hostess asked. "This isn't the Haiti where you used to live."

A refrain I heard again and again.

One of the other guests, an architect modestly active in promoting civilian government, said he would drive me back. When we arrived at his Honda, we found the windshield neatly removed, razored out, but oddly enough, nothing touched inside the car.

Cursing, then laughing, my friend said, "Okay, tonight it's fine, the air is fresh, it feels nice. But what am I going to do tomorrow? I'll have to wear goggles and a leather helmet."

He thought again.

"What the devil do they want with my windshield?"

Pacot at night now seemed eerily deserted. The evening strollers were inside their gates. I could hear the familiar Port-au-Prince dogs barking, earnestly celebrating dog communication, but the city was otherwise silent. Since people couldn't specify the exact causes of the dangers in the streets, perhaps this unnatural silence was not political. A bit of grit blew into our faces.

When the architect dropped me off, he said, "I guess I'll have to look for a macoute with very large glasses on his nose." He was laughing again. "Sorry, Herb. A *former* macoute."

DELIA AND Jean Weiner, the children of my old friend, came to sit one morning over cups of dark Haitian coffee and talk about their father. I said that I cared for him—he was someone unique in Haiti, in life, in my life. They asked if I wanted to visit his grave. I asked if they would be hurt if I didn't. I told them I wanted to remember him as the angry, amused, kind man who looked for meanings in his history, even as far away as his Jewish grandfather from Vienna. They said they knew about this, too. Ti-Jean said his father would have voted against himself if he had run for President. Delia said his standards were too high. She also said he had been too good-looking; he had been spoiled by women all over the world. Ti-Jean didn't comment on this.

Ti-Jean, an electrical engineer like his father, has built an ice plant. Puffing on his brown cigarette, he said he was not as tall or as good-looking as his father, but he had learned something his father never learned—that politics is useless in a man's life but ice keeps people cool and healthy in the sweltering summers.

And after his somber brooding as we spoke, I suddenly saw the hilarious grief of his father break through when he threw back his head, revealed his teeth, and laughed about the concept of expressing friendship by visiting a grave.

I wasn't traveling in Haiti; I was strangely at home. Sometimes, when I was with my children here, we tried to make sense of where an American family had lived because the mother and father happened upon the place. Our own very different history was touched by the intransigent one of Africans brought as slaves to a French island colony and confused by their fate for hundreds of years now.

I was like a happy orphan clinging to new parents in Haiti. Gradually, like a bruised orphan, I came to judge my community. Since nosiness is almost a sacrament, a part of the traveler's metabolism, I began to treat this world of strange as if it were really mine. In some way it became so. After repeated journeys, long friendships, griefs marking out stringent failures, rediscoveries of blessings left intact, angers because a people suffers and shouldn't suffer so much, I have no choice. Haiti is here and so am I. Jean Weiner is gone—he became family, it seemed—so are Fortuné Bogat, Jacques Large, and Monsieur Noh, now gone, and I must draw the inference for myself. I bring my children to Haiti because I need their help in the enterprise of remembering.

I used to think the Haitian people were indomitable. Now everyone knows that all peoples are domitable. Yet some innocence of hope still survives here, just because the air can be sweet in Kenscoff, or fragrant with charcoal smoke and flowers in the hillside neighborhoods of Port-au-Prince, or salty and seaborne in Jacmel and the other villages sloping up from the jagged harbors of this island. The sun is strong, gardens grow on the steepnesses, the children clamor on their way to school, if there is a school, and their parents proudly take them by the hands. In the midst of murder and an unending chaotic decline of the fragile structures of society, a chamber music group gives its concert, a voodoo priest paints his visions, a peasant farmer washes each carefully nurtured tomato, a song rises with the drumsound over a misty field as neighbors band together in the coumbite rite of putting together a house. People still share all they truly possess—their naked spirit.

Sometimes a shout or a laugh breaks the air, cutting into heat and fume, or a child calls to a parent over the cacophonies of blaring radios, street traffic, barkings, and cockcrows. I stop on the street, sweating, and remember what I loved—the defenselessness of the human presence; the literal nakedness of people washing in a stream, joking, teasing, and busy; the nakedness of need. My own neediness as a young man finding my way in this world thirty-seven years ago is surely a part of the pleasure I can't let go. I keep coming back.

Krik. Krak.

Now it's time again.

HERBERT GOLD is the author of numerous works of fiction, including *Fathers, A Girl of Forty,* and *Dreaming.* He was awarded the Sherwood Anderson Prize for Fiction in 1989. He lives in San Francisco.